UTOPIA LTD.

Historical Materialism Book Series

More than ten years after the collapse of the Berlin Wall and the disappearance of Marxism as a (supposed) state ideology, a need for a serious and long-term Marxist book publishing program has risen. Subjected to the whims of fashion, most contemporary publishers have abandoned any of the systematic production of Marxist theoretical work that they may have indulged in during the 1970s and early 1980s. The Historical Materialism book series addresses this great gap with original monographs, translated texts and reprints of "classics."

Haymarket Books is proud to be working with Brill Academic Publishers (http://www.brill.nl) and the journal *Historical Materialism* to republish the Historical Materialism book series in paperback editions. Current series titles include:

Utopia Ltd.

Ideologies of Social Dreaming in England 1870–1900

Matthew Beaumont

Haymarket Books
Chicago, Illinois

First published in 2005 by Brill Academic Publishers, The Netherlands
© 2006 Koninklijke Brill NV, Leiden, The Netherlands

Published in paperback in 2009 by
Haymarket Books
P.O. Box 180165
Chicago, IL 60618
773-583-7884
www.haymarketbooks.org
ISBN: 978-1-608460-21-2

Trade distribution:
In the U.S., Consortium Book Sales, www.cbsd.com
In the UK, Turnaround Publisher Services, www.turnaround-psl.com
In Australia, Palgrave Macmillan, www.palgravemacmillan.com.au
In all other countries, Publishers Group Worldwide, www.pgw.com

Cover design by Ragina Johnson. Cover image by Antonia Sofronova, 1932.

This book was published with the generous support of the Wallace Global Fund.

Printed in the United States.

Entered into digital printing January, 2018.

Library of Congress Cataloging-in-Publication Data is available.

To Natasha Shallice

It seems as if the new century, this gigantic newcomer, were bent at the very moment of its appearance to drive the optimist into absolute pessimism and civic nirvana.

– Death to Utopia! Death to faith! Death to love! Death to hope! thunders the twentieth century in salvos of fire and in the rumbling of guns.

– Surrender, you pathetic dreamer. Here I am, your long awaited twentieth century, your 'future'.

– No, replies the unhumbled optimist: You – you are only the *present*.

L.D. Bronstein
'On Optimism and Pessimism: On the Twentieth Century and on Many Other Issues' (1901)

Contents

Acknowledgements

'To spend months recording the dreams of a better future, of an "ideal" society, devouring the unreadable – what a windfall! I hasten to add that this tedious literature has much to teach, and that time spent frequenting it is not entirely wasted'. That at least is how the notoriously pessimistic essayist E.M. Cioran portrayed the satisfaction of his 'penitential longings' to understand the 'Mechanism of Utopia'. It is thanks to the support that I have received from a number of people that the time I spent attempting to satisfy these longings was positively pleasurable. My greatest debt is to Kate Flint, who supervised my Oxford University D.Phil. thesis on this topic. I am also deeply indebted to Terry Eagleton and Sally Ledger, my two examiners, both of whom have provided encouragement in the course of its subsequent gestation. Nick Shrimpton and Helen Small both read drafts of the present work, in earlier phases of its development, and I am extremely grateful for the detailed and insightful comments that they offered me. More recently, Darko Suvin and Andrew Hemingway were generous enough to read it in typescript and volunteer their support, which I greatly value. Sebastian Budgen, to whom I am particularly indebted, has helped to guide this book into print; as have Kim Fiona Plas, Regine Reincke and Joed Elich at Brill, to whom I am also extremely grateful. For reading parts of the typescript, or simply for being supportive, I want in addition to thank Amelia Beaumont, Michael and Joanna Beaumont, Dinah Birch, Stathis Kouvelakis, Josephine McDonagh, Jane Shallice, and Susan Watkins. My son Jordan somehow seems to have made its composition possible, despite his attempts to distract me and deprive me of sleep. Naturally, I blame any errors that remain on him. Inadequacies in the argument itself are of course my own responsibility.

Introduction

'At the present day', wrote the Secularist G.W. Foote in 1886, 'social dreams are once more rife'.[1] Around and *à propos* of utopia, there is a veritable discursive explosion at the end of the Victorian period. This is most obvious in the field of fiction. In the final thirty years of the nineteenth-century, hundreds of novels and short stories – each one prophesying a future society from whose imaginary standpoint the present state of affairs seemed manifestly unsatisfactory – were printed in Britain and the United States.[2] In lesser quantities, fictional utopias were published in other parts of the world at this time too: after 1870, in Russia and Japan as well as throughout Europe, an unprecedented amount of utopian literature appeared.

The popularity of utopian fiction at the *fin de siècle*, particularly in England, the country on which this study is centred, and in North America, is confirmed by the sales figures for the more famous examples of the form. *Looking Backward* (1888), Edward Bellamy's celebrated 'state-socialist' utopia, sold two hundred thousand copies in the United States during its first year in print, as well as spawning numerous imitations. In England, it proved almost as successful: seventeen reprints of its first English edition had

---

[1] Foote 1886, p. 190.
[2] See Sargent 1988.

been issued by the end of 1889, and in early 1890 the *Review of Reviews* reported sales of some one hundred thousand copies.[3] In his short survey of 'The Utopian Romance', published in 1898, the English economist J.A. Hobson singled it out for consideration because of 'the popular testimony to the critical and constructive power of its teaching'. 'Taking the test of direct intellectual influence upon numbers', he announced, 'we must account "Looking Backward" as one of the most important literary events of the century'.[4]

Other utopias benefited from the climate created by the success of Bellamy's unlikely blockbuster. By 1895, for instance, George Noyes Miller's *The Strike of a Sex* (1890) had sold thirty-one thousand copies in its American edition; while Theodor Hertzka's *Freeland: A Social Anticipation* (1890) had, according to contemporary advertisements, sold seventy thousand copies in its German edition. Commercial statistics for most of the utopian pot-boilers published at this time have disappeared, but there can be little doubt that English publishers printed utopian and science fiction in such quantities because they were confident that they could exploit an interested readership – especially after 1894, when the single-volume novel was established as the standard form of publication. Final proof of the fashion for utopian fiction at the *fin de siècle* is furnished in 1898, at the height of H.G. Wells's early success, by one of a series of articles in the *Academy* on 'What the People Read'. 'A Wife' is asked whether she likes 'novels about the future': 'She pondered a moment, wrinkling her brows. "Well, I can't say that I exactly *like* them", she said; "but one has to read them, because everyone talks about them"'.[5]

The fictional fantasy of the future was not the only incarnation, in the late nineteenth-century, of what two influential critics termed the 'utopian impulse'.[6] A utopian impulse palpitates in 'non-literary' as well as 'literary' texts of the time, so that 'any attempt to define the boundaries of utopia by purely literary criteria speedily ends up in absurdity'.[7] This is the import of Foote's article from 1886, which is not primarily interested in 'paper Utopias'. He deliberately alludes to 'social dreams' in order to accommodate the fact that 'Lassalle and Marx have hundreds of thousands of followers in Germany . . . Russia has its

---

[3] Marshall 1962, pp. 87–8.
[4] Hobson 1898, p. 179.
[5] Anonymous 1898, p. 293.
[6] See Manuel and Manuel 1979.
[7] Kumar 1987, p. 26.

Nihilists . . . France has its Socialists and Anarchists . . . England has its *Justice* and its *Commonweal*'.[8] According to many contemporary commentators, utopianism is an almost atmospheric effect of the social climate at the *fin de siècle*. As one essay published in Foote's journal *Progress* put it in 1884, in frankly inflationary terms, it 'is the great spiritual motive power of the world, and is rapidly rising to high-pressure'.[9] In the face of a widespread perception that capitalist society had arrived at some sort of historical turning point, the end of the last century was permeated with anticipatory or utopian consciousness.

My conception of utopian consciousness corresponds to what Raymond Williams described as a 'social experience in solution', that is, the 'structure of feeling' symptomatic of an 'emergent social formation'. At certain times, Williams argued, 'the emergence of a new structure of feeling is best related to . . . contradiction, fracture, or mutation within a class (England, 1780–1830 or 1890–1930), when a formation appears to break away from its class norms, though it retains its substantial affiliation, and the tension is at once lived and articulated in radically new semantic figures'.[10] The final decades of the nineteenth-century represent the pre-history of the modernist moment to which Williams points. A realignment of the middle classes occurred from the early 1870s, in reaction to the adaptations of British capitalism on the one hand, and the uneven development of the labour movement on the other. This ideological drama was played out, most markedly, in the political and intellectual impact of socialism on middle-class consciousness. Socialism appealed to intellectuals of the middle class to the extent that it opened up the possibility of ameliorating the capitalist system; but it tended to appal them to the extent that it threatened to overthrow it altogether. The generalised expression of this tension was the utopian structure of feeling typical of the late-Victorian epoch. In the dehiscent climate of the time, the future itself functioned as a new semantic figure in which this tension was articulated.

The proliferation of literary utopias in the late-Victorian period is broadly explained therefore by the peculiar socio-economic conditions in which they were produced. The early 1870s heralded an epoch of economic uncertainty

---

[8] Foote 1886, pp. 190–91.
[9] Britton 1884, p. 121.
[10] Williams 1977, pp. 133–35.

and political instability. The so-called 'Great Depression', from the mid-1870s to the mid-1890s, exposing the decline of Britain's industrial supremacy, fissured the confidence of the middle class in the capitalist system. The apparition of the spectre of communism, the most ominous of the utopian futures on offer at the time, reinforced this effect. The Parisian Communards' experiment with proletarian democracy in 1871 momentarily dramatised the possibility of an historical alternative to capitalism. And, during the riots and industrial unrest in England during the later 1880s, when the 'New Unionism' and the nascent socialist movement were in their ascendancy, memories of the Commune rematerialised. In this climate, there was a widespread sense, across the political spectrum, that some sort of systematic social transformation was afoot.

Of course, this was not ultimately the case. History did not deliver a new civilisation. Instead, as the dramatic events that culminated in 1914 seemed to demonstrate, it had merely aborted the old one. The period from roughly 1870 to 1900 appeared to contemporaries to be suspended between two distinct orders, an individualist and a collectivist one. This delicately balanced state of historical postponement probably provided the optimum conditions of possibility for utopian publications. Fredric Jameson has recently argued that it is necessary 'to posit a peculiar suspension of the political in order to describe the utopian moment'.[11] No doubt this is an overstatement, as Perry Anderson has indicated.[12] However, Jameson offers a convincing evocation of the political ambivalence that characterises times of explosive utopian activity (among others he gives the example of 'the great utopian production of the populist and progressive era in the United States at the end of the nineteenth-century'): 'These are all periods of great social ferment but seemingly rudderless, without any agency or direction: reality seems malleable, but not the system; and it is that very distance of the unchangeable system from the turbulent restlessness of the real world that seems to open up a moment of ideational and utopian-creative free play in the mind itself or in the political imagination'.[13] Utopian discourse functioned at the *fin de siècle* as a means of understanding these uncertain political conditions, those of a social experience

---

[11] Jameson 2004, p. 45.
[12] Anderson 2004, p. 69.
[13] Jameson 2004, pp. 45–6.

in solution; and as a means of shaping the hopes and fears that it raised, fears and hopes that finally remained unfulfilled.

'The prophetic romance is indeed becoming a feature of the literature of to-day', George Goschen commented in 1891; 'but we must note that as a rule it is also propagandist romance'.[14] Fictional and non-fictional utopias alike performed a distinct ideological role at the *fin de siècle*. Social reformists wanted to steer Western civilisation between the Scylla of a spiritually bankrupt bourgeoisie and the Charybdis of a potentially anarchic working class. Utopias consequently served as an imaginary resolution of the social contradictions of capitalist society. On the one hand, they tried to decipher traces of the occult future secreted in the social and cultural conditions of the present; and, on the other, they sought to conjure away the spectre of communism that threatened to destroy the prospect of a peaceful evolution to the coming social order. This double ideological burden is embodied in the narrative strategy of *The Time Machine* (1895), a text that I do not discuss in any detail in this book. H.G. Wells's portrait of a dystopia in which proletarian primates prey off an effete super-human species is a dire warning to the bourgeoisie of what will happen to it if it does not implement minimal social reforms in the present – but one which, at the same time, takes fright at the deterrent image of the future that it flaunts. It is finally spooked by the historical implications of its picture of the present as one in which a proletarian future is already a latent, a tendent reality.

This book is above all an attempt to set late nineteenth-century utopianism in its historical and ideological context. Evidence that hitherto this has not adequately been achieved, despite the quantity of academic work in the field, is provided by Edward James's recent 'Introduction to English-Language Science Fiction in the 19th Century'. Volunteering reasons for the 'great increase in the production of science fiction, above all in the last fifteen years of the century', James cites 'the influence of specific books' by Bulwer-Lytton, Chesney and Bellamy. Sensing that this partly displaces the problem, he weakly claims that 'there must also have been wider cultural changes which allowed for the rapid growth of these new categories of literature, most of which had something to do with historical change'.[15] This is too vague. I am concerned

[14] Goschen 1891, p. 28.
[15] James 1995, p. 37.

to examine precisely what utopian literature had to do with historical change. But, in conducting this enquiry, it needs to be stated at the outset, I necessarily present a partial and incomplete account of late nineteenth-century utopianism. So, in terms of content, I do not explore the religious and scientific influences on utopian fiction in the late-Victorian period. And, in formal terms, I do not offer an account of the literary history of utopia.[16]

My concern is to excavate some of the political presuppositions, or ideological coordinates, that underpin the social dreams of the time, and to explore the implications of this approach for an understanding of utopianism more generally. In the late nineteenth-century, when most examples of the utopian genre are of doubtful literary merit, and consequently manifest their ideological function all the more clearly, the fictional utopia is, in a phrase taken from Ernst Bloch, the pre-eminent Marxist philosopher of the utopian function, 'seismographic' – it 'reflects cracks under the social surface'.[17] It is on this assumption that I follow the example of the Rev. Kaufmann, the author of *Utopias; or, Schemes of Social Improvement, from Sir Thomas More to Karl Marx*, published in 1879. 'The aim of the writer', he announces in his insightful preface, 'has been throughout to present the several schemes for social improvement in the light of contemporary history, to show how far they reflect the spirit of the times, and what were the causes in the condition of the people which gave rise to the Utopian speculations they contain'.[18] I can scarcely think of a better formula for a materialist history of utopian fiction at the *fin de siècle*.

What specific tasks does this book seek to execute? It begins with an investigation of the historical conditions in which utopian literary discourse emerged in the late nineteenth-century. In Chapter 1, I sketch a period in

[16] Darko Suvin, for whom 'utopian fiction' is a subset of 'science fiction', has provided a uniquely rich and well-researched overview of the field in the late nineteenth-century, and my work is at least partly premised on the unrivalled bibliographical, biographical and sociological insights that he uncovers in Suvin 1983. Kumar 1987 is an excellent introduction to the broader topic, especially for the non-specialist reader. On the theoretical trajectory of utopia, see Levitas 1990. For a recent account of the literary history of utopian fiction, see Ferns 1999. Freedman 2000 and Wegner 2002 offer sophisticated Marxist accounts of various aspects of utopian literature, and they have been extremely useful to me. For an invaluable survey of the critical literature on utopia over the last thirty or forty years, see Moylan 2000, Chapter 3.

[17] Bloch 1986, p. 1088.

[18] Kaufmann 1879, p. vi.

Ch. 1

which dramatic socio-economic instability raised expectations of social transformation that were to remain unsatisfied. I offer an exploratory account of the *fin de siècle* in relation to the Great Depression, before diagnosing what I describe as the period's 'culture of expectancy'. In a final section, I propose that the emerging conditions of modernity, which entailed the dramatic acceleration of everyday life, and consequently rendered the present inaccessible or even (in phenomenological terms) absent, created a crisis of representation to which the utopian novel was a response. It was used by social reformists to arrive at an historical understanding of their own times from the critical perspective of a redemptive or retributive future. In its ideal-typical form, it is probably most easily grasped as a subspecies of the historical novel, grappling with the problem of apprehending the present in all its opacity.

Chapter 2 interrogates the ideological role played by utopian thought in Ch. 2 the socialist movement of the time. Taking William Morris's review of *Looking Backward* as its point of departure, it contends that the 'state-socialist' utopia, the dominant political utopia of the period, was the product of the ideological outlook, or 'temperament' (in Morris's terms), of reformist intellectuals. I follow a familiar practice among labour historians in assuming that the term 'reformism', in the late nineteenth-century, 'went under a variety of different names, with rather different connotations: social reform, revisionism, economism, opportunism, etc.', and that 'what they had in common was defined by exclusion; they were deviations from the revolutionary politics of the class struggle'.[19] This chapter maintains that utopian novels such as *Looking Backward* performed two tasks, which were conditioned by the class position and political outlook of their producers. On the one hand, they provided the basis for a forceful critique of the status quo; and, on the other, they reassured their largely middle-class readers that social change could occur without seriously altering the present system. In this sense, for all their futurist perspective, they constituted what Marx called 'sophistical rationalisations of existing society'.[20] Like some of the non-fictional texts that I examine, by H.M. Hyndman for example, they performed, at least partly, a 'prophylactic' function, in protecting the middle classes from revolutionary socialism. I explore this function in some detail, looking in particular at Bellamy's novel,

---

[19] Beetham 1987, p. 130.
[20] See Hook 1936, p. 316.

which, despite being published in America, manifests many of the characteristics typical of the ideology of a domestic state-socialist tradition, as its popularity and influence in England implies.

Chapter 3 focuses on feminist utopianism. It argues that its real import in the late nineteenth-century lay less in its manifest content, its blueprints for a future matriarchy or gynocracy, than in its latent content, its more modest fantasies of a like-minded community of women in the present. The feminist-utopian novel's political charge was conducted by the dream of an ideal fellowship of women writers and readers. This is because feminist-utopian fiction at the turn of the twentieth-century – by Jane Hume Clapperton, Gertrude Dix and Isabella Ford for example – was a product of the contradictory character of feminist politics at that time. Late-Victorian feminism was caught, historically, between what might be called the 'identity politics' of the New Woman and the mass movement that the suffrage campaign subsequently became. This chapter demonstrates that claim by exploring the socialist-feminist movement at the *fin de siècle* in relation to the 'politics of fellowship'. It also examines the appearance of feminist utopianism in response to a self-consciously anti-feminist form of political fantasy. It concludes with a detailed discussion of Elizabeth Corbett's *New Amazonia* (1889), in terms of its attempt to offer heuristic 'proof' of the possibility of an egalitarian future.

Chapter 4 traces the emergence of a 'cacotopian' form in the last three decades of the nineteenth-century. It claims that one of the ways in which conservative ideologues countered the perceived threat of the nascent socialist movement in England was by reformulating what the *Manifesto of the Communist Party* (1848) had called 'the nursery tale of the spectre of communism' – in terms of an imaginary history of revolutionary social upheaval in the present or the near future. The cacotopian future history, as the ensuing analysis makes clear, drew on the polemical rhetoric of anti-communism, recently reinvigorated by the spectacle of 'mob rule' provided by the Paris Commune of 1871. It applied the dystopian generic conventions pioneered by Colonel Chesney in *The Battle of Dorking* (1871) to the field of class conflict. The cacotopia comprises a utopian sub-genre that specialises in apocalyptic images of the proletariat. Bracebridge Hemyng's polemic, *The Commune in London* (1871), is prototypical. I also explore the tropes deployed in a number of later cacotopian novels, from William Delisle Hay's *The Doom of the Great City* (1880) to Charles Gleig's *When All Men Starve* (1898). Like all utopian fiction, these cacotopias, in spite of their reactionary content, were compelled by their form to interrogate the relations between present and future, and hence to question the stability and immutability of the *status quo*.

In Chapter 5, I analyse *News from Nowhere* (1891), by William Morris, as a utopian fiction that, in sharp contrast to other contemporary examples of the form, experimented with a dialectical relationship between present and future. Morris portrays the socialist future as a realm in which the alienating effects of commodity culture have been triumphantly overcome, and in which, consequently, the present is not absent, as it is in capitalist society, but present to itself. In *News from Nowhere*, Morris realises a consciousness of the present that, in Walter Benjamin's phrase, shatters the continuum of history. Developing an argument broached in Chapter 1, I begin by examining the problem of the perception of the present under capitalist relations of production, and proposing that utopian thought is an imaginary solution to it. Then I interpret Morris's Nowhere as a society characterised by a form of social fulfilment that is structurally alien to the reified culture of late nineteenth-century England. In a brief final section, I reflect on the political implications of Morris's exploration of the relationship between the future and the present.

In conclusion, I scan the various forms of fictional utopia at the *fin de siècle*, and infer that, irrespective of their particular political affiliations, all of them posit a readership to which they ascribe an important, even decisive historical role. The late-Victorian utopian novel secretly invests in its readers the hope that, collectively, they will form the nucleus of the ideal society that it has outlined. For all its supposedly exotic claims about the future, therefore, the literary utopia is in fact a relatively parochial form of political discourse. The somewhat cryptic title of this book – a satirical echo of an operetta by Gilbert and Sullivan, *Utopia (Limited); or, The Flowers of Progress* (1893), in which a utopian colony is turned into a joint stock company[21] – anticipates that particular contention. But it should be apparent that I believe that the prevailing limits of the late-Victorian political imaginary do not prevent William Morris, in *News from Nowhere*, from making a provocative demand on his readers' capacity for producing social dreams of their own – as part of a moment of utopian praxis.

[21] Gilbert 1893.

This book is intended as a contribution not only to the literary history of the utopian novel, and to the cultural history of the late nineteenth-century, but also to the Marxist critique of utopian thought. It is no doubt already evident that it does not attempt to revive the discourse of late-Victorian utopianism as an instrument of emancipatory politics today. On the contrary, it tries to demonstrate that, at the turn of the last century, the conception of the future that structured utopian thought was for the most part complicit, ideologically speaking, with the prevailing capitalist model of history as an evolutionary process of social improvement – even as this model of history entered into the state of crisis that, emblematically, I identify as the *fin de siècle*. To make this kind of claim is not however to imply that utopian thought at this time was inescapably conservative. That would obviously be absurd. Utopian novels like *Looking Backward*, which endeavoured to historicise the present from the perspective of the future, would not have been so popular if they had not responded to people's acutely felt anxieties about contemporary capitalism, and if they had not codified them in the form of powerful polemical attacks on its social depredations. It is instead to assert that the ideological content of late nineteenth-century utopian thought has received less scholarly attention than its critical content.

William Morris's intervention in the debate about the political value of utopian fantasy, in various lectures and reviews as well as in his own vision of a socialist society, is indispensable, because – like the philosophical criticism of Karl Marx in the 1840s – it provides the tools for a dialectical and materialist critique of this ideological content. It is the intellectual and political tradition marked out by Marx and Morris in the nineteenth-century, and by Benjamin and Bloch in the twentieth-century, that informs this book's enquiry into the relations between history and utopia at the *fin de siècle*. Although it constantly has to be reinvented, it is, I believe, this tradition that offers the most sophisticated framework for understanding the spirit of utopia that has recently flared up in the anti-capitalist movement at the turn of the twenty-first century.

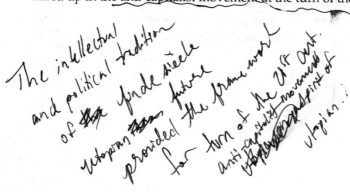

Chapter One

History and Utopia at the *Fin de Siècle*

I. Introduction

The political imaginary of Europe at the *fin de siècle* was haunted by spectres of a utopian future. In England prophets and fantasists of all kinds, confronting a decadent culture in a state of disquieting transformation, excitedly codified their social dreams of a different world order. In slightly jaded tones, the popular socialist Edward Carpenter noted in 1884 that 'it seems to be admitted now on all hands that the social condition of this country is about as bad as it can be', and that, in consequence, 'many schemes, more or less philanthropic or revolutionary, are proposed for its regeneration'. His own particular doctrine, one of 'human brotherhood', heralded the Democratic Age that would emerge, like a germinating flower, from the 'fierce parturition-struggle' of contemporary social conflict.[1] It had to compete with innumerable other utopian schemes promoted at this time.

Contemplating the apparently disproportionate number of utopian publications that populate 'the history of the development of political criticism', Antonio Gramsci insisted on starting 'with the attitude that this is a social phenomenon'. 'Does the (relatively)

---

[1] Carpenter 1885, p. 3.

mass publication of such literature coincide with definite historical periods, with the symptoms of deep socio-political upheavals?', he asked.[2] This chapter asks a similar, if more specific question: What are the historical preconditions for the reappearance of utopian fiction at the end of the nineteenth-century in England? As a preliminary step, it is important to explain the historical span covered by this book. Karl Mannheim warned that 'to fix the beginning of a movement at a given point in the stream of historical events is always hazardous and signifies a neglect of the forerunners of the movement'. He went on to advise, however, that 'the successful reconstruction of what is most essential in historical development depends upon the historian's ability to give the proper emphasis to those turning-points which are decisive in the articulation of phenomena'.[3]

What is the turning point for the development of utopian discourse at the end of the Victorian period? Throughout Europe, E.H. Carr once remarked, 'the failures and disillusionments which followed the revolutions of 1848 created a climate unpropitious to Utopias'.[4] In England, the 1850s and 1860s were affluent decades for the middle classes. For the working classes, concomitantly, they were decades of political retrenchment after the demise of Chartism: capitalism was experienced as a relatively stable system, to be accommodated rather than challenged directly. The social conditions in which utopian thought tends to thrive – which can be crudely characterised in terms of a manifest historical tension between dominant and emergent class forces – only arose when this consensus started to founder from the late 1860s and early 1870s.

The 1870s, I.F. Clarke confirms, represent 'the alpha point of modern futuristic fiction, when a new college of prophets and predictors first began to describe the new machines, the new societies, and the new wars that would follow in the next decade or the next century'. More specifically, Clarke has contended that 'the utopian literature of the last century divides sharply about the climacteric of 1871', after which point utopian novels and pamphlets are published almost every year. In fact, he has traced the birth of late-Victorian utopian fiction to a particular day in 1871, the first of May. On that date,

---

[2] Gramsci 1985, p. 238.
[3] Mannheim 1936, p. 190, n. 1.
[4] Carr 1969, p. 15.

In a period of challe... to fue accepted capitalist norm | utopia = alternative pursuit

when Samuel Butler left the manuscript of *Erewhon* (1872) at Chapman and Hall, both Bulwer-Lytton's *The Coming Race* (1871) and Chesney's *Battle of Dorking* (1871) were published.[5] These publications established a 'pattern of expectation' for the next thirty or forty years. They are premature symptoms of the fact that, especially during the Great Depression, of approximately 1873 to 1896, 'optimism about a future of indefinite progress gave way to uncertainty and a sense of agony, in the classical meaning of the word'.[6] A crisis of legitimation for the capitalist system prised open glimpses of an alternative future.

It is more difficult to define the outer limit of my object of study. Utopian fiction continued to be published in some quantity until the outbreak of global conflict in 1914. At that point, history intervened decisively to stop the blood supply that had hitherto sustained utopian thought. Social development was dramatically interrupted, collapsing the supports on which the troubled late-Victorian dream of progressive evolution had rested. In Europe in the 1910s, the technological power of the capitalist system was pressed into the service of a military-industrial crusade at once soterial and suicidal. Its structural contradictions induced a cataclysm. In such circumstances, the new machines and new societies of the late nineteenth-century prophets and predictors suddenly appeared in an obscene light, like a form of technological or sociological pornography. And, in this sense, the nineteenth-century utopia – Utopia (Limited); Or, The Flowers of Progress – was only finally buried beneath the feet of soldiers fighting trench warfare.

There is however some justification for claiming that the demise of utopian fiction occurred at an earlier date. Darko Suvin identifies himself 'with those who plump for the beginning of the 20th century', on the (admittedly vague) grounds that 'parallel to international and national economic developments, at that time had come into being those patterns of both bourgeois and working-class life which were to characterize Britain until the 1960s'.[7] Here, I take the turn of the century as an approximation for the end of an epoch in the production of utopian fiction. For symbolic purposes, H.G. Wells's *A Modern Utopia* (1905), a text that, like his other novels, this book alludes to only

---

[5] Clarke 1995, p. 1; Clarke 1958, p. 80; and Clarke 1979, p. 144.
[6] Landes 1969, pp. 240–41.
[7] Suvin 1983, p. 262.

incidentally, can be interpreted as a postscript to this particular tradition: Frank Manuel says that it was 'the last of the 19th-century utopias', and so the last important example of the old dream of progress that had embraced socialist as well as capitalist ideology in the previous century.[8] Wells drafted *A Modern Utopia* from 1903, when he fell in with the Fabians. And Fabianism itself, as A.L. Morton has written, 'is in a sense the last attempt to provide capitalism with a forward-looking body of ideas': 'after Wells there are not . . . any more Fabian Utopias, or any Utopias at all of a positive character'.[9] The early 1900s represent the point at which the utopian impulse of the late nineteenth-century, hitherto stimulated by the instability of the capitalist system, starts to peter out.

The period between 1870 and 1900 can be portrayed in terms of the space opened up between the collapse of two utopias of progress: first, that of an unfettered, free-trade capitalism; and second, that of a reformist socialism premised on the belief that systematic transformation can occur within the framework of the existing social order. It was a no-man's-land between two worlds, one apparently dying, the other powerless to be born. In 1909, the 'New Liberal' C.F.G. Masterman filed an obituary for the former utopia:

> The science which was to allay all diseases, the commerce which was to abolish war, and weave all nations into one human family, the research which was to establish ethics and religion on a secure and positive foundation, the invention which was to enable all humanity, with a few hours of not disagreeable work every day, to live for the remainder of their time in ease and sunshine – all these have become recognised as remote and fairy visions.[10]

At the time of the demise of this dream, the state-socialist utopia, built on a comparable faith in the progressive evolution of an increasingly technocratic society, was also enfeebled (like some poor relation whose life is irretrievably tied to the fortunes of a more senior member of the same family). Throughout Western Europe, 'intellectuals and artists who had been drawn to a broad, vaguely defined movement of workers by the general air of hope, confidence, even utopian expectation which it generated around itself now faced

---

[8] Manuel 1973, p. 80.
[9] Morton 1952, p. 193.
[10] Masterman 1909, pp. 214–15.

a movement uncertain of its future prospects and riven by internal and increasingly sectarian debates'.[11] In England, the formation of the Labour Party, 'a name which designates not an ideal society . . . but an existent interest', was, ironically, confirmation of this fact.[12]

In this chapter, I examine the socio-economic mutations of capitalism at the time of the Great Depression, and then explore the 'culture of expectancy' that germinated in this ominous climate. In the final section, I propose that utopianism is the symptomatic product of a period in which the present comprises a problem for representation. Under the conditions of modernity, utopian discourse tries to understand the transitional epoch in which it is produced from the pseudo-historical perspective of its imaginary futures.

II. The Great Depression

What explains the appearance of three important utopias in the spring of 1871? Suvin has claimed that, despite the socio-political complexity of this period, 'there is no doubt that the immediate stimuli were the Franco-Prussian War and the Paris Commune of 1871, and in a more diffuse way the political regroupings in the UK attendant upon the 1867 suffrage reform'. As he insists, 'deeper reasons must be sought in a crisis of confidence in societal values and stability, which – significantly enough – began already during the economic boom of the early 1870s, *predating* the onset of the 1873–1896 economic depression'.[13] The historical coordinates of this economic, political and cultural crisis need to be plotted with some care. Let us start by iterating the point that, in the early 1870s, throughout the theatre of capitalist production, the 'era of liberal triumph' that had been founded on the defeated revolutions of 1848 stuttered and faltered.

The events in France of 1870 and 1871 felt like a tremor. In effect, they were the warning of a fault-line that would finally reconfigure the global balance of power. As the Liberal historian G.M. Trevelyan was to write in 1944: 'The Franco-Prussian war of 1870 was the first shock. And during the three following decades America and Germany rose as manufacturing powers rival to our

[11] Hobsbawm 1998, p. 134.
[12] Anderson 1992, p. 37.
[13] Suvin 1983, p. 325.

own. The immensely greater natural resources of America, the scientific and technical education provided by far-sighted governments in Germany, told more and more every year'.[14] On the one hand, the Franco-Prussian War announced the climax of German unification – at a time when new nation-states were reconstituting territory throughout Europe. On the other hand, 'the Paris Commune was a signal that registered all over Europe' – at a time when 'the strength of independent labor movements indicated the rise of the working class as a dynamic factor and increased widespread middle-class anxieties'.[15] The concatenation of these events – the fact, in brief, that the War eventuated in a revolution – meant that, for the ruling class in England, from the start of the 1870s, the external threat of economic supersession was inextricably entwined with the internal threat of social revolution.

This helps to explain the apparent paradox of a crisis of confidence in societal values and stability that *anticipates* an economic depression. Not unlike the rapacious Parisian proletariat, or the arrogant German army, the consequences that attended the realignment of international capital on the continent threatened to assault the ideological bastions of free trade and libertarian individualism. Chesney's invasion-scare story, *The Battle of Dorking*, with its anxious allusions to communism and economic decline, is an early indication that the crisis that was to last intermittently from 1873 until the mid to late 1890s, is already descending on England. 'We thought we were living in a commercial millennium, which must last for a thousand years at least', the narrator ruefully remarks as he recalls his country's ruination.[16] As Eric Hobsbawm has insisted, the term 'Great Depression' is misleading, and not least because 'it was on balance a period of extraordinary advance rather than stagnation'. It is accurate, he claims, only if '"depression" indicates a pervasive . . . state of mind of uneasiness and gloom about the prospects of the British economy'.[17] The malaise was social as well as economic. It signifies a society hunched in uncertain expectancy, flinching before the prospect of capitalist crisis or working-class revolt. In this sense, the Great Depression predated the Great Depression. It is as if the *fin de siècle* arrived early in the nineteenth-century.

---

[14] Trevelyan 1944, p. 557.
[15] Kocka 1999, p. 246.
[16] Chesney 1871, p. 63.
[17] Hobsbawm 1968, pp. 103–4.

For all that, the character of the late-Victorian epoch is ultimately determined by the economic slump. The Great Depression 'has come to be regarded as forming a watershed between two stages of Capitalism: the earlier vigorous, prosperous and flushed with adventurous optimism; the latter more troubled, more hesitant and, some would say, already bearing the marks of senility and decay'.[18] Up to this point, Britain's reputation as a progressive nation had been underpinned by its role as the pioneer of industrial capitalism's productive forces. It had also depended on the peculiar political compromise of 1832, whereby, in the absence of a working-class electorate, the aristocracy applied the policy of the manufacturing class. Between the mid-1860s and the mid-1890s – despite the partial recoveries of 1880 and 1888 – these privileges disappeared. British capital was increasingly ill-equipped to cope with the country's immense productive system: on the one hand, it expanded production so as periodically to flood all the markets with produce; and on the other, it was less and less capable of holding its own against foreign competition. The depression of prices and profits, and the advance of strong nation-states in Germany, Japan and the USA, conspired to upset Britain's pre-eminent position on the world stage. In short, Britain became the first casualty of the capitalist mode of production's law of uneven development – the process whereby relative latecomers to the capitalist system, because they can modernise their economies without being constrained by an established industrial base, overtake nations previously dominant in the world market.

The economic era of the Great Depression was characterised by trends towards monopolisation, mass production, and international competition. It was under the conditions of this so-called 'second industrial revolution' that Britain struggled to contend with its rivals, who were richer in natural resources than it was. Instead, Britain consolidated its role in the underdeveloped world, as the dominant commercial power and the greatest source of international loan capital. This was the epoch of empire. The early 1870s can serve as historiographical shorthand for the incipient phase of monopoly capitalism. This was defined by the concentration of production, and of finance capital, in the form of monopolistic cartels, and by 'a colonial policy of monopolist possession of the territory of the world'.[19] The expansion of the role of the

[18] Dobb 1963, p. 300.
[19] Lenin 1968, p. 233.

state at home, and the prosecution of a pugnacious protectionism abroad, was, at the same time, a symptom of the collapse of the principles of unlimited competition and a response to the problem that it represented. So a socio-economic sea-change underlies the tidal sense of transitivity characteristic of the late-Victorian period.

To many commentators at the time, it seemed as if, for better or worse, the so-called 'Collectivist' economy was starting to evolve from the chrysalis of an 'Individualist' economy. In 1890, the American economist David Wells quoted a letter sent to him by an 'economic thinker and writer' of his acquaintance:

> What are the social and political results to follow the sweeping reconstruction of our material prices and our labor system? Are we not unconsciously, and from the sheer force of these new elements, drifting fast into a form of actual socialism – if not exactly such as the *doctrinaire* reformers preach, yet a reform which in respect to material interests swallows up individualism in huge combinations? . . . And if so, to what sort of social construction is it likely to lead?[20]

England bristled with this question in the 1880s. Its pressing importance appeared to be confirmed by the popularity of Henry George, the influential North-American author of *Progress and Poverty* (1879), which championed land reform on the basis of a 'Single Tax'. During his lecture tour of England and Ireland in 1882, radicals and reformist intellectuals heralded him as the prophet of a new political economy. The formation of the Democratic Federation and the Fabian Society in the early 1880s intensified this sense of a subterranean social shift.

Most importantly, perhaps, the comparative radicalism of Liberal policies such as the Irish Land Acts of 1881 deepened a widespread impression that there was state opposition to private property. The state's protrusion into public affairs, and the fading influence of *laissez-faire* principles, was interpreted as irrefutable proof that, as Robert Blatchford put it in 1893, 'Socialism has begun'.[21] 'A new sense of urgency characterised discussions of the extent to which current legislation was, albeit in a covert and piecemeal way, embracing

---

[20] Wells 1890, p. 326.
[21] Blatchford 1893, p. 105.

Socialism and abandoning the older principles of limited state-intervention'. Collectivism, according to Stefan Collini, was a general description of this tendency towards what appeared to be a new sort of social construction.[22]

Back in 1879, the English economist William Cunningham had tried to console the readership of the *Contemporary Review* with his claim that it is 'not as a remedy for the miseries of the poor, but rather as an alleviation of the cares of the rich that Socialism is coming upon us'.[23] During the social disturbances of the following decade, this statement must have seemed naïve as well as cynical to many socialists. For in the late 1880s and early 1890s in particular, the state came under considerable pressure from below – from both the unemployed and the organised proletariat – to provide a remedy for the miseries of the poor. These years were marked by rioting and demonstrations, as well as by the rise of the 'New Unionism'. So, if the working class was 'still an embryo, of which no one can yet quite forsee the final development', as Matthew Arnold said in 1868, it nonetheless displayed signs of independent activity.[24] Politically speaking, it was becoming prehensile. Like the Chartists almost half a century earlier, certain sections of the working class in the late nineteenth-century were starting to demand control over their destinies.

It is in the context of this advance in working-class consciousness that Cunningham's consolation to his immediate audience of middle-class readers looks so canny. It is revealing, because it articulates the logic according to which, increasingly, the ruling class tried to steer the nation through its economic and social crisis. The free market was to be tamed or domesticated by the state. The political compromises of the period were designed to appease the disproportionate demands of the populace. 'The first steps in the creation of a mass democratic culture', from the 1884 Reform Act to the 1888 Local Government Act, were the product of a 'passive revolution', intended to forestall more fundamental social transformation.[25] The 'transition' of the late nineteenth-century was only another turn of the screw. Even at the height of *laissez-faire*, the hand of the state had intervened to protect the free play of

---

[22] Collini 1979, p. 33.
[23] Cunningham 1879, p. 252.
[24] Arnold 1965, p. 132.
[25] Hall and Schwarz 1985, p. 25.

the market, so collectivist policy in any case scarcely marked a radical break with liberal economic practice. Moreover, as Hobsbawm confirms, the period of the Great Depression produced no real change in either social or economic policy, 'for (to the lasting misfortune of Britain) the depression eventually passed before business and politics had been sufficiently frightened. It merely raised the question whether traditional orthodoxy, and especially its quasi-religious symbol Free Trade, should be abandoned'.[26]

The confidence of the ruling class, in other words, was shaken, and not shattered. Under pressure from increased international competition and reduced profit margins, employers were aggressive in their attempts to impose low wages and rigid discipline on workers in the 1890s. But this did not mean that capitalism had triumphed. George Bernard Shaw, writing in 1892, was not the only commentator to assume that 'insurrectionism will reappear at the next depression of trade as surely as the sun will rise to-morrow morning'.[27] A subjective state of insecurity persisted throughout the last ten years of the nineteenth-century, and continued into the twentieth-century. In the years before the First World War, 'wisps of violence hung in the English air, symptoms of a crisis in economy and society which the self-confident opulence of the architecture of Ritz hotels, pro-consular palaces, West End theatres, department stores and office blocks could not quite conceal'.[28] So the Great Depression also outlasted its allotted time. The capitalist system continued to be haunted by the spectre of its own eclipse.

It can be concluded that, throughout the last three decades of the nineteenth-century, the socialist alternative served as a determinate absence, a non-event that was nonetheless decisive. As Stephen Yeo emphasises, 'the fact that the breakthrough did not occur should not blind us to the reality of the possibility as perceived at the time'.[29] At the peak of the 'Socialist Revival', in August 1889, the month in which the Dock Strike started in the East End, David Wells surveyed the English economic crisis from across the Atlantic and risked a prognostication: 'Out of these changes will probably come further disturbances, which to many thoughtful and conservative minds seem full of menace of a mustering of the barbarians from within rather than as of old from without,

---

[26] Hobsbawm 1968, p. 202.
[27] Shaw 1892, p. 10.
[28] Hobsbawm 1968, p. 163.
[29] Yeo 1977, p. 20.

for an attack on the whole present organization of society, and even the permanency of civilization itself'.[30] 'Big with destiny', as Edward Carpenter half-satirically put it, it is scarcely surprising that turn-of-the-century capitalism, at least in its *laissez-faire* form, appeared to have come to its term.[31] The closing decades of the nineteenth-century comprised a period of expectancy.

III. The culture of expectancy

'Expectancy belongs by nature to a time balanced uneasily between two great periods of change', Masterman commented in 1905; 'on the one hand is a past still showing faint survivals of vitality; on the other is the future but hardly coming to birth'.[32] Utopianism is symptomatic of an era in which there is this widespread perception that one epoch of history is in its decline and another is announcing its ascendancy.

The diffuse sense of foreboding that accompanies this perception at the turn of the twentieth-century is not incompatible with utopianism. On the contrary, a certain suspension of the political is one of the latter's preconditions. For a utopian structure of feeling is the product of social and ideological conflict. The hegemonic culture of any society that consists of contradictory class forces will reflect the fears of the dominant class for its future history; and these fears, in a refracted form, will reflect the hopes of the dominated classes that inform them. Culture is, after all, a composite relation between its dominant, residual and emergent elements. Any epoch is therefore a dialectical cultural process shaped by 'the complex interrelations between movements and tendencies both within and beyond a specific and effective dominance'.[33] For this reason, in Ernst Bloch's phrase, 'there is no hope without anxiety and no anxiety without hope, [and] they keep each other hovering in the balance'.[34] In the late-Victorian period, utopianism is not some simplistic counter-cultural optimism that emerges as a response to the pessimism of official culture. It is a symptom of the fact that the future cannot be foretold, and that the present cannot be interpreted, for all the signs of social

---

[30] Wells 1890, p. vi.
[31] Carpenter 1916, p. 247.
[32] Masterman 1905, p. xii.
[33] Williams 1977, p. 121.
[34] Bloch 1986, p. 333.

transformation. It is the product of an emergent culture characterised by expectancy – an unstable compound of hope and fear that is in part dependant on the dominant culture of *apprehension*.

If 'every age has had its hopes', as William Morris pointed out in 1885, then 'those hopes have been stronger not in the heyday of the epoch which has given them birth, but rather in its decadence and times of corruption'. He continued as follows:

> In sober truth it may well be that these hopes are but a reflection in those that live happily and comfortably of the vain longings of those others who suffer with little power of expressing their sufferings in an audible voice: when all goes well the happy world forgets these people and their desires, sure as it is that their woes are not dangerous to them the wealthy: whereas when the woes and grief of the poor begin to rise to a point beyond the endurance of men, fear conscious or unconscious falls upon the rich, and they begin to look about them to see what there may be among the elements of their society which may be used as palliatives for the misery which, long existing and ever growing greater among the slaves of that society, is now at last forcing itself on the attention of the masters.

For Morris, the optimism that permeates the spirit of the time is an abstract reflection of the concrete aspirations that animate the people. The hopes of the age, 'hopes that look to something beyond the life of the age itself, hopes that try to pierce into the future', are a gleam emitted by middle-class culture as it dully mirrors and distorts the desires of the working class.[35] The utopian temper of the late-Victorian period is in a relation of relative autonomy to the mood of the humble mass. Many middle-class socialists, for whom this mass was not the fundamental instrument of social transformation, as it was emphatically for Morris, were more or less fearful of a full-blooded expression of the aspirations of the people to whom they appealed for help on the more or less triumphant pathway to the future. So, if hope was indissociable from the fear of its historical betrayal, it was also inseparable from the fear of its total fulfilment.

I explore this ideological contradiction in Chapter 2, where I interpret the period's state-socialist utopian politics as a product of the discrepant social

---

[35] Morris 1915a, p. 59.

position of reformist intellectuals. In the present context, it is sufficient to emphasise that, as an emergent structure of feeling associated with a social sub-formation that 'appears to break away from its class norms, though it retains its substantial affiliation', utopianism is a compound of hope and anxiety.[36] At the turn of the last century, utopian discourse was predicated on an underlying concern that, in the face of socio-economic crisis, civilisation itself would collapse into pandemonium. As David Wells observed:

> One of the remarkable features of the situation has been the tendency of many of the best men in all countries to rush, as it were, to the front, and appalled by some of the revelations which economic investigators everywhere reveal, and with the emotional largely predominating over their perceptive and reasoning faculties, to proclaim that civilization is a failure, or that something ought immediately to be done, and more especially by the state, without any very clear or definite idea of what can be done, or with any well-considered and practical method of doing.[37]

The futurist literature of the period, for all that it is superficially rationalist or even positivistic in its outlook, is apocalyptic in tone to the extent that, more or less implicitly, it pushes a dystopian prospect of the development of society into proximity with a utopian one.

Typically, the central, utopian, tableau of Bellamy's *Looking Backward* (1888) is framed by two fragmentary images of dystopia. The first is the brief glimpse – afforded by the utopian tour-guide Dr. Leete's reference to the 'followers of the red flag' in the twentieth-century – of revolutionaries 'burning, sacking, and blowing people up'. The second is the hero Julian West's nightmare about the Boston he has left behind him, a world of rampant commercial competition that amounts to a state of siege ('these mills and shops were so many forts, each under its own flag, its guns trained on the mills and shops about it, and the sappers busy below, undermining them').[38] These crepuscular images, of socialists and plutocrats respectively, are the side panels of a triptych whose central vision is the secular equivalent of a sight of the heavenly city.

If utopia 'is primarily a vision of the orderly city and of a city-dominated society', as Northrop Frye has claimed, then *Looking Backward* is the summit

---

[36] Williams 1977, pp. 134–35.
[37] Wells 1890, pp. 428–29.
[38] Bellamy 1888, pp. 352–53, 448.

of this tradition because it confronts the disorderly reality of the city, symbolic of the crisis of civilisation itself, more clearly than its precursors.[39] In particular, the apocalyptic quality of West's nightmare of returning to the nineteenth-century stems from the force of Bellamy's parabolic description of the city as the epitome of a specifically modern form of alienation. Boston's streets and rookeries, which 'reek[ ] with the effluvia of a slave ship's between-decks', nurture a race of thanatoids. Confronting 'the festering mass of human wretchedness', West is forced to bear witness to what he identifies as another Golgotha.[40] In utopian thought at this time, the city serves as a metaphor for the power of industrial society to redeem or destroy the promise of Western civilisation. It is the repository of social reformists' hopes and fears because, if it is a dystopic space, where individuals are reduced to monadic fractions of the 'festering mass', it is at the same time utopic in its capacity for forging 'the new collective conscience which is the social product of the urban experience'.[41] The *fin-de-siècle* city was above all the battlefield on which the fate of humanity was finally to be determined. It stood at what Bloch called the 'Front of history' – whether the Victorians envisaged its abolition, its effortless sublation or, less grandly, its gradual transformation into a garden suburb.

Naturally, the nation's social tensions were conducted by its cities. The agricultural crisis of the early 1870s, which had been caused by falling prices and the flight of capital to industry, led to casualisation in the countryside and epidemic unemployment in towns throughout Britain. Their atmosphere crackled with socio-political static – particularly when the threat of industrial conflagration intensified in the later 1880s. But it was London that dominated the utopian and anti-utopian imaginary in the late nineteenth-century. In *After London* (1885), an extraordinary pastoral fantasy by the naturalist Richard Jefferies, the city is a pestilential swampland, the noxious site of some half-forgotten holocaust that has transformed human destiny irredeemably. It is the book's obscure, half-absent symbolic centre. London is the emblematic setting too for *News from Nowhere* (1891), a utopian fiction that, in its portrayal of the city as a civic environment furtively recovered by primeval woods and

---

[39] Frye 1973, p. 27.
[40] Bellamy 1888, pp. 456–58.
[41] Williams 1973, p. 272.

meadows, deliberately redeems the disaster of which Jefferies dreamed. As Krishan Kumar testifies, 'in its bewildering contrasts of the extremes of wealth and poverty, glitter and squalor, West End and East End, it seemed, like the new industrial society as a whole, to be pregnant with as many glorious possibilities as frightful disasters'.[42]

From the mid-1880s, the West and the East End of London, symbolic of what the *Quarterly Review* called 'the complete separation of the residences of different classes of the community', were convulsed with contractions of the body politic.[43] But despite this breach (commemorated in the appendix to Charles Booth's *Life and Labour of the People of London* (1889), a map of the metropolis in which the poor areas are a dark smear against the red and gold background that represents the respectable parts of the city centre), their connections were becoming increasingly clear. 'If you want to see the origin and explanation of an East London rookery', Carpenter wrote with stark simplicity in 1884, 'you must open the door and walk in upon some fashionable dinner party at the West End'.[44] In the East End, an 'Outcast London' was excavated in the course of social investigations carried out by strangely engrossed members of the middle class. In the West End, riots and demonstrations revealed the murky depths of society to the horrified gaze of the 'respectabilities'. On these occasions, when the brutal social contradictions with which the city bristled culminated in what Marx had described as 'the shock of body against body', the 'final denouement' of capitalist society suddenly seemed at least imaginable.[45]

The apocalypse did not take place – to the relief as well as the frustration of many socialists and social reformists. In fact, the most dramatic of these episodes, 'Bloody Sunday', when the police and army ruthlessly suppressed a demonstration against the Irish Coercion Act on 13 November 1887, marked an impasse. Exposing 'the true face of reaction', it precipitated 'the turn towards Fabianism and gradualism, the spread of disillusionment in revolutionary organization and tactics'.[46] In this way, it fortified reformist trends within the socialist movement. It had become apparent that the climactic process by

---

[42] Kumar 1987, p. 171.
[43] Quoted in Briggs 1963, p. 314.
[44] Carpenter 1885, p. 9.
[45] Marx 1976c, p. 212.
[46] Thompson 1977, p. 502.

which capitalism was to mutate into socialism would not commence tomorrow. Consequently, a gradualist strategy or long game now seemed fully justified to many on the Left. For Bernard Shaw, the 'defeat' of Bloody Sunday confirmed that 'the way was clear at last for Fabianism'.[47] It was not that capitalism would not be superseded by socialism, but that it would happen slowly and peacefully, as part of a well-nigh natural process, when people's hearts and minds were prepared for it. The end was not in doubt, only the means. Insurrectionism had manifestly failed.

This interpretation of events reinforced the influence on the Left of what Yeo has identified as the 'religion of socialism'. For if it was at present useless to try to seize the historical initiative, it was still certain that, in relation to the hidden hand of history, these were 'special times'.[48] If the apocalypse had been postponed, a spirit of apocalypticism persisted. 'All the time the Socialist clock was really going forward', as Carpenter hopefully affirmed, and 'the nation steadily and almost unconsciously became saturated with the new ideas'.[49] An undercurrent of expectancy persisted. And, in the absence of any deeper proof of an immediate social transformation, faith in a different future fed off itself, as doubt does. It is as if the emergent culture had overlooked the fact that it was merely 'pre-emergent' – 'active and pressing, but not yet fully articulated'.[50] This is in part because, in the political mainstream, a prospective spirit quickened contemporary debates about the construction of a new state capable of controlling mass forces. More importantly, though, it is because of the peculiar nature of the politics of the cultural periphery. Utopianism is the quite predictable feature of a period in which, as the novelist W.H. Hudson phrased it, 'ten thousand fungoid cults . . . sprung up and flourished exceedingly in the muddy marsh of man's intellect'.[51]

Unofficial culture was itself a kind of muddy marsh at the *fin de siècle*, in which positivists and anti-vivisectionists, socialists and theosophists, freely cross-fertilised, 'participating in a common quest for a new unity amid the bewildering changes of modern life'.[52] The syncretic quality of this late-

---

[47] Shaw 1892, p. 10.
[48] Yeo 1977, p. 19.
[49] Carpenter 1916, p. 247.
[50] Williams 1977, p. 126.
[51] Hudson 1887, p. 265.
[52] Pierson 1979, p. 26.

Victorian counter-culture is evoked, in a tone of revealing and faintly comic gravity, in one description of a meeting of the Liverpool branch of the Land Nationalization Society, made up of Bellamy's British supporters, in 1891: 'There were present Socialists, Trade Unionists, Co-operationists, Anti-Co-operationists, Good Templars, Theosophists, gentleman holding important positions under government, Traders, thus making in all a very sound representative meeting'.[53] Morris's friend Ernest Belfort Bax fulminated against the 'mephitic social atmosphere' in which these ideologies flourished alongside his particular brand of scientific socialism. But, like others in the movement for social reform, he identified it as an effect of 'the rank overgrowth of an effete civilization', and hence as proof of the fertility of history, of its readiness to produce some more virile alternative.[54]

This farraginous culture thus performed a compensatory function for those who were disappointed by the unpunctuality of history. Utopian promise is especially important when the opportunity to implement real social change momentarily comes to seem slightly more remote. Parousiamania, so to speak, is a symptom of disappointment as well as hope. It is not perhaps surprising, therefore, that, from 1889, there was a considerable increase in the number of utopias published in the English-speaking world. Nor is it anomalous that a small practical utopian movement, 'in part a reflection of political disillusionment', sprang up at this time.[55] The 1880s and 1890s provided the perfect conditions for utopian thought, because they reinforced the sense in which, like the background against which the classical utopias were composed in the sixteenth-century, 'the age was at once an age of new hopes, and of new despair as these hopes were continually frustrated'.[56]

If the air was thick with utopian thought, this tended to obscure the objective likelihood of social transformation in the future. Late nineteenth-century utopianism was disproportionate to the socio-political conditions that produced it. In a sense, though, this disproportion is a structural property of utopia. By definition, as Jameson emphasises, 'Utopian visions are not yet themselves a politics'.[57] This is, at the same time, the strength and weakness of utopian

---

[53] 'An Echo from the Mersey' 1891, p. 126.
[54] Bax 1891, p. x.
[55] Pierson 1973, p. 224.
[56] Morton 1990, p. 81.
[57] Jameson 1991, p. 159.

thought: it goes beyond its age and it lags behind it. To the extent to which the utopian impulse is not tied to an instrumental political force, it is condemned to outrun reality only to have to wait for reality finally to catch up with it. It overleaps itself and falls on the other side.

In the late-Victorian period, utopian thought is a product of the fact that revolutionary social change was, to all extents and purposes, impossible. Perry Anderson rightly asserts that 'the very insignificance of socialism as a political force in England, at a time when no mass labour movement existed to pose urgent day-to-day problems of mobilization, encouraged a tendency to futurism'.[58] The existing system was in crisis; but, in the absence of a mass movement capable of replacing it with something else, it overcame its own contradictions, or suspended them at least. The Great Depression 'was a moment of truth' for British capital, but it 'was soon shut out again'.[59] One consequence of this was that an alternative to the competitive system became, briefly, conceivable. It too was shut out even as it was opened up. In spite of some apocalyptic posturing by men such as Hyndman, and the occasional panic of the middle classes, the end of capitalism was not a real historical possibility. So, while humankind 'inevitably sets itself only such tasks as it is able to solve', as Marx remarked, it also dreams of solutions for which the material conditions do not yet exist.[60]

The socialist utopians of the *fin de siècle* were idealists – in the political sense that they were optimists, but also in the philosophical sense that they set out 'from what men say, imagine, conceive, [and] from men as narrated, thought of, imagined, conceived, in order to arrive at men in the flesh'.[61] Morris himself, for all his philosophical materialism, is not immune to this claim. His 'Foreword' to Thomas More's *Utopia* (1893), in which he claimed that 'the change of ideas concerning "the best state of a publique weale" . . . is the great event of the end of this century', is symptomatic of this tendency.[62] But Norman Britton, writing in *Progress* about 'Socialism as a tendency, an aspiration', provides a better example of the temptation to interpret ideas as the determining influence on historical development: 'With Utopianism for

---

[58] Anderson 1980, p. 171.
[59] Hobsbawm 1968, p. 168.
[60] Marx 1987, p. 263.
[61] Marx and Engels 1976a, p. 36.
[62] Morris 1936, p. 289.

its propeller and Science at the helm', he proclaimed, 'Humanity cannot but speed forward to a new heaven and a new earth'.[63]

In the light of Britton's boastful announcement, a critical kernel can still be recovered from his editor G.W. Foote's somewhat curmudgeonly essay on 'Social Dreams' in the same journal, *Progress*: 'Let those who have a taste for such things remodel society according to their fancy; and let us, if we are so disposed, entertain ourselves with their schemes. But do not let us think that fancies are easily translated into facts. Nature, although kind, is also stern; and she has designed that, if our imaginations may soar, our hands must strive and our feet must plod'.[64] Many of Foote's contemporaries forgot that, for all the ferment of the end of the century, tick followed tock for the workers on the factory floors. Inflationary rhetoric of the kind that he quietly criticises is a recurrent feature of memoirs of the 1880s and 1890s. Carpenter recalled that these years 'marked the oncoming of a great new tide of human life over the Western World': feminism, socialism, anarchism and 'the Theosophic movement' – 'all constituted so many streams and headwaters converging, as it were, to a great river'.[65] This efflorescence on the surface of society was widely taken as confirmation of a more profound transformation. Effects were confused with causes. Amidst the messianic excitement, utopian writing entreated: 'To announce oneself . . . is that not already to be there in some way?'.[66]

Utopian thought, in other words, rounded upon itself as proof of the imminence of fundamental social transformation. History was at this time saturated with the utopian claims of the imagination. The illusory effect of this was that, as in the 1960s, according to Herbert Marcuse, 'the utopian claims of the imagination [seemed to] have become saturated with historical reality'.[67] Engels observed in 1883 that 'with every great revolutionary movement the question of "free love" comes in to the foreground'.[68] In the mid-1890s, at the time of the controversy surrounding the New Woman's ascendancy, it is as if, in a reversal of logic, feminists and socialists interpreted

---

[63] Britton 1884, p. 121.
[64] Foote 1886, p. 194.
[65] Carpenter 1916, p. 245.
[66] Derrida 1994, p. 36.
[67] Marcuse 1956, p. 156.
[68] Engels 1883, p. 113.

the proliferation of discussions about sex and sexual equality as positive evidence of the spectral presence of some alternative future. But history proceeded instead by its bad side. The subjective and objective conditions for revolutionary change did not coincide.

According to Bloch, during the 'sentimental or angry red dawn' of the Russian Narodniks in the late nineteenth-century, the conversations of revolutionaries 'utopianized on the dusty boulevards of Russian provincial towns', helping to create the revolutionary climate in which, 'later in the big cities, with increasing socialist clarity', the ideal of equality could be made concrete. The dreams of the English socialist utopians, by comparison, failed to pass from the prefiguration of a peripheral, heterogeneous culture 'to a more or less socially sharpened, socially mandated premonition'.[69] The utopian structure of feeling at the *fin de siècle* described what was, finally, only a phantom pregnancy.

IV. Modernity and utopia

The late nineteenth-century, an epoch of unprecedented expansion in the advertising industry, was a period in European history when the adjective 'new' was applied to almost every product of artistic and commercial culture. In the 1890s, in particular, the rhetoric of marketeers and critics – announcing the arrival of the new art, the new literature, the new fiction, the new journalism, the new humour, the new criticism, the new hedonism, the new morality and the new woman – mimicked the vocabulary of an ever more articulate commodity. 'That very word "new," strikes as it were the dominant note in the trend of present-day thought, present-day effort and aspiration', Emily Morgan-Cockerell commented in an article of 1896.[70] It was the semiotic of a capitalist society steeped in a sense of its exceptional historical status.

It is, of course, crucial not to take the cultural commentators of the *fin de siècle* at their word. 'The new is the longing for the new, not the new itself', Theodor Adorno once observed: 'that is what everything new suffers from'.[71] The concept of the new, as Morgan-Cockerell's opinion testifies, is inescapably

[69] Bloch 1986, p. 117.
[70] Morgan-Cockerell 1896, p. 339.
[71] Adorno 1997, p. 32.

shaped by a utopian impulse. When Havelock Ellis proclaimed, in *The New Spirit* (1890), that 'the growth of social organization is now beginning to open up possibilities which a few years ago would have seemed Utopian', he simply expressed a hope. The inter-imperial conflicts of capitalism in its monopolistic phase scarcely constituted a fertile climate for the international community of which he dreamed. The possibilities that he had in mind – the 'disappearance of war' for example – were finally a form of wish-fulfilment fantasy.[72]

But to point this out is not to accept that the hopes expressed in *The New Spirit*, and in contemporaneous publications by utopians, were completely unrealistic. The development of industrial technology, as well as the expansion of popular education, had created socio-economic conditions in which the capitalist division of labour was not, in fact, imperative. Moreover, the advent of an organised labour movement made it evident that capitalism was, at least potentially, susceptible to popular revolution. One historian has insisted that, in order to understand the moods of late nineteenth-century socialists in Britain, it is important to appreciate 'that such a day was indeed no dream but had a real basis'.[73] It might be more dialectical to claim that such a day was indeed a dream, but that it was a dream founded on a real basis. Utopian fantasy was germinated in the loam of material possibilities at the *fin de siècle*, however implausible the fulfilment of those possibilities remained under the contemporary capitalist social formation.

In spite of its utopian impulse, or perhaps because of it, the concept of the new is haunted by the image of homogeneous, empty time. Certainly, it is noticeable that its ascendancy in end-of-the-century England coincided with the decline of the possibility of replacing capitalism with a different system. But it is not the case that, as Adorno elsewhere contended, 'the cult of the new, and thus the idea of modernity, is a rebellion against the fact that there is no longer anything new'.[74] It does not necessarily admit to the end of history. The 'new', to repeat, is a longing for the new. It is the symptomatic product of contradictory historical circumstances in which rapid changes are taking place in a system that is ultimately secure from

[72] Ellis 1890, pp. 18, 19.
[73] Yeo 1980, p. 122.
[74] Adorno 1974, p. 235.

systematic transformation. The discourse on modernity and the new in the later nineteenth-century describes an optimistic attempt to come to terms with the discrepant nature of capitalist society, which opens up historical opportunities even as it closes them down. So the late-Victorian period was one of those 'moments in history [in which] the topic "modernity" might be used just as an attempt at self-definition, as a way of diagnosing one's own present'.[75]

The experience of modernity at this time, premised on the acceleration and concentration of European capital at a time of imperial expansion, can be adumbrated in terms of a double movement: the opening up of geographical space, under the impact of capitalism in its imperial phase; and, correspondingly, the contraction of social space, as a result of rapid developments in the technology of transport and telecommunication. The corollary of this was 'the discovery of world-wide simultaneity' at the turn of the century: 'the present was everywhere and one could communicate with people all over the place'.[76] This 'radical readjustment in the sense of time and space in economic, political, and cultural life', a form of 'time-space compression', occasioned what David Harvey calls a 'crisis of representation'. First manifest from the 1840s and 1850s, but reinforced to particularly dramatic effect at the *fin de siècle*, this crisis affected classical forms across the arts. In the field of literary production, the realist novel, which had been premised on the assumption that stories can be chronicled as if events occur in a coherent, consecutive order, seemed inconsistent with a world marked by spatial and temporal insecurity.[77]

In *Degeneration* (1895), his bitter diatribe against *fin-de-siècle* culture, Max Nordau registered this crisis when he described the neurotic consequences of living in modern urban society. He complained about 'the vertigo and whirl of our frenzied life, the vastly increased number of sense impressions and organic reactions, and therefore of perceptions, judgements, and motor impulses, which at present are forced into a given time'.[78] The aesthetic movements that he decried in this hectoring tract were precisely those that,

NORDAU

Critique on the culture

---

[75] de Man 1983, p. 143.
[76] Novotny 1994, p. 27.
[77] Harvey 1990, pp. 260–63.
[78] Nordau 1895, p. 39.

in addition to displaying symptoms of moral corruption, tried to reproduce the mental and physiological effects of 'time-space compression' in their formal experiments: the proponents of Mysticism (symbolists such as Stéphane Mallarmé), of Ego-mania (Henrik Ibsen and his acolytes), and of False Realism (the school of Emile Zola) are subject to especially splenetic complaint. Utopianism at this time did not find expression in experimental literary forms. It was reliant on narrative structures that reflected a quite conventional view of history as a consecutive process, and it was therefore incapable of capturing the impact of modernity on the experience of social life. But like the radical aesthetics cursed by Nordau, it was a literary response to the challenge to grasp a present simultaneously new and not-new, at once rapidly changing and stubbornly static. The discourse of utopia was used to read an unreadable reality, a disoriented world that, because of the accelerated metabolism of modern society, seemed at the same time too abstract and too concrete to be understood.

Utopian fiction attempted to historicise the present from the perspective of a fantastical future. It was an exercise in what might be called 'historicity'. For Fredric Jameson, historicity is the attempt to grasp the contemporaneous as part of an historical process. It is 'neither a representation of the past nor a representation of the future (although its various forms *use* such representations): it can first and foremost be defined as a perception of the present as history; that is, as a relationship to the present which somehow defamiliarizes it and allows that distance from immediacy which is at length characterized as a historical perspective'.[79] In utopia, the present is the past of a specific, fictional future. Time-travelling to the future, it transpires, is about the return journey to the present traced by the forward motion of the time machine itself. As Morris wrote, 'no age can see itself: we must stand some way off before the confused picture with its rugged surface can resolve itself into its due order, and seem to be something with a definite purpose carried through all its details'.[80] Utopia provides an historicist perspective – a meta-perspective – from which the present appears in its approximate proportions. It is, to quote Paul Ricoeur, 'an empty place from which to look at ourselves'.[81]

---

[79] Jameson 1991, p. 284.
[80] Morris 1915a, p. 21.
[81] Ricoeur 1986, p. 15.

Utopian thought is eccentric; or, as Ernest Belfort Bax phrased it in his *Outlooks from the New Standpoint* (1891), it is 'a hybrid pseudo-reality . . . which is neither past, present, nor future'. Bax complained that contemporary utopian romances represented a pointless attempt to escape the inescapable opacity of the lived present:

> When we ourselves are part and parcel of a social state, when we ourselves are a portion of the reality of a given society, bathed in its categories and inhaling its atmosphere, our imagination cannot transcend it to any appreciable extent, if at all. Our logical faculty can, indeed, pierce through, or, as it were, dissolve the reality for abstract thought, and show the lines on which the new principle growing up within it is going, but our imagination is quite incapable of envisaging the reality in its final and complete shape. We can just as little conceive how the men of the future will envisage our civilisation of to-day – how they will represent to themselves our thoughts and feelings, aspirations and antipathies – for when all this social life has become objective, with all its categories stiff and lifeless, it will be seen in its true proportions and significance.[82]

Bax's comparison between, on the one hand, utopian thought, and, on the other, the hopeless attempt to conceive 'how the men of the future will envisage our civilization of to-day', is instructive. It provokes a suspicion that these imaginative gestures are in fact mutually complicit. To think a future civilisation is to think the future of civilisation – that is, to picture civilisation in an historical context. It is an effort to freeze the flow of contemporary social life in order to identify its posterior significance. But the present is peculiarly resistant to this interpretative discipline. And in spite of his close attention to the darkness of the lived moment, Bax is insensitive to the fact that, as Bloch indicates, 'the lived darkness is so strong that it is not even confined to its most immediate nearness'.[83] Not even the passing of time can be relied upon to resolve the present into its proper shape.

Most importantly, Bax fails to appreciate that utopia may be an important part of the attempt to pierce reality. The utopian wager is that the imaginative faculty furnishes a more effective means than the logical faculty for penetrating

---

[82] Bax 1891, pp. viii–ix.
[83] Bloch 1986, p. 296.

what Morris called 'the murky smoked glass of the present condition of life amongst us'.[84] The best utopian fiction, according to Suvin, is about 'clairvoyance – literally, clear seeing – of what's hidden yet advancing upon us'.[85] To quote Morris once more, it tries to detect 'the silent movement of real history which is still going on around and underneath our raree show'.[86] In this sense, it is less about the future (as a distinct category in opposition to the past), than it is about 'the Front', the outer limit or horizon of the present. Utopia tries to occupy this Front. It prises open a caesura in the present. It is an internal distantiation of the present – 'distance, right within'.[87]

This utopian perspective – that of a point of retrospection pleated into the outer limit of the present – can be explained in terms of the figure of anamorphosis. Anamorphosis 'is any kind of construction that is made in such a way that by means of an optical transposition a certain form that wasn't visible at first sight transforms itself into a readable image'.[88] The most famous example of anamorphosis is no doubt the distorted death's head superimposed by Holbein on his painting of *The Ambassadors*: the skull's form only emerges when the spectator stands askance to the picture. 'We must throw the entire painting out of perspective in order to bring into perspective what our usual mode of perception cannot comprehend'.[89] Utopia is a fictional future from which the stain of the present assumes an intelligible historical form. Bloch describes this stain as a 'blindspot in the mind, this darkness of the lived moment'. And in his characteristically cryptic, expressionist style, he explains that, from the prospect of utopia, 'a sudden, not historically horizontal, but vertically striking light then falls on immediacy so that it almost appears to be mediated, though without ceasing to be immediate or overclose nearness'.[90]

In 1895, Grant Allen published *The British Barbarians*, a utopian satire on nineteenth-century social conventions from the vantage point of a visitor from

---

[84] Morris 1994, p. 338.
[85] Suvin 2001, p. 237.
[86] Morris 1914, p. 315.
[87] Bloch 1988, p. 207.
[88] Lacan 1992, p. 135.
[89] Greenblatt 1980, p. 19. Greenblatt argues that the narrative displacements of More's *Utopia* 'are the closest equivalent in Renaissance prose to the anamorphic' (p. 22).
[90] Bloch 1986, pp. 290, 294.

the twenty-fifth-century. He subtitled this book 'A Hill-top Novel'. Frustrated with the censorious influence of magazine editors after the controversy surrounding his bestseller *The Woman Who Did* (1895), Allen formulated the phrase to identify novels that had not been interfered with before their publication. These novels were to be marked, he claimed, by their independence and 'purity'. It is no accident that he coined the term in conjunction with a fiction set in the future. As Allen explained, he picked his emblematic image because he wrote from a study high up above the city in the pellucid air of a hill-top: 'But away below in the valley, as night draws on, a lurid glare reddens the north-eastern horizon. It marks the spot where the great wen of London heaves and festers. Up here on the free hills, the sharp air blows in upon us, limpid and clear from a thousand leagues of open ocean; down there in the crowded town, it stagnates and ferments, polluted with the diseases and vices of centuries'.[91] The hill-top is a romantic vantage point from which contemporary society can be comprehended in its totality. It therefore functions as the spatial equivalent of a future temporality. The same principle shapes the symbolic landscape of Havelock Ellis's 'Dialogue in Utopia', *The 19th Century* (1900), a novel that is set on a hill-top emblematically 'crowned by an observatory'.[92] The hill-top symbolises the objectivity of perspective realised in the anamorphic gaze of both Allen's alien visitor from the twenty-fifth-century and Ellis's twenty-first century student of nineteenth-century culture.

This is the totalising, historicist perspective of utopia, the 'critical-utopian' gaze that, in a metaphor taken from Goethe, Bloch described as 'a view from the roof', one that enabled the observer 'not only to see far, but particularly to see the vicinity around the house more clearly'.[93] It is tempting to term the late-Victorian utopian novel, irrespective of its critical property, a 'rooftop novel'. Utopian novelists were the inheritors of a Victorian romantic tradition: their forays into a fictional future are equivalent to those 'long, deep plunges into the past' taken by Tennyson and Browning, by Arnold and Carlyle, in the course of their search for 'an observatory from which to survey their own epoch'.[94]

---

[91] Allen 1895, pp. xvii–xviii.
[92] Ellis 1900, p. 1.
[93] Bloch 1988, p. 222.
[94] Kiernan 1989, p. 147.

In the late nineteenth-century, utopian novels are often identified by subtitle as 'imaginary' or 'alternative' histories. A review of Edward Maitland's first 'imaginary history', *By and By: An Historical Romance of the Future* (1873), confirms that it is in comparatively common usage from the early 1870s.[95] Utopian fiction is historiographical at the *fin de siècle*. If the historical novel transforms the present into the post-history of the past, the utopian novel transforms the present into the pre-history of the future. Dr. Aerius Pott, the protagonist of a 'Political Utopia' by William Stanley, published in 1903, avers that 'the direction that thought must take in order to attain the prophetic must be in a historical vein, as the scale of the future must follow in the continuity of the past through the present and onwards'.[96] The political utopia of this period speculates that the converse is also the case, and that the direction that thought must take in order to attain the historical must be in the prophetic vein. Looking backward from a fictional future serves to construct a frame from within which the present, obfuscated by the vertigo and whirl of a frenzied life, concentrated and exploded by the culture of time-space compression, can be calmly apprehended.

Lecturing in 1938, H.G. Wells talked about the need to create 'the illusion of reality' – which he paraphrased as the effect of 'an historical novel, the other way round' – in fiction about the future.[97] A number of subsequent critics, most recently Carl Freedman, have proposed that utopian or science fiction is comparable to the historical novel.[98] Jameson, to take an influential example, argues that science fiction emerges in the late nineteenth-century as a genre that 'registers some nascent sense of the future, and does so in the space on which a sense of the past had once been inscribed'. But although he refers indefinitely to 'a mutation in our relationship to historical time itself', he fails to offer a sufficient explanation for the fact that fiction about the future surfaces at the *fin de siècle*.[99]

This mutation – the partial eclipse of the present – was a product of the 'time-space compression' precipitated by the imperial expansion of the realm of capital at this time. It was also the product of the crisis of capitalism during

---

[95] Anonymous 1977, p. 308.
[96] Stanley 1903, p. 14.
[97] Wells 1980b, p. 247.
[98] See Freedman 2000, pp. 44–62; and Nellist 1995.
[99] Jameson 1982, pp. 149–50.

the Great Depression, when economic decline and social disorder upset the idea that, as Morris so pungently put it, 'what the idiots of our day call progress would go on perfecting itself'.[100] In these circumstances, an optimistic history of the future acted as a kind of ideological insurance against the destruction or decline of capitalist civilisation to which Morris looked forward with such fervour. For the hopeful temper of utopianism in the late-Victorian period, and particularly of socialist utopianism, represses a furtive suspicion that history itself might betray the promise of a socialist future. When the times are in decay and in labour at the same time, it is always possible that civilisation might simply collapse into barbarism instead of superseding itself. This prospect is all the more alarming if one's politics, like those of the state socialists, are founded on the evolutionist belief that socialism will one day triumph of its own accord. For, if history functions as the hidden hand of destiny, then, by definition, there is no social force capable of forestalling the catastrophe. In some of the most confident prophecies of the late nineteenth-century, the fear that history will miscarry, and that socialism will be stillborn, exercises a powerful fascination.

The historiographical form of utopian fiction offered its reading public a comforting wish-fulfilment fantasy as well as an opportunity to criticise and come to terms with the imperfections of the present. Particularly when it was the product of a reformist political consciousness, as is most frequently the case, the utopian novel of the late-Victorian period employed what W.T. Stead termed 'the historico-prophetic method'. His utopian projection of Chicago as 'the ideal city of the world', in *If Christ Came to Chicago!* (1894), is founded on the belief that 'the majority of the social changes wrought in the social economy of the city have been realized piecemeal elsewhere'. A little mental effort is therefore all that is required to make his modest hopes materialise. As Stead reassures his readers, 'in describing Chicago as it might be in the twentieth-century, I have refrained from colouring the picture by introducing any element that is not well within the grasp of her citizens, if only they would give their minds to the task of obtaining it'.[101] In this characteristic apparition, the spectre of utopia assumes a comforting, familiar form. It assumes, like Aerius Pott, that history is a continuous process, and that 'the

---

[100] Morris 1987, p. 436.
[101] Stead 1894, p. 409n.

scale of the future must follow in the continuity of the past through the present and onwards'. In this manifestation of the utopian impulse, the future is simply not fantastical enough to force the reader into a disquieting, dialectical relation to the present.

If utopian fiction tried to apprehend a present the historical physiognomy of which had been obscured by the dynamic insecurity of modern life, it rarely risked what Wells later called 'breaking the Frame of our Present'.[102] In Chapter 2, I ask why the dominant species of utopianism in the late nineteenth-century, state socialism, was virtually incapable of developing, in Walter Benjamin's phrase, 'a consciousness of the present that shatters the continuum of history'.[103]

[102] Wells 1936, p. 48.
[103] Benjamin 1979, p. 352.

Chapter Two

State Socialism and Utopia

I. Introduction

'The key to the intelligibility of utopias', according to Karl Mannheim, 'is the structural situation of that social stratum which at any given time espouses them'.[1] This is a helpful starting-point for any attempt to apprehend the politics of utopia in the late nineteenth-century. It is important to ask who promoted utopian solutions to social problems in this epoch, in order to diagnose the ideological conditions of which utopianism, or the dominant strain of utopianism, is a symptomatic expression. In 1889, William Morris grappled with precisely this question in a review of the American Edward Bellamy's celebrated novel *Looking Backward* (1888). *Looking Backward* was a product of the populist and progressive era in the United States; but its incalculable impact on debates about socialism on the other side of the Atlantic make it central to any discussion of utopianism in late-nineteenth-century England, as Morris acknowledged. It functions as a focal point of reference for this chapter because Morris's remarkable critique of it – which deserves closer analysis than it has so far received[2] – effectively

---

[1] Mannheim 1936, p. 187.

[2] Certain statements from Morris's review have been cited by critics often enough, if in frankly misleading contexts, as Dentith 1990 indicates (p. 124); but its methodology has not been closely interrogated.

establishes it as the emblematic instance of contemporary reformist utopianism in Britain as well as in North America. It served as the talisman of the movement for social reform in London quite as much as in Boston, where it was first published.[3]

Writing in *Commonweal*, the organ of the Socialist League, Morris argued that 'the only safe way of reading a utopia is to consider it as the expression of the temperament of its author'.[4] At first sight, this insistence on the personal nature of utopian fiction is not entirely helpful. Of course, utopian fiction frequently served in the nineteenth-century as the literary equivalent of a soapbox hurriedly set down at Hyde Park Corner, a rough platform from which politically eccentric individuals voiced their opinions in a more or less homiletic, more or less hectoring tone. But, if fictional utopias were expressive of their authors' political idiosyncrasies, they also expressed, more significantly, the political contradictions of the epoch in which they were produced.

Ernst Bloch, who averred that 'however privately [a] dream rises it contains the tendency of its age and the next age expressed in images', is correct to emphasise that the dream's 'social mandate', as he formulates it, 'is always stronger than the individual characteristics of the utopians'.[5] This is in part because utopian fiction describes an impossible attempt to historicise the present in spite of its impenetrability. And it is in part because the temperament of the utopian writer is itself a product of the social mandate (though that is not to say that 'each of us is but an automatic mouthpiece' of the spirit of the age, as Grant Allen assumed).[6] To pose the problem of how safely to read utopia in terms of an alternative between two external forces, the personality of the writer and the epoch in which it is written, as Morris superficially appears to do, is implicitly to misunderstand the dynamics of literary production. A literary text, which is inevitably reproduced by the process of its consumption, is the overdetermined product of a dialectical interaction between several modes of formation, from the writer's biography to the system of social relations in which, mediated by contradictory ideological conditions, that biography unfolds. Morris, who was a committed historical materialist, had in fact a clear grasp of these dynamics, as he repeatedly

[3] See Marshall 1962.
[4] Morris 1994, p. 420. Further references are given after quotations in the text.
[5] Bloch 1986, pp. 479–80.
[6] Allen 1895, p. xxiii.

demonstrated in his essays and lectures on art and society in the 1880s and 1890s. It transpires, on closer inspection, that to interpret the admittedly deceptive term 'temperament' in relation only to the author's personality is to misconstrue its critical potential.

Morris's influential instruction to the reader of utopian literature has all too often been misinterpreted. Lifted from its context, his emphasis on 'temperament' seems to ratify a purely psycho-biographical interpretation of utopia. In fact, Morris is interested in the subjectivity of the writer only to the extent that it is itself symptomatic of some more fully social phenomenon. The remarks in which he amplifies this claim to the effect that utopia is 'the expression of the temperament of its author' are quoted less frequently than the phrase itself:

> And of course his [Bellamy's] temperament is that of many thousands of people. This temperament may be called the unmixed modern one, unhistoric and unartistic; it makes its owner (if a Socialist) perfectly satisfied with modern civilization, if only the injustice, misery, and waste of class society could be got rid of; which half-change seems possible to him. (pp. 420–21).

In an abrupt shift of perspective, Morris pulls back from Bellamy's individual temperament and pans across the corporate temperament of which it is a representative part. Bellamy is typical of a particular ideological outlook, 'the unmixed modern one, unhistoric and unartistic', because as a relatively unsophisticated writer of fiction he is incapable of exploring its contradictions in an innovative or creative form. 'There are some writers who are chiefly interesting in themselves', H.G. Wells affirmed in a preface to Thomas More's *Utopia*, 'and some whom chance and the agreement of men have picked out as symbols and convenient indications of some particular group or temperament of opinions'.[7] If More belongs to the latter category, as Wells argued, there can be little doubt that, as far as Morris was concerned, so too does Bellamy.

In his critique of *Looking Backward*, Morris's presentation of Bellamy in terms of his 'temperament' is consistent with the approach he adopts when composing a self-portrait in 'How I Became a Socialist' (1894). There, he insists that an autobiographical account of his conversion to socialism can only be justified 'if my readers will look upon me as a type of a certain group of

---

[7] Wells 1980, p. 234.

people'. Insisting on his status as a renegade from the affluent bourgeoisie, he defines this 'type of a certain group of mind' in opposition to those of a '*Whig* frame of mind' – that is, those for whom capitalism is a completely acceptable state of affairs so long as it is improved 'by getting rid of a few ridiculous survivals of the barbarous ages'. The Morrisians are from a different school of radical critique – historic and artistic, so to speak. Like their precursors, John Ruskin in particular, they are inspired by 'hatred of modern civilization' and 'hope of its destruction'.[8] They are part of the polemical tradition of romantic anti-capitalism. The Bellamyites, for their part, are defined by a 'Whig frame of mind': they remain 'perfectly satisfied with modern civilization'.

In this chapter, I examine the dominant paradigm of utopian thought at the end of the nineteenth-century, that of socialist reformism – the aim of which, according to Morris, was 'to make concessions to the working class while leaving the present system of capital and wages still in operation'.[9] I try to grasp the politics of utopia in terms of what, in a lecture on 'Art under Plutocracy', Morris called 'the social position of the producers'.[10] I identify this social position, in Section II, as that of the intelligentsia, the class perspective of which, as I explain in Section III, is structurally equivalent to the outlook of the petty bourgeoisie. In Section IV, I then scrutinise the 'unmixed modern' temperament of state socialism in terms of its underlying ideological contradiction, which can be characterised as a dialectic of utopianism and reformism. In Section V, I analyse *Looking Backward* as an exemplary instance of the 'prophylactic' function of reformist utopianism, which displaced revolutionary attitudes towards capitalism in the late-nineteenth-century labour movement. Finally, in Section VI, I discuss the dialectic of critical and ideological dynamics that tends to structure utopian productions.

I am, of course, conscious that the apparent imprecision of the term 'petty-bourgeois', which has all too frequently been thrown about as an insult rather than theorised as a critical concept, presents a risk for the argument sketched out in this chapter. It is I believe imperative however to iterate Jameson's claim from some twenty years ago that 'ideological analysis is inconceivable without a conception of the "ultimately determining instance" of social class'.[11]

---

[8] Morris 1984, pp. 240, 242.
[9] Morris 1996, p. 7.
[10] Morris 1915, p. 166.
[11] Jameson 1977, p. 201.

In his recent article on 'The Politics of Utopia', Jameson has underlined the importance of understanding 'not only that all utopias spring from a specific class position, but that their fundamental thematization . . . will also reflect a specific class-historical standpoint or perspective'. Jameson goes on to argue that the utopian 'imagines his effort as one of rising above all immediate determinations in some all-embracing resolution of every imaginable evil and misery of our own fallen society and reality'; but that 'no matter how comprehensive and trans-class or post-ideological the inventory of reality's flaws and defects, the imagined resolution necessarily remains wedded to this or that ideological perspective'.[12] This precept guides my detour through Marx's critique of reformist socialism in the 1840s, as well as through Morris's critique of it in the 1880s, in subsequent sections of this chapter. It seems to me that, despite the polemical contexts in which Marx and Morris constructed their respective critiques, both of which are focused on 'the social position of the producers', they continue to offer an important example for the materialist analysis of utopianism. To the extent though that my argument homogenises the ideological positions of utopians from a class background that is ultimately more variegated than I seem to suggest, this chapter must be read merely as a preliminary attempt to theorise the class-historical standpoint of the utopian thinkers that dominated discussion of the society of the future at the end of the nineteenth-century.

---

[12] Jameson 2004, p. 47. For a perceptive, if not completely up-to-date analysis of Jameson's views on utopia, see Moylan 2000, pp. 89–101, 139–45. See Chapter 3 of Moylan's important book for a comprehensive survey of developments in the critical literature on utopianism over the final quarter of the twentieth-century. It should be noted at this point that, throughout the chapter, I neglect the formal aspects of utopia that have of course been a central preoccupation of critical studies of the utopian genre. Carl Freedman explores the relevant debates with perceptiveness in Freedman 2000, pp. 62–86. It would be deceptive to claim that in these pages his argument about the utopian genre simply complements my analysis of its ideological preconditions in the late-Victorian period, but his distinctly critical précis of the 'characteristics of the literary utopia' can nonetheless stand in for a thorough discussion of formal questions in this chapter: 'The detailed schematization of an alternative society – the ready-made representation of a no-place that is generated as if directly *willed* from the brain of the author as individual – amounts, on the one hand, to a generally monologic authorial style that tends to forestall any properly novelistic clash and heterogeneity of different voices, and, on the other hand, to a largely static and spatial form of narrative construction inhospitable to historical temporality and characterological typicality' (p. 80).

II. Utopia and the intelligentsia

Support for Morris's point about the impossibility of separating the writer's personality from the period in which she lives is provided by the novelist Maurice Hewlett in his review of *News from Nowhere* for the conservative *National Review* in 1891. Hewlett starts with a precept which, so he claims, 'no one can reasonably refuse: namely, that the interest of paper paradises is mainly biographical'. A slippage from the personal to the political emerges though in the following sentence: 'Nobody cares to discuss the potentialities of the *Republic* or the *Utopia* from the present, or any past, point of view; but both have a high interest historically as gauges of contemporary polity'.[13] Proposing that Plato's utopia is a reflection of contemporary polity is not unlike proposing that Bellamy's utopia is a reflection of contemporary politics.

As a materialist, Morris makes the point more powerfully. He is not really bothered by Bellamy's biography. He is interested in *Looking Backward* to the extent that it is symptomatic of the intellectual and social conjuncture in which it is produced and read. As he said soon after writing his review, 'the success of Mr Bellamy's utopian book, deadly dull as it is, is a straw to show which way the wind blows'.[14] Morris is concerned with the cognitive and imaginative impact of *Looking Backward* on the movement for social reform from which it surfaced. In this context, 'temperament' indicates some sort of ideological formation. It denotes the ideology of a class, or of a particular section of a class. The concept of a collective temperament collapses the individual into the ideological contradictions of his specific position within the social relations of production. Far from promoting an interpretation of utopian fiction in terms of the writer's subjectivity, Morris's review of *Looking Backward* recommends a class-based analysis of the form. To overstate the matter, we might say that Morris silently erects a well-known notice: 'Individuals are dealt with only in so far as they are . . . embodiments of particular class relations and class interests'.[15]

What is the class position of the 'owner' of an unmixed modern temperament, as Morris puts it? Bellamy, who pursued a career as a professional journalist and writer, though he had qualified for the law, was representative of a social

---

[13] Hewlett 1973, pp. 343–44.
[14] Morris 1994, p. 493.
[15] Marx 1996, p. 10.

stratum that Max Adler once delineated not as a class but as an 'inter-class group' – the intelligentsia. In a critical review of Adler's book on *Der Sozialismus und die Intellektuellen* (1910), Leon Trotsky alluded to what he called the 'class psychology' of intellectuals.[16] This concept, which is comparable to Morris's notion of a corporate temperament, provides an important point of entry to an understanding of the ideological framework of utopian fiction in the late nineteenth-century. My basic contention is that, in this period, the majority of utopian writers are reformist intellectuals whose political perspective is significantly shaped by their peculiar class position, their place in the social division of labour, which is equivalent to that of the petty bourgeoisie. In particular, state-socialist utopias exemplify the petty-bourgeois temperament typical of much of the socialist movement in this period.

These claims are substantiated by Darko Suvin's literary sociology of nineteenth-century science fiction and its 'socio-political subgenre', utopian fiction. Suvin carefully stratifies the class affiliations of some seventy writers. These writers – from Lord Lytton to the London plasterer Thomas Lee – cover a wide spectrum of class positions. But they tend to be concentrated in distinct strata of the social system. It transpires that, up until approximately 1886, 'various groups of professionals in general and men/women of letters in particular were the *principal social addressors* of Victorian fiction in general and [the] S-F corpus in particular'; and that, thereafter, 'the dramatic increase of publication brings an influx of lower-class or Grub Street writers'.[17] This influx is fuelled by the formation in the late nineteenth-century of what Sidney Webb called *la nouvelle couche sociale*. In terms borrowed from Pierre Bourdieu, the shift can be characterised as one from 'bohemians of the upper bourgeoisie' to 'petty-bourgeois institutional servants'. Despite the clear differences between these two categories, intellectuals and artists in both of them 'occupy a dominated position in the field of power'.[18] It is important to emphasise that, in the face of a widespread sense of social crisis, individuals from quite different class fractions wrote utopian fiction. They did so in order to foreclose the prospect of European civilisation's collapse – either in the common ruin of the contending classes, or in what for many amounted to much the same

---

[16] Trotsky 1966, pp. 4–5.
[17] Suvin 1983, pp. 242, 248.
[18] Bourdieu 1993, p. 125.

thing, that is to say, the revolutionary reconstitution of society on the basis of communist principles.

H.G. Wells, who conflates these two outcomes in the fictional future of *The Time Machine* (1895) – first demonstrating that what seems to be a communist society is in fact founded on a radical class polarisation, and second demonstrating that this state of affairs is itself underpinned by the dictatorship of a parasitic proletariat, in the form of the so-called Morlocks – is an exemplary petty-bourgeois utopian. Along with Sidney Webb and a number of other members of the Fabian Society, which he joined in 1903, Wells formed 'a contingent recruited from *la nouvelle couche sociale*, the rising stratum of modestly placed professional men, civil servants, journalists, teachers, scientists and technicians'.[19] He was part of the 'intellectual proletariat'.[20] This is the import of Christopher Caudwell's portrait of Wells, which depicts him as a typical petty bourgeois, split between the hope of improving himself, 'of getting a step nearer the good bourgeois things so far above [him]', and the fear 'of falling from respectability into the proletarian abyss which, because it is so near, seems so much more dangerous'.[21]

But what about Edward Bulwer-Lytton, who was a Tory peer and a Member of Parliament? *The Coming Race* (1871) is his popular dystopian fantasy of a subterranean people, the Vril-ya, who have used an all-powerful energy source, Vril, in order to construct an alternative civilisation. This race has built its society on the basis of 'the extinction of that strife and competition between individuals, which, no matter what forms of government they adopt, render the many subordinate to the few, destroy real liberty to the individual, whatever may be the nominal liberty of the state, and annul that calm of existence, without which, felicity, mental or bodily, cannot be attained'.[22] In practice, it is a kind of bionic, Carlylean English aristocracy. With its mysterious spiritual technology, it has the power to beat the industrial bourgeoisie at its own game (Civilization™ might be one name for it) – but without making a hideous mess of it, or getting its hands too dirty in the process. In this sense, it is analogous to the technocratic solution of *A Modern Utopia* (1905), Wells's

---

[19] Harrison 1987, p. 42.
[20] Wolfe 1975, p. 157.
[21] Caudwell 1938, p. 76.
[22] Lytton 1871, p. 121.

Fabian fantasy of a world state run by the *samurai*, a meritocratic caste that is nonetheless 'something of an hereditary class'.[23] As Marie-Louise Berneri mused in one of the first critical studies of utopia, *The Coming Race* is 'a curious attempt to reconcile certain socialist principles with laissez-faire capitalism'.[24]

Lytton was, after all, a professional writer, who had been forced to earn a living from the late 1820s (when his mother, who disapproved of his marriage, cut him off from his allowance), and who had furthermore been forced to finance expensive court cases after separating from his wife. He was also a member of the declining class of landowners, squeezed by agricultural recession and hustled by electoral reform; a class that felt comparatively cramped and pinched in the late-Victorian period, and, in this particular sense, therefore seems analogous to the petty bourgeoisie. It is not perhaps surprising that, squinting at the workers as well as at the manufacturing class, he should finally catch a glimpse of the monstrous Morlocks of *The Time Machine*, calmly coming towards him. The penultimate sentence of the novel, written in the narrative present, registers a sharp shift of perspective, because it implicitly associates the coming race with the industrial miners past whom the narrator must climb in order to return to the surface of the earth: 'Only, the more I think of a people calmly developing, in regions excluded from our sight and deemed uninhabitable by our sages, powers surpassing our most disciplined modes of force, and virtues to which our life, social and political, becomes antagonistic in proportion as our civilisation advances, – the more devoutly I pray that ages may yet elapse before they emerge into sunlight our inevitable destroyers'.[25] A dystopian future is uncannily concealed within an obscure crack in the apparently serene surface of present-day society. The capitalist order is secretly undermined by its opposite.

In his notes on the utopias and 'politico-philosophical constructions' of the Counter-Reformation, Antonio Gramsci urged the following generalisation: 'Utopias are created by individual intellectuals who in formal terms go back to the Socratic rationalism of Plato's *Republic*, and in terms of substance reflect, greatly misshapen, the conditions of instability and rebellion latent in the

---

[23] Wells 1905, p. 299.
[24] Berneri 1951, p. 242.
[25] Lytton 1871, p. 292.

popular masses of the age. They are basically the political manifestos of intellectuals who want to create the optimum state'. This statement can be translated into the historical context of the nineteenth-century without its central insight seeming anachronistic. In the late-Victorian period, it continues to be the case that 'through utopias individual intellectuals attempted to solve a series of problems of vital importance to the humble masses, that is, they tried to find a link between intellectuals and people'.[26] Although the physiognomy of Western class society underwent a dramatic transformation between the early seventeenth and the late nineteenth centuries – and not least because the humble masses started to make history on their own terms in this time – the steady advance of capitalism ensured a considerable continuity within the tradition of utopian thought. Wells, for instance, traced the ancestry of his 'scientific utopias' back to Francis Bacon. Both were practitioners of what, in a slightly clumsy phrase, we can identify as 'utopianism-from-above'.

This term denominates almost the entire literary tradition of utopia since the time of Thomas More. 'The modern utopia', Kumar comments, 'is egalitarian, affluent and dynamic'.[27] Certainly. Even in its socialist variants, however, it is habitually underwritten by the idea that equality and affluence, to quote Hal Draper's description of 'socialism-from-above', 'must be *handed down* to the grateful masses in one form or another, by a ruling elite which is not subject to their control in fact'.[28] Preliminarily, this tradition can be characterised in terms of its opposition to a putative 'utopianism-from-below'. The latter current is less a literary institution than a collective response to alienated social conditions. It derives not from the form of Socratic rationalism in Plato's Republic, but from that of the carnivalesque in the Land of Cokaygne, the feudal serf's fantasy of a world in which suffering is forgotten in the face of the free gratification of physical needs. From the dream of Cokaygne onwards, this current, according to A.L. Morton, 'persisted as an almost secret tradition under the surface, while the main stream of utopian thought passed through other channels'.[29]

This politics of utopian play is repudiated in all the 'paper paradises' of the late-Victorian period, with the exception of News from Nowhere, which

---

[26] Gramsci 1985, pp. 239–40.
[27] Kumar 1987, p. 32.
[28] Draper 1992, p. 3.
[29] Morton 1952, p. 171.

Morton has summarised, in my opinion correctly, as 'the first Utopia which is not utopian', principally because of its concern not with the mechanics of the state in the ideal society but with its 'quality of life'.[30] 'The power of Morris's utopia', Miguel Abensour has subsequently argued, 'stems from there being no ideal or plan for the moral education of humanity and, furthermore, from the impossibility of there being one. The rupture with utopian model-building implies a radically antipedagogical effect, to the extent that any model necessarily contains an educational method and vice-versa'.[31] Morris's utopia is offered as a contribution to the spirited political debate described in its opening chapter, not as a programme for social reform. It is heuristic. Consequently, it does not aspire to be representative of its readers, despite its obvious intention to shape their imaginative engagement with socialist theory. This is in marked contrast to a utopia such as Looking Backward, which is precisely about utopian model-building, concerned as it is in particular with the mechanics of the state. In terms of Morris's critique of 'practical' socialists, Bellamy fails to see into the future 'except through the murky smoked glass of the present life amongst us'. The 'epoch of rest' depicted in News from Nowhere proposes instead 'that such a stupendous change in the machinery of life as the abolition of capital and wages must bring about a corresponding change in ethics and habits of life'.[32] As I propose in Chapter 5, it evokes 'the present pleasure of ordinary daily life', which is finally redeemed from the reification of the present under capitalism.[33]

To take another example of the dominant reformist trend, Robert Blatchford's Merrie England (1893), indubitably one of the most popular textbooks of socialist theory published in the later nineteenth-century, is quite uninterested in 'habits of life'. It declares that socialism is 'a scientific scheme of national Government, entirely wise, just and practical', explicitly repudiating the disruptive utopia of play: 'Socialism is not a wild dream of a happy land where the apples will drop off the trees into our open mouths, the fish come out of the rivers and fry themselves for dinner, and the loom turns out ready-made suits of velvet with golden buttons without the trouble of coaling the

---

[30] Morton 1952, p. 164.
[31] Abensour 1999, p. 131.
[32] Morris 1994, p. 338.
[33] Morris 1912, p. 72.

engine'.[34] *News from Nowhere* does not, of course, embody a social dream of this kind, but it is nonetheless committed to conceiving the possible pleasures of ordinary life under socialism. Blatchford's book is, by contrast, unconcerned with the lived texture of the everyday in an ideal society, and this arguably makes it a doubtful directory of the anti-capitalist dreams of nineteenth-century workers. Morton is surely right to assert that, in general, 'the great literary utopias are the work of the learned . . . reflecting indeed historical development but only indirectly and in a distorted form the struggles and hopes of the people'.[35]

In the late nineteenth-century, utopian fiction is one means by which reform-minded intellectuals try to find a solution to the social contradictions that they encounter. The concept of the intellectual, however, presents a preliminary semantic problem. The terms 'intelligentsia' and 'intellectual' are products of the middle and later nineteenth-century: the former, imported from Poland, appeared in the 1860s in Russia, where it designated students who criticised the Tsarist system in the name of Enlightenment ideals; the latter came into common parlance in France in the 1890s, when it was employed as a term of abuse for supporters of the campaign to free Dreyfus. But it must be emphasised that these associations with the Left are in one significant sense misleading, because one of the most striking characteristics of intellectuals is their political heterogeneity. Putting their leftist affiliations to one side, we might identify intellectuals, provisionally, in terms of their social position, as 'a particular component of the new middle class, the one that performs cultural, ideological, and mental functions in the complex division of labor of a capitalist society, on the basis of qualifications acquired in higher education'.[36]

In the late nineteenth-century, intellectuals are men and (to a lesser extent) women who produce ideas outside the patronage system that, from the late eighteenth-century onwards, capitalism had progressively extirpated. They are forced to sell their sacred ideas over a counter in a corner of the profane marketplace. It is only in this sense that they can be considered at all 'free-floating' (in Alfred Weber's famous phrase). The intelligentsia is recruited from a range of social classes, certainly; and one cannot, in consequence,

---

[34] Blatchford 1893, p. 99.
[35] Morton 1952, p. 171.
[36] Eley 1996, p. 74.

ascribe it a singular class consciousness. But, contrary to Mannheim's insistence, they are not an 'unanchored, *relatively* classless stratum'.[37] If intellectuals do not form a class, then, as Michael Löwy says, they are nonetheless 'a *social category*, defined not by their place in the production process, but by their relation to non-economic instances of the social structure'. It is only because, as 'the "creative" sector of a broader mass of "intellectual" (as opposed to "manual") workers', they are 'the section of this mass furthest removed from economic production', that they appear to be independent.[38]

In fact, sociologically as well as ideologically speaking, the intelligentsia is homologous with one class in particular: the petty bourgeoisie. As Löwy demonstrates, this is for two fundamental reasons:

> First, the majority of the intelligentsia is recruited from the petty bourgeoisie, or to be more precise, from the sector of 'intellectual workers' as opposed to other members of that class such as small traders and small peasants. We should therefore neither ignore nor overestimate the bond of social origin that undeniably links a major fraction of this social category to the petty bourgeoisie. Second, the intellectual professions of writer, teacher, artist, and others, as well as the means of labour and subsistence offered to intellectuals, have traditionally fallen to the petty bourgeoisie, and in particular to members of the liberal professions. (Of course, a minority of intellectuals have nevertheless belonged, by occupation and social position, to the bourgeoisie, the aristocracy, and even the working class.)[39]

These comments need to be situated in relation to the historical emergence of the intelligentsia. It was the late nineteenth-century, especially, that witnessed the dilation of that section of the petty bourgeoisie from which most intellectuals were enlisted – that is to say, the 'white-collar' lower-middle class, or 'salariat'. And it was above all in Britain – where the imperialist expansion of trade temporarily counterpoised the impact of industrial decline – that the extension of financial, commercial, and administrative sectors of the economy created the conditions out of which this stratum of salaried employees appeared. What this 'new petty bourgeoisie' of non-productive wage-earners has in

---

[37] Mannheim 1936, p. 137.
[38] Löwy 1979, p. 15.
[39] Löwy 1979, p. 16.

common with the 'traditional petty bourgeoisie' of small-scale producers and owners, as Nicos Poulantzas proposes, is 'the fact that they neither belong to the bourgeoisie nor to the working class'.[40]

Arno Mayer summarised the emergence of the lower-middle class as the 'second birth of the petite bourgeoisie'; and he added that, throughout Europe, it 'coincided with and was stimulated by the swift growth of government bureaucracies, schools, hospitals, and armies'. In England, this process accelerated from the late 1860s and early 1870s, when there was an increase in centrally controlled obligations for local government, including the Education Act of 1870. These institutions were the training centres of an intelligentsia that, as Mayer suggests, continued to be conditioned by 'lower-middle-class realities'.[41] The quotidian existence of this intelligentsia equated with that of the less literate strata of the petty bourgeoisie. For if, on the one hand, it was partitioned from the proletariat, because it had the privilege of education, then, on the other hand, and to the extent that popular education was expanding, it was also proletarianised. Paul Lafargue – fulminating against the fact that capitalism transformed 'intellectual faculties into merchandise' – referred in 1900 to 'a swarming and famishing throng of intellectuals whose lot grows worse in proportion to the increase of their numbers'.[42]

In other words, the insecure character of their daily life is the direct consequence of their petty-bourgeois class position, which Engels typified in terms of an 'intermediate position between the class of larger capitalists, traders, and manufacturers, the bourgeoisie properly so-called, and the proletarian or industrial class'. This contradictory class position – 'aspiring to the position of the first, the least adverse turn of fortune hurls the individuals of this class down into the ranks of the second' – helps to explain the vacillatory politics of the petty-bourgeoisie. Engels went on to argue that, as a social group, it 'becomes seized with violent democratic fits as soon as the middle class has secured its own supremacy, but falls back into the abject despondency of fear as soon as the class below itself, the proletarians, attempts an independent movement'.[43]

---

[40] Poulantzas 1975, p. 206.
[41] Mayer 1975, pp. 417, 430.
[42] Lafargue 1907, p. 79.
[43] Engels 1933, pp. 13–14.

Karl Kautsky confirmed that it is this ambivalence, derived from 'the ambiguity of its social position', that unites the 'old petty bourgeoisie' and the new intelligentsia: 'While today it protests against the greediness of capital, tomorrow it will look down on the bad manners of the proletariat. While today it appeals to it to defend its human dignity, tomorrow it will try to preserve social peace by stabbing it in the back'.[44] This ideological contradiction is analysed in cross-section by Poulantzas, when he submits that the political stance of the new petty bourgeoisie is 'anti-capitalist but leans strongly towards reformist illusions'. A typical expression of this reformist politics, he says, is the demand 'for a "rationalization" of society that would enable "mental labour" to develop fully, without the shackles of the profit-motive, i.e. in the form of a left-wing technocracy'.[45] The state-socialist movement in late-nineteenth-century England needs to be understood in terms of precisely this position.

It is certainly no coincidence that the organisations associated with the so-called 'socialist revival' of the 1880s and 1890s tended to be dominated, on the one hand, by bohemian members of the bourgeoisie, and, on the other, in far greater number, by members of the lower middle class. In this sense, the Fabian Society is only a caricature of the composition of other groupings, such as the Social Democratic Federation and the Independent Labour Party: as Hobsbawm remarks, 'the mass of middle-class members falls into two somewhat different groups: members of the traditional middle classes who had developed a social conscience, a dislike of bourgeois society, or some other form of dissidence, and the much more interesting body of self-made professionals'. Further, the example of the Fabian Society offers a reminder that, in the late nineteenth-century, the word 'socialist' signified everything opposed to *laissez-faire*. It is in view of this elastic definition that Hobsbawm has tried to situate the Fabians 'not as an essential part of the socialist and labour movement (however effective or ineffective, reformist or radical), but as an "accidental" one': 'Their history must be written not in terms of the socialist revival of the 1880s, but in terms of the middle-class reactions to the breakdown of mid-Victorian certainties, the rise of new strata, new structures,

---

[44] Kautsky 1983, p. 22.
[45] Poulantzas 1975, pp. 290–91.

new policies, within British capitalism: as an adaptation of the British middle classes to the era of imperialism'.[46]

Utopia is a semantic figure generated by this historical conjuncture. Utopian writers in the late-Victorian period are a product of the process whereby a bourgeois belief in progress is increasingly challenged. They are reformists in the broadest sense, because they work for the amelioration of the poor within the framework of the existing social order. It is towards this inclusive category of reformist intellectuals that Morris gestures when he intimates that the unmixed modern temperament 'makes its owner (*if a Socialist*) perfectly satisfied with modern civilization' (emphasis mine).

III. Petty-bourgeois socialism

Morris's comments on *Looking Backward* cannot, of course, supply us with a key that can unlock the ideological secret of late-Victorian utopian thinking. After all, the pastoral utopias written by Richard Jefferies and W.H. Hudson, *After London* (1885) and *A Crystal Age* (1887) respectively, are not the products of an 'unmixed modern' temperament. They are part of the romantic anti-capitalist tradition that I characterised in the introductory section of this chapter as suspicious of modern civilisation (if from a more conservative current of it than Morris himself). But Morris's polemic does point to the ideological contradictions typical of many of the utopian intellectuals who were part of the wider movement for social reform at the time, for all the heterogeneity of their individual views on the most effective means of achieving an alternative society to that of free-market capitalism. Morris portrays this temperament thus:

> It makes its owner (if a Socialist) perfectly satisfied with modern civilization,
> if only the injustice, misery, and waste of class society could be got rid of;
> which half-change seems possible to him. The only ideal of life which such
> a man can see is that of the industrious *professional* middle-class men of
> to-day purified from their crime of complicity with the monopolist class,
> and become independent instead of being, as they now are, parasitical.
> (pp. 420–21.)

[46] Hobsbawm 1964, pp. 257, 266.

Capital without capitalism: in this phrase we might sum up 'the universal reign of moderate bourgeois society which some have dreamed of', as Morris sarcastically puts it in another context.[47]

It is a fantasy that corresponds to the economic theory that Marx mocked in the 1840s as 'the *philanthropic* school'. Condemned 'to make an abstraction of the contradictions that are met with at every moment in actual reality', this school consequently advances a version of 'idealised reality'. The philanthropists, Marx argued, 'want to retain the categories which express bourgeois relations, without the antagonism which constitutes them and is inseparable from them'.[48] In 1884, Morris himself attacked what he called the 'economical kind' of philanthropist. He distinguished between the 'preaching Philanthropists', who are 'very specially callous and stupid rich men soaked through and through with middle-class prejudice'; and 'philanthropists proper', who play an active part in the movement for social reform (though 'they to a great extent accept the doctrines of the preacher philanthropists'). He lamented the latter in particular, complaining of 'their wizened scheme for the regeneration of Society', premised on the assumption 'that the basis of society cannot be altered'.[49] As Morris testified, there was intense hostility between socialists and philanthropists at the *fin de siècle*. This was because of and not in spite of the close kinship, ideologically speaking, between philanthropy and reformist socialism at this time.

To put it polemically, we might say that reformism was a radical form of philanthropy. In 1884, Wolfe maintains, the first Fabians were a group of 'radical philanthropists with vague, melioristic aspirations'.[50] These followers of Thomas Davidson, for whom socialism was something of a fad, were influenced by the self-proclaimed Marxist H.M. Hyndman as well as by the social investigators Mearns and Stead. But despite his fearsome appeals for social transformation, Hyndman himself initially offered a conspicuously philanthropic version of socialism. In his 1881 essay for the *Nineteenth Century*, 'Dawn of a Revolutionary Epoch', he defined 'genuine Communism' as the principle 'that the well-to-do should provide for the poor certain advantages

---

[47] Morris 1915, p. 187.
[48] Marx 1976, p. 177.
[49] Morris 1994, pp. 75–6.
[50] Wolfe 1975, p. 164.

whether they like to do so or not'.[51] And, if he subsequently adopted a far more aggressive posture, he and his acolytes, according to Wolfe, 'were really reformists in revolutionary garb and used the rhetoric of violent revolution chiefly to stimulate enthusiasm among their sluggish followers and to fill the leisure class with fear'.[52]

The values of philanthropy profoundly infected the socialist movement of the late-Victorian period. In the context of late-nineteenth-century literary fiction, these values can be identified with naturalism. Indebted to the recent tradition of social investigation, the 'older form of naturalism', as Jameson says, 'let us briefly experience the life and the life world of the various underclasses, only to return with relief to our own living rooms and armchairs: the good resolutions it may have encouraged were always, then, a form of philanthropy'.[53] In an aside made during a discussion of George Gissing in a different context, Jameson suggests that the failure of the 'philanthropic strategy' formulated by the novelist of the late nineteenth-century 'throws off a new (or reinvented) subgenre, the Utopian novel, which displays renewed vitality throughout this period'.[54] I contend instead that utopian literature, rather than being merely 'thrown off' by the failure of the philanthropic strategy, represented its apotheosis. Utopian fiction totalised the partial solutions of a philanthropic reformism. In *Looking Backward*, for example, philanthropy is a diffuse function of what is, in effect, a perfectly functioning welfare state: 'The idea of charity on such a scale', comments the protagonist, 'would have made our most enthusiastic philanthropists gasp'.[55]

The utopian future portrayed in *Looking Backward* is the *terminus ad quem* of more modest and pragmatic philanthropic projects. Anna Swanwick's account of *An Utopian Dream and How It May Be Realized* (1888), published in England in the same year as Bellamy's book, exemplifies their politics. It represents an appeal to fellow philanthropists to support the People's Palaces in South London: for 'in liberating their brethren at home from the bondage of ignorance and sin', it pledges, 'drunkeness and other ghastly horrors will

---

[51] Hyndman 1881, p. 12.
[52] Wolfe 1975, p. 102.
[53] Jameson 1991, p. 286.
[54] Jameson 1981, p. 196.
[55] Bellamy 1888, p. 183. Further references are given after quotations in the text.

disappear, and "the moral desert will bloom as the rose"'.[56] The provision of moral education to the deserving poor in a humane environment will create an island of Christian brotherhood in the flooded delta of London's spiritual and material poverty. Reform, to alter the metaphor, is to be handed down from above, and received deferentially.

It is no accident that philanthropic projects were frequently associated with the dismissive sense of the word 'utopian' in this period. One anonymous writer noted in 1894 that '"utopian fancy" is the comment with which alike the heartless unimaginative Philistine, and the cool-headed reasoner, dismiss the eager schemes of too enthusiastic, too unpractical, well-meaning – nay, best-meaning – philanthropists'.[57] It was, presumably, in part because of this association of philanthropy and utopianism, and of utopianism with socialism, that Morris was repeatedly compelled to define his politics in opposition to philanthropists and reformists. 'When things are done not *for* the workers but *by* them', he insisted, 'an ideal will present itself with great distinctness to the workers themselves, which will not mean living on as little as you can, so as not to disturb the course of profit-grinding, but rather living a plentiful, generous, un-anxious life, the first quite necessary step to higher ideals yet'.[58]

Marx identified what he called 'philanthropic illusions' with the specific class outlook of the petty bourgeoisie.[59] According to him, the contradictory class position of the petty bourgeoisie accounts for the split optic of its social perspective: because of his situation, '*a petty bourgeois* is dazzled by the magnificence of the upper middle classes and feels compassion for the sufferings of the people'.[60] And this petty-bourgeois outlook, as I have implied, is a plausible interpretation of Morris's use of the term 'temperament' in his review of *Looking Backward*. In particular, it is the point of his portrait of the ideal life of an unmixed modern man, 'that of the industrious *professional* middle-class men of to-day purified from their crime of complicity with the monopolist class'. If the intelligentsia, as Kautsky claimed, 'tends to consider itself above the narrow-mindedness of class interests, [and] to be under the

[56] Swanwick 1888, p. 33.
[57] Perrycoste 1894, p. 5.
[58] Morris 1994, p. 77.
[59] Marx and Engels 1976a, p. 457.
[60] Marx and Engels 1984, p. 215.

idealistic illusion that it is somehow superior and not affected by momentary and particular interests', then Morris's figure of a politically purified professional describes a standard wish-fulfilment fantasy. To the extent that this is socialism, as Kautsky continued, it is 'a kind of socialism which unhappily is very similar to [Marx and Engels's] conception of "true socialism"'.[61]

In the *Communist Manifesto*, Marx had characterised the current of 'German, or "True", Socialism', in relation to the social pressure experienced by the petty bourgeoisie: The industrial and political supremacy of the bourgeoisie threatens it with certain destruction; on the one hand, from the concentration of capital; on the other, from the rise of a revolutionary proletariat. 'True' socialism appeared to kill these two birds with one stone.[62] 'True Socialism' played an important part in Bellamy's political formation. According to the writer's brother, his letters from Germany in the late 1860s were 'full of German Socialism'.[63] In the spirit of 'true socialism', the utopians of the late nineteenth-century presented imaginary solutions to their perception of the contradictory class position of the petty bourgeoisie in industrial society.

Disquiet at the prospect of an ascendant proletariat and a hesitant distrust of the brutal administration of the bourgeoisie are the distinctive features of late nineteenth-century reformism. Ideologically, it seeks a third way between the anarchy of *laissez-faire* capitalism and the anarchy of socialist revolution – between the Gold International and the Red International. This ambivalence of attitude is petty-bourgeois to its bootstraps. Whether an intellectual or a shop-owner articulates it, petty-bourgeois ideology in the late-Victorian period is the product of 'a supplementary part of bourgeois society', a class that senses it is caught between the monopolists and the proletariat.[64] The capitalist economy equivocates with this class. It makes and it mars the members of the petty bourgeoisie. The action of competition in turn pulls them up into the bourgeoisie proper, and pushes them down into the working class. Petty bourgeois are therefore particularly well placed to experience the contradictions of capitalism, in spite of their peripheral relation to the conflict between capital and labour.

[61] Kautsky 1933, pp. 22–3.
[62] Marx and Engels 1976c, p. 512.
[63] See Morgan 1944, p. 369.
[64] Marx and Engels 1976c, p. 509.

The petty bourgeoisie, in other words, is, on the one hand, crucially important to the development of class society, and on the other strangely irrelevant to its day-to-day struggles. Its identity as a class depends upon the outcome of a social conflict that it cannot directly determine. So the political paradox of the petty-bourgeois reformist is that he cannot afford to care too much about the very social conflicts that ultimately affect him so profoundly. He can hope for a society in which the vicissitudes of capitalist competition are ironed out, and in which everybody is assimilated to the pristine culture of the middle class, but he cannot do much about it. Like the narrator of *A Modern Utopia*, he is a sedentary world-mender rather than a brisk activist.[65] This is because he perceives only two possibilities to which the development of capitalist civilisation is open: either progress will in the end abolish competition and poverty, in which case taking one side or another in the class conflict is unnecessary; or poverty and competition will extinguish progress, in which case, once again, partisanship is superfluous. His position approximates to that of a slightly supine Calvinist, who strives to qualify for the elect in his everyday life, despite the fact that his status as one of the saved or damned has already been decided. He is at the mercy of what Engels once called 'predestination (alias chance)'.[66]

IV. Utopianism and reformism

Utopia, which operates as both a stimulant and a tranquilliser, may thus be the perfect expression of the petty-bourgeois reformist's political consciousness. If 'the contradiction of all utopianism', as Eagleton suggests, is 'that its very images of harmony threaten to hijack the radical impulses they hope to promote', then, for the reformist intellectual, impotent to alter the course of history, this is perhaps its secret virtue.[67] 'For the truth is', as Morris said of the archetypal late-Victorian radical, '[his] hope is a languid one'.[68] Reformist utopianism acts as a political opiate as well as an inspiration. Bloch characterises this 'abstract utopianism' in the course of a discussion of its opposite, which

---

[65] Wells 1905, p. 66.
[66] Engels 1998, p. 895.
[67] Eagleton 1990, p. 371.
[68] Morris 1994, p. 63.

he calls 'concrete utopianism'. 'Because it regards the future as something which has long since been decided and thus concluded', he says in *The Principle of Hope*, abstract utopianism 'is only a reprise of contemplative quietism': 'Confronted with the future-state which stands like an agreed consequence in the so-called iron logic of history, the subject can just as easily lay his hands in his lap as he once folded them when confronted with God's will'.[69] This is not so much a form of militant optimism as of acquiescent hopefulness.

It is this disposition that underlies the deterministic politics of the Second International, which Löwy depicts in terms of 'optimistic fatalism'.[70] The German Social Democrats, the dominant party in the International by dint of their considerable electoral support in the 1880s and 1890s, subscribed to the theory that at this time capitalism confronted its inevitable and more or less imminent 'breakdown' [*Zusammenbruch*]. In the conditions of the Great Depression, the 'historical tendency' towards terminal crisis that Marx had identified as a feature of the capitalist economy was translated into an iron law of social evolution. Kautsky, the most important theoretician of the Second International, made this exemplary prediction in 1892: 'Irresistible economic forces lead with the certainty of doom to the shipwreck of capitalist production. The substitution of a new social order for the existing one is no longer simply desirable, it has become inevitable'.[71] On the one hand, this position sanctions a reformist acceptance of the *status quo* – because there is scarcely any point in a socialist playing an active part in the class struggle if socialism is a fatal necessity. On the other hand, it licenses a clandestine strain of utopian thought – because a state of political passivity frees the socialist to fantasise about her future society.

Utopianism is thus the perfect complement to reformism. August Bebel's *Woman in the Past, Present and Future* (1879), a political treatise into which utopian speculation is carefully plaited, owed its immense popularity not only to its attempt to answer the so-called 'woman question', but to its confident assumption that socialist society is an historical certainty in the future. 'Socialism is not arbitrary destruction and reconstruction', the German Social Democrat argued, 'but a natural process of development'. He entreated

---

[69] Bloch 1986, p. 198.
[70] Löwy 1993, p. 92.
[71] Kautsky 1910, p. 117.

'that all the elements of dissolution on the one hand and of growth on the other, are factors which act because they cannot do otherwise, [and] that neither "statesmen of genius" nor "demagogues who stir up revolt", can guide the course of events according to their will'.[72] This serene yet self-contradictory conviction that politics is effectively irrelevant to the historical development of society is seductive because it frees socialists to console themselves for the frustrations encountered by the labour movement in the present with a heavenly vision of the future. It is only when some sort of historical transformation seems well-nigh inevitable, but at the same time remains obstinately absent, that one can indulge in what Marx, noting the resurgence of utopian socialism in the German labour movement of the late 1870s, dismissed, no doubt exaggeratedly, as 'playing with fancy pictures of the future structure of society'.[73]

This dialectic of utopianism and evolutionism is the object of critique in Walter Benjamin's twelfth and thirteenth 'Theses on the Philosophy of History'. In the latter, he criticises the Social Democrats' faith in the march of progress for being complicit with the procession of 'homogeneous empty time'. In the former, he deplores their abandonment of Marx's insistence that the task of the working class is to avenge a past that is founded on brutal human exploitation: 'Social Democracy thought fit to assign to the working class the role of the redeemer of future generations, in this way cutting the sinew of its greatest strength. This training made the working class forget both its hatred and its spirit of sacrifice, for both are nourished by the image of enslaved ancestors rather than that of liberated grandchildren'.[74] In late-Victorian Britain, state-socialist utopian fiction provided the framework for an image of liberated grandchildren that, if it served as an incentive to working-class action, also served as a deterrent to it. To dream of the freedom of one's grandchildren is to risk forgetting the enslavement of one's ancestors. Hobsbawm claims that 'the ideal of a new society was what gave the working class hope' in Europe in the late nineteenth-century.[75] But it must be added that, in its reformist variant, the ideal of a new society played a part in

---

[72] Bebel 1885, p. 257.
[73] Marx and Engels 1934, p. 350.
[74] Benjamin 1970, p. 262.
[75] Hobsbawm 1987, p. 133.

preventing the realisation of this hope too. Middle-class socialists in the movement – those for whom the image of enslaved ancestors was at most a distant memory – tended to nourish their occasionally anaemic politics with the image of liberated grandchildren.

Morris emphasized this class difference in his poem about the Paris Commune, 'The Pilgrims of Hope' (1885), which addressed the difficulty confronting the worker who tries to hold 'the hope of the morning of life' before him, in the face of mounting immiseration. The worker is punished both for dreaming about the future and for fighting to fulfil the dream. In brutal contrast, 'he who is rebel and rich may live safe for many a year / While he warms his heart with pictures of all the glory to come'.[76] Morris is acutely sensitive not only to the privileges of his own class position, but also to the iniquities of those for whom utopian speculation is a luxury. Not everyone can afford to fantasise about the future. Morris reinforces this point in Old Hammond's account of 'How the Change Came' in *News from Nowhere*. There, Hammond reports that 'the great motive-power of the change was a longing for freedom and equality'. Morris knows that want induces want, that lack induces desire. And he knows that this compulsive utopianism is no empty impulse – it is a forceful repudiation of the pain and suffering of the present. The visceral longing of the workers is 'akin if you please to the unreasonable passion of the lover; a sickness of heart that rejected with loathing the aimless solitary life of the well-to-do educated men of that time' (pp. 104–5). Their hatred shows that, if both spiritually and physically they pine for a society in which their grandchildren will feel liberated, their politics are still nurtured by the bitter experience of a society that has enslaved their ancestors.

Hammond stresses that 'though they could not look forward to the happiness or peace of the freeman, they did at least look forward to the war which a vague hope told them would bring that peace about' (p. 106). This passion is a manifestation of concrete utopianism. In Morris's ideal scenario, the workers look forward to the specific conditions of their self-emancipation – the revolutionary phase of the class struggle. So, if their hope is badly defined, it is scarcely abstract. According to Bloch, 'there is never anything soft about

---

[76] Morris 1915b, p. 395.

conscious-known hope, but a will within it insists: it should be so, it must become so'. Abstract utopianism, by contrast, is compensatory and escapist. 'An abstract utopia, even the so-called socialist state of the future, namely that which is for our grandchildren, very rarely knows any real danger; even its victory, not just its path, then seems undialectical'.[77]

In late-Victorian Britain, abstract utopianism dominates the perspective of social reformists on the future state of society. It is the obverse of evolutionism, particularly in its Fabian variant. In a discussion of the Fabians and their influence on the revisionist current of German social democracy after the First World War, Bloch characterises their reformism in the following way:

> Upheaval then takes place gently and is merely called evolution, private property is abolished when the time for it is as safe as a man with a bank account. Thus the decisive act is again and again left to children and grandchildren, and it is characteristic of this kind of postponement that the path becomes all, the goal nothing. . . . Socialism for the preachers of wine and drinkers of water is or was always only future, always only a country for their children, and the path itself knows no decisions but only a thousand provisos.[78]

A compensatory utopia creeps into this apparently hard-headed and practical approach to politics, because evolutionist solutions cannot offer people an active part in determining their historical destiny.

'The Fabians, though proclaimedly empirical, were by no means averse to sounding the millennial note', as Raphael Samuel emphasises.[79] Contributors to the *Fabian Essays* of 1889, including Sidney Webb, invoked the collectivist future, in triumphalist rhetoric, as an historical inevitability. And this passive reliance on a vision of the peaceful evolution of society concealed the fact that they had no idea how to implement the specific measures that they so frequently drafted, like the Constitution of a Socialist Commonwealth or the New Reform Bill. The Fabians' policies were therefore effectively written in the future perfect tense. But this mood served as an excuse for their failure to explain the practical implementation of these policies, and not as a source

---

[77] Bloch 1986, pp. 147, 477.
[78] Bloch 1986, p. 941.
[79] Samuel 1985, p. 26.

of political inspiration. Reform, for them, finally signified the minimum amount of social engineering necessary to make everybody a member of the middle class. 'Their highest ideal', one historian confirms, 'was to generalize their own modest life-style and to make it possible for all to achieve their own sure sense of social usefulness'.[80] Here, once more, is Morris's unmixed modern temperament. It was not that, in spite of appearances, Fabianism had no utopia; it was that, like the utopia later embraced without embarrassment by the Webbs, the Stalinist myth of the Soviet Union, 'it was unfortunately lacking in most attributes of desire'.[81]

The temperament or mentality of the petty-bourgeois socialist can also usefully be identified in the writing of Hyndman, the former Tory who, as leader of the Democratic (later, Social-Democratic) Federation, popularised Marx's writings on political economy for the English labour movement. At first sight, as I indicated when discussing the philanthropic profile of his apparently revolutionary aspect, Hyndman seems an unlikely bedfellow of the Fabians. From 1884, the year in which the SDF was formed, he spiced his speeches with references to violent revolution, in rhetorical flourishes entirely foreign to the polite tone of Fabian politics. This rhetoric was screwed to its sticking-point in Hyndman's speech to the unemployed agitation of 8 February 1886. On that occasion, portions of the press held him responsible for the fact that, a short time later, on being jeered at from gentlemen's clubs in Pall Mall, some demonstrators retaliated with a spot of indiscriminate looting. But, for all that he 'was filled with a kind of fervour of revolutionary anticipation', as Edward Carpenter was to put it, Hyndman was a political opportunist whose grasp of history was finally passive and progressivist: 'We used to chaff him because at every crisis in the industrial situation he was confident that the Millennium was at hand – that the S.D.F. would resolve itself into a Committee of Public Safety, and that it would be for him as Chairman of that body to guide the ship of the State into the calm haven of Socialism!'.[82] The Hyndmanites, Wolfe writes, 'were really reformists in revolutionary garb'.[83] It is no accident that Carpenter's parodic description

---

[80] Harrison 1987, p. 43.
[81] Weeks 1984, p. 76.
[82] Carpenter 1916, p. 246.
[83] Wolfe 1975, p. 102.

is also applicable to the Fabians' conception of social transformation. Hyndman too saw the future in terms of the timely administration of socialism from above. Morris hinted in 1885 that behind the latter's histrionic calls to action, 'all these theatrical boasts and warnings about immediate violent revolution', he was completely supine – 'waiting about to see what can be made of the political situation, if perhaps at the best one may attain to a sort of Bismarkian State Socialism, or as near it as we can get in England'.[84] For Hyndman, in contrast to Morris, the working class was ultimately an inert historical force, merely the raw material for a socialist future. His socialism was defined by an élitist strain of reformism.

There is thus a secret pact between Hyndman, with his messianic conception of the collapse of capitalism, and the Fabians, with their melioristic conception of the rise of socialism. Hyndman is a Fabian in clothing that has been fleeced from Marx. His politics are simply the flipside of the politics of 'practical' socialism, in which, as Morris claimed, 'the wolf of Socialism gets clad in the respectable sheeps-skin [sic] of a mild economic change'.[85] This can be seen in *The Historical Basis of Socialism in England* (1883):

> When we know that such a force as Niagara, such a power as the tides, such an agent as the wind, such a universal and all-pervading force as the heat of the sun, may be turned to account and stored for human use within the next few years, the portals of the future open wide before us and we gaze upon a long vista of golden ages for mankind. . . . Doubtless centuries may pass before the goal is reached; but that is no reason to question that the last great class struggle has begun nor why we should be deterred from helping on the evolution as far as we may.

Hyndman's reformism is exemplified by the phrase 'helping on the evolution'. The upheaval Hyndman imagines may be more or less violent or pacific, depending on the political climate, but history is a passive evolution. There is no sense here of the historical imperative by which, in Marx or Morris, the proletariat is forced to fight for socialism. Earlier in this volume, Hyndman wrote that 'society is undergoing a great and crucial revolution within, which may show itself openly either five, 10, or 50 years hence, but which cannot

---

[84] Morris 1987, p. 368.
[85] Morris 1994, p. 337.

in the nature of the case be delayed beyond a calculable period'.[86] This revolution resembles nothing so much as a natural process. It is a 'revolution within', an underground transformation that will finally reconfigure the surface of the earth. It is not surprising that the slightest social disturbance sent him into apoplexies of excitement.

At once voluntaristic and fatalistic, Hyndman's vision of the future is a version of what Stephen Yeo identifies as an historical narrative defined by 'ungradual inevitability' – either 'because of an evolutionary view with these years as a qualitative leap: or because of a widely-shared sense of crisis in the political and party machines, socialism was going to happen'. This faith was central to the *Fabian Essays* of 1889, and to Blatchford's political project, as Yeo emphasises.[87] It defines the beliefs of much of the Left at this time. For this reason, Morris's review of Sidney Webb's Fabian Essay of 1889 can also be read as an effective critique of the passage from Hyndman's *Historical Basis of Socialism* that I cited above: 'He is so anxious to prove the commonplace that our present industrial system embraces some of the machinery by means of which a Socialist system *might* be worked, and that some of the same machinery is used by the present municipalities, and the bureaucratic central government, that his paper tends to produce the impression of one who thinks we are already in the first stages of socialistic life'.[88] In a sense, late nineteenth-century socialist reformism inherited the contradictions of an earlier utopian socialism. For all their revolutionary experiments in inter-personal freedom, the Owenite schemes of the first half of the century described a dialectic of 'reformist premises and utopian aspirations'.[89] This dialectic is a subterranean current in the 'socialist revival', the dreams of which, like those of its precursor, can seem at the same time romantic and banal. The socialist utopias of the *fin de siècle* project an idealised version of municipal capitalism into a future free of social conflict.

The socialism of the late nineteenth-century therefore tends to be both reformist and utopian – the two apparently contradictory attitudes, close-sighted and long-sighted respectively, are inseparable parts of a single optic.

---

[86] Hyndman 1883, pp. 469, 452.
[87] Yeo 1977, pp. 21–2.
[88] Morris 1994, p. 458.
[89] Taylor 1983, p. 7.

Engels was manifestly aware of this when in 1887 he typified the politics of 'petty-bourgeois socialism' in the German Social-Democratic Party:

> While the fundamental views of modern socialism and the demand for the transformation of all the means of production into social property are recognised as justified, the realisation of this is declared possible only in the distant future, a future which for all practical purposes is quite out of sight. Thus, for the present one has to have recourse to mere social patchwork, and sympathy can be shown according to circumstances, even with the most reactionary efforts for so-called 'uplifting of the labouring class'.[90]

The reformist defers the socialist society to a future so far removed from the present as to invalidate the need to fight for it with revolutionary means. But, for all that, this society does not seem impossible, because it does not posit any break with the system as it stands. On the contrary, it is plausible, and (in the colloquial sense) 'practical' rather than 'utopian', to the precise extent that it conforms to the patchwork reform of present society. But this understanding of history is premised on the supposition that society is static, and ultimately unalterable, except in terms of a trajectory internal to its structure – rather than something that is constantly reproduced by struggle.

Morris argues on the contrary that 'it is utopian to put forward a scheme of gradual logical reconstruction of society which is liable to be overturned at the first historical hitch'. And it is in order to reinstate the role of the class struggle in history that he includes a lengthy account of 'How the Change Came' in his utopian fiction. His stress on human beings as historical actors making their own history, though not in circumstances of their own choosing, is a supreme example of militant optimism. It contrasts starkly with the pessimistic assumption underpinning the apparent optimism of a reformist politics that regards the development of socialism as an evolutionary inevitability. Morris's speculation, as a Marxist, 'that in destroying monopoly we shall destroy our present civilization', amounts to a wager – a wager that, 'if you tell your audiences that [in a socialist society] you are going to change so little that they will scarcely feel the change, whether you scare anyone or not, you will certainly not interest those who have nothing to hope for in the

---

[90] Marx and Engels 1984, p. 167.

present Society, and whom the hope of a change has attracted towards socialism'.[91]

As Morris suggests, the effect of a reformist politics is precisely to stop the bourgeoisie from feeling petrified by what he defiantly refers to as 'too brilliant pictures of the future of Society'.[92] The reformist utopia, in other words, is partly cultivated in order to choke the vital germs of thought that, shooting up in the present, point to a radically different future for the oppressed. Perry Anderson is correct to assert that, 'for Morris, utopian images of the future were indispensable for revolutionary struggle against *reformism* in the present'. And he is right too to quote in support of this assertion the following statement from *Socialism – Its Growth and Outcome* (1886–1888): 'It is essential that the ideal of the new society should always be kept before the eyes of the working classes, lest the *continuity* of the demands of the people should be broken, or lest they be misdirected'.[93] But what needs to be added is that, for Morris, as his polemic against reformism implies, the function of utopianism is to combat – utopianism. That is to say, it is to combat utopianism to the extent that it is not utopian, but presents the 'idealised reality' of which Marx complained. The influence of a reformist and idealist utopianism, a utopianism of the negative sort defined by Engels as unscientific, has to be effaced by a revolutionary and materialist utopianism. 'Elaborate utopian schemes for the future', Morris says, must be supplanted by 'dreams for the future' that can 'put a man in a fit frame of mind to study the reasons for his hope'.[94]

News from Nowhere, which, as I explain in Chapter 5, sets out to realise a future state that is qualitatively different from the idealised reality evoked by some of his contemporaries, is an attempt to defuse the power of *Looking Backward*. It cancels out one promissory note with another. Bellamy's book, so Morris says in his review, presents 'a twofold danger': to those who are inspired by it, the danger is that 'they will accept it with all its necessary errors and fallacies (which such a book *must* abound in) as conclusive statements of facts and rules of action, which will warp their efforts into futile directions'; and to those who are depressed by it, especially if they are 'enquirers or very

[91] Morris 1994, p. 341.
[92] Ibid.
[93] Anderson 1980, p. 174.
[94] Morris 1973, pp. 188–89.

young Socialists', the danger is that 'they also accepting its speculations as facts, will be inclined to say, "If *that* is Socialism, we won't help its advent, as it holds out no hope for us"' (p. 420).

V. *Looking Backward*

Morris provides an indispensable introduction to the preventative function of reformist utopianism at the *fin de siècle*. Utopia-from-above pre-empts utopia-from-below. In one 'Prospective History' of *The English Revolution of the Twentieth Century* (1894), this dynamic is presented in terms of a choice between two models of political change: 'From the top, by a fearless and brave reform, or from the nethermost by horrid revolution'.[95] At this time, the utopian form is deployed by reformist intellectuals who want to deter their readership from arriving at the conclusion that capitalism must be systematically destroyed if socialism is to stand a chance of solving the contradictions of class society. Like the socialists castigated by Marx in *The Poverty of Philosophy*, these utopians 'want the workers to leave the old society alone, the better to be able to enter the new society which they have prepared for them with so much foresight'.[96]

In his study of Fabianism in the 1880s, Wolfe identifies an influential strain of socialist politics that he defines as 'the "prophylactic theory" of Socialism: Socialism to prevent revolution'.[97] A symptomatic expression of this politics is the prophylactic function of the utopian form at this time. Utopia acts as a vaccination against the germ of revolution. This is apparent in the quietly assertive subtitle to the first edition of Ebeneezer Howard's utopian plan, *To-morrow: A Peaceful Path to Real Reform* (1898). In its second edition, Howard altered the title to *Garden Cities of To-morrow* (1902). But, in the late 1890s, when political discourse still echoed with the incendiary rhetoric of the socialist revival, it served surreptitiously to parody a short-lived Marxist journal published in the mid-1880s, *To-day: The Monthly Magazine of Scientific Socialism*. For 'Scientific Socialism', read 'A Bloody Path to Sham Reform'. Howard affirms in his chapter on the 'Difficulties' of social reform that 'no reader will

---

[95] Lazarus 1894, p. 9.
[96] Marx 1976b, p. 210.
[97] Wolfe 1975, p. 69, n. 7.

confuse the experiment here advocated with any experiment in absolute Communism'.[98]

The prophylactic function of utopian fiction is also identifiable in *Looking Backward*, a book that exercised a profound influence on Howard, who claimed to have persuaded the radical publisher William Reeves to pirate the first English edition.[99] Bellamy's politics had a close affinity to those of the Fabian Society: Annie Besant praised 'the ingenious author of "Looking Backward, from A.D. 2000"' in her article on 'Industry under Socialism' for the *Fabian Essays;*[100] and Bellamy reciprocated the compliment in 1894, when he edited the first American edition of the *Essays*. Paul Meier has claimed convincingly that, in the articles and lectures that he wrote after the publication of *Looking Backward*, Bellamy 'very faithfully reproduced the Fabian programme of municipal socialism'.[101]

When Beatrice Webb was researching her history of trade unionism in 1895, she apparently wanted to write a novel entitled 'Sixty Years Hence'. She promised that it would not be a utopian novel but a story about what society will look like 'if we go on "evoluting" in our humdrum way'.[102] Bellamy's book had in effect already made this plan redundant. *Looking Backward*, which purports to be a retrospective survey of the evolution of American society from an anarchic capitalist system in the late nineteenth-century to a rationally controlled state-socialist one in the twentieth-century, was the utopian novel never written by the Fabians.

The novel's narrator is Julian West, a wealthy insomniac who, with the help of a hypnotist, falls into a deep sleep one night in Boston in 1887. His insomnia is manifestly a physiological symptom of the feverish social unrest disturbing the confidence of the terrified middle classes at this time. America is prostrated by a 'great business crisis'. It is disabled too by 'disturbances of industry': 'the working classes had quite suddenly and very generally become infected with a profound discontent with their condition, and an idea that it could be greatly bettered if they only knew how to go about it' (pp. 19, 20–1). An 'impending social catastrophe' is expected. West's desperate

---

[98] Howard 1898, p. 96.
[99] Howard 1926, p. 133. See Beaumont 2003, p. 100.
[100] Besant 1889, p. 160.
[101] Meier 1978, p. 78.
[102] Cited in Showalter 1991, p. 63.

retreat into his unconscious is an escape from the 'nervous tension of the public mind' (p. 7). It is also a flight from history itself: West sleeps until the year 2000.

West does not merely dream that he has slept until the turn of the twenty-first century – he has in fact slept until the turn of the twenty-first century. After the initial shock, he settles into the future quite quickly. In the space of few months, he falls in love (conveniently enough, with a descendent of his old fiancée) and finds employment (appropriately enough, as an historian of the nineteenth-century). He is therefore uniquely qualified to offer 'a more definite idea of the social contrasts between the 19th and 20th centuries', as the book's preface indicates (p. iv). Cast in the form of an autobiographical account of his experiences in the Boston of the future, the bulk of West's narrative comprises a history of the development of the city's infrastructure and a tour of its superstructure, both of which are conducted by a Ciceronian character called Dr Leete.

West's first question to Leete, the point from which Bellamy's portrait of the future unfolds, concerns 'the labour question', which he calls 'the Sphinx's riddle of the 19th century'. He tells his interlocutor that when he went to sleep 'the Sphinx was threatening to devour society, because the answer was not forthcoming' (p. 66). Leete responds with some complacency that 'the solution came of the result of a process of industrial evolution which could not have terminated otherwise' (p. 67). He then proceeds to explain this 'process of industrial evolution'. In the 1880s, he recalls, 'the organization of labour and the strikes were an effect, merely, of the concentration of capital in greater masses than had ever been known before' (p. 71). In subsequent decades, 'the absorption of business by ever larger monopolies continued'. This 'era of corporate tyranny' widened the gap between the rich and the poor, but it also demonstrated that, 'as a means merely of producing wealth', capital is efficient 'in proportion to its consolidation' (p. 76).

Early in the twentieth-century, Leete reports, monopoly capitalism naturally developed into state capitalism:

> The industry and commerce of the country, ceasing to be conducted by a set of irresponsible corporations and syndicates of private persons at their caprice and for their profit, were intrusted to a single syndicate representing the people, to be conducted in the common interest for the common profit. The nation, that is to say organized as the one great business corporation

in which all other corporations were absorbed; it became the one capitalist
in the place of all other capitalists, the sole employer, the final monopoly in
which all previous and lesser monopolies were swallowed up, a monopoly
in the profits and economies of which all citizens shared. (pp. 77–8.)

The labour problem was solved because competition was abolished when the
nation became the sole capitalist. The introduction of socialism was then,
ironically, 'thanks to the corporations themselves' (p. 80). This development
was sponsored by public opinion. 'The popular sentiment towards the great
corporations and those identified with them', Leete proclaims in satisfied
tones, 'had ceased to be one of bitterness, as they came to realize their necessity
as a link, a transition phase, in the evolution of the true industrial system'
(p. 79). It is, presumably, this happy consensus that permitted the nation to
apply 'the principle of universal military service' to the problem of labour,
and to turn the people into an 'industrial army' (p. 86). The 'industrial army'
is the foundation for the entire superstructure in the state-socialist future.
Production is organized with a regimental efficiency analogous to that of 'the
German army in the time of Von Moltke' (p. 340); and this system informs
all aspects of life in the twenty-first century, from the provision of leisure to
the preservation of order. If the utopian programme of Looking Backward is
egalitarian, it is also aggressively utilitarian.

As Philip Wegner has recently reminded us, 'Bellamy differed little from
most late-19th-century, middle-class, progressive thinkers in his fear of the
consequences of direct action on the part of the workers'.[103] He called his
scheme 'Nationalist' in order to purge it of the slippery and sometimes pungent
associations of the word 'Socialist', which, as he piously remarked in a letter
to William Dean Howells, 'smells to the average American of petroleum,
suggests the red flag, with all manner of sexual novelties, and an abusive
tone about God and religion'.[104] It is clear from Looking Backward that he was
keen not to be accused of any relation to revolutionary politics. In the course
of his ongoing historical account of the creation of the state-socialist system
in the nineteenth and twentieth centuries, Leete stresses that 'the red flag
party' almost sabotaged the entire enterprise, because its assorted anarchists
and communists 'were paid by the great monopolies to wave the red flag

---

[103] Wegner 2002, p. 68.
[104] Quoted in Morgan 1944, p. 374.

and talk about burning, sacking, and blowing people up, in order, by alarming the timid, to head off any real reforms' (pp. 352–3). This image, which partially realises the restless fears of cataclysmic class warfare from which West suffers before he finally falls asleep at the *fin de siècle*, is restaged in the form of a gruesome melodrama in the fictions generated by the contemporary anti-socialist imagination. There is, in fact, a dystopian aspect to Bellamy's book, and it consists in its attempt to conjure away the spectre of communism. In a dark irony therefore, the dystopia or cacotopia, which is at this date frequently only a coarse portrait of social anarchy, luridly coloured with the crudest caricatures of working-class militancy, exhibits the political unconscious of *Looking Backward*, the archetypal socialist utopia of the late nineteenth-century.

It is Bellamy who, invoking the prospect of revolutionaries 'burning, sacking, and blowing people up', attempts 'to head off any real reforms', that is to say, any systemic transformation. As his praise for the creative potential of monopolistic corporations in *Looking Backward* makes evident, Bellamy's politics were in important aspects far closer to those of the capitalists than to those of self-styled communists and anarchists. On the first anniversary of the Boston Nationalist Society, in 1890, he underlined his opposition both to 'the money power' and to the power of the masses. But his attitude is asymmetrical, as a rhetorical flourish no doubt indicates: 'Let no mistake be made here', he concluded, 'we are not revolutionists, but counterrevolutionists'.[105] Scattered references to the red flag party aside, *Looking Backward* acts as an ideological deterrent not by demonising revolutionary chaos, but by canonising the notion of an industrial economy that is controlled entirely by a equalitarian state. Nationalism, the novel announces, in the tone of a letter to potential shareholders, or 'stake-holders' perhaps, is as desirable as it is inevitable.

In terms of its ideological function, *Looking Backward* is the fictional equivalent of *The Coöperative Commonwealth*, the popular utopian tract by the Danish socialist Laurence Gronlund, which was published in the United States in 1884 and later edited in England by Shaw. Gronlund's book is a socialist primer, the purpose of which was clearly to appease the panicky concern of the British and American middle classes. It sets out its object, like a contract,

---

[105] Thomas 1967, p. 77.

in an address 'To the Reader': 'I hope to show you that Socialism is no importation, but a *home-growth*, wherever found; to give you good reason to suppose that this New Social Order will be indeed a happy issue to the brain-worker as well as to the hand-worker, woman as well as man; and to justify my conviction that it must come to that, here as elsewhere, within a comparatively short period, or to barbarism'.[106] In a double sense, this passage is speculative. For if it conjectures that the 'New Social Order' is a settled outcome for society some time in the more or less immediate future, it promotes socialism not as a political commitment but as a sort of ideological investment – one that will be renumerated later, profitably enough, in the form of socio-economic security. Gronlund seeks to reassure a readership to which the term 'socialism' evokes incendiary associations that civilisation as they know it will remain untouched by the transition to a cooperative commonwealth.

Looking Backward builds on this basis by fabricating a socialist society that seems at the same time glamorously futuristic and comfortingly familiar. It constructs a kind of architect's model for a project to modernise the outmoded design of capitalism – it is all clean lines and gleaming white surfaces. Nationalist Boston, with its 'side-walk coverings', which turn the city into a corridored interior when the climate is inclement (p. 210), is like a pavilion at a contemporary world exposition. And this is scarcely an accident, since, as Susan Buck-Morss writes, 'the message of the world exhibitions as fairylands was the promise of social progress for the masses without revolution'.[107] *Looking Backward* enshrines a consumerist utopia. The city's neo-classical department store, its portal presided over by a statue of 'Plenty, with her cornucopia', is a secular cathedral (p. 140). It looks uncannily familiar today:

> I was in a vast hall full of light, received not alone from the windows on all sides, but from the dome, the point of which was a hundred feet above. Beneath it, in the centre of the hall, a magnificent fountain played, cooling the atmosphere to a delicious freshness with its spray. The walls and ceiling were frescoed in mellow tints, calculated to soften without absorbing the light which flooded the interior. Around the fountain was a space occupied

---

[106] Gronlund 1892, p. 5. On Gronlund and Bellamy, see Morgan 1944, pp. 389–92.
[107] Buck-Morss 1989, p. 86.

> with chairs and sofas, on which many persons were seated conversing.
> Legends on the walls all about the hall indicated to what classes of
> commodities the counters below were devoted (pp. 140–41).

West experiences his most profound epiphany on entering the sacrosanct
interior of this impressive store, from which the commodity itself has been
effaced. He discovers that one acquires goods simply by scrutinising printed
descriptions of them, and then discreetly placing an order with a courteous
clerk, who communicates through 'pneumatic transmitters' with the wholesale
department (p. 147). This is a temple dedicated to celebrating the power of
capital without capitalism, a commodity culture in which the commodity is
occluded. Concomitantly, the act of labour, and the scene of production, are
also notably absent from Bellamy's book. In Wegner's compelling account of
its ideological content, he argues that 'the utopia of *Looking Backward* figures
a society ordered according to the logic of the commodity, a consumerist
paradise wherein the dilemmas of industrialism have been wished away,
a world of reified commodities from which every trace of labor has been
expunged'.[108] Unsurprisingly, Bellamy's bland Bostonian heroine, West's
companion Edith, is less a pioneer of some post-capitalist social ethic than
she is 'an indefatigable shopper', the embryonic symbol of late-nineteenth-
century capitalism's emancipatory promise (p. 137).

As we have seen, *Looking Backward* starts out in the nineteenth-century from
a social situation in which 'the relation between the workingman and the
employer, between labor and capital, appeared in some unaccountable manner
to have become dislocated' (p. 20). Bellamy's accent on the 'unaccountable'
character of this fact, which presents the class conflict at the centre of capitalist
relations of production in terms of something outside human control, sanctions
his subsequent story of capitalism's 'industrial evolution' into its apparent
opposite. It is a simple matter of submitting to the charms of the absolute
spirit as it slowly uncoils through time: 'All that society had to do was to
recognize and cooperate with this evolution, when its tendency had become
unmistakable' (p. 67). History does everything, humanity nothing. There is
little point in enquiring 'how the change came', as Morris's emissary from
the nineteenth-century does in *News from Nowhere*.

---

[108] Wegner 2002, p. 80.

Despite its frequently powerful anti-capitalist polemic, Bellamy's utopia therefore 'lies flawlessly in the line of extension of the modern world', as Bloch says; 'it is fundamentally satisfied with the disposition of capitalist civilization'.[109] This was confirmed at the time by a member of the Liberty and Property Defence League, who remarked in his assessment of the book that 'at best State Socialism is but our present artificial materialism reduced to a huge despotic cast-iron system, and worshipped as the *summum bonum*'.[110] Nationalism is a utopian adaptation of the principal devices employed by capital to combat the Great Depression: protectionism, monopolisation, and 'Taylorist' management. Twenty-first-century Boston offers a redemptive version of the capitalist reformation of the economic sphere at the *fin de siècle*.

Morris analysed the 'conservative instinct' of contemporary reformist politics in the following manner:

> Many among the middle class who are sincerely grieved and shocked at the condition of the proletariat which civilization has created, and even alarmed by the frightful inequalities which it fosters, do nevertheless shudder back from the idea of the class struggle, and strive to shut their eyes to the fact that it is going on. . . . They propose to themselves the impossible problem of raising the inferior or exploited classes into a position in which they will cease to struggle against the superior classes, while the latter will not cease to exploit them. This absurd position drives them into the concoction of schemes for bettering the condition of the working classes at their own expense, some of them futile, some merely fantastic.

'The greater part of these schemes aim', he concluded, 'though seldom with the consciousness of their promoters, at the creation of a new middle class out of the wage-earning class, and at their expense'.[111] Morris picked up these themes in a letter published in *Commonweal* one month later. 'The whole system of palliation', he repeated, '[tends] towards the creation of a new middle class to act as a buffer between the proletariat and their direct and obvious masters; the only hope of the bourgeois for retarding the advance of Socialism lies in this device'. I want to underscore the acuity with which

---

[109] Bloch 1986, p. 613.
[110] O'Brien 1892, p. 73.
[111] Morris 1973, pp. 177, 179.

Morris prises the utopian kernel of late-Victorian reformism from its critical shell. 'Shall the ultimate end of civilization be the perpetual widening of the middle classes?' he cries despairingly.[112] 'Yes!' is Bellamy's spontaneous response in *Looking Backward*. It is a response encrypted into most of the maps of utopia printed in this period.

Georges Sorel, who pointed out the failure of socialists to attack 'the senseless hope which the Utopists have always held up before the dazzled eyes of the people', complained in 1916 that the 'ridiculousness' of Bellamy's novels had not been sufficiently highlighted. His contempt for Bellamy's success was derived from his sense that 'they presented to the people an entirely middle-class ideal of life'.[113] In Morris's terms, this makes them 'practical'. Bellamy embodies the dialectical unity of utopianism and pragmatism. Morris's complaint about the 'practical' socialist is that, because and not in spite of the fact that he is 'anxious that some step towards socialism should be taken at once', he presents the middle classes with a socialism transmogrified from a terrifying spectre into a 'sham amiable monster'. 'Is it conceivable', he splutters, 'that the change for the present wage-owners will simply mean hoisting them up into the life of the present "refined" middle-classes, and that the latter will remain pretty much what they are now, minus their power of living on the labour of others?'.[114]

It is this reformist fantasy – of 'the existing state of society minus its revolutionary and disintegrating elements'[115] – that seems 'inconceivable' to the militant materialist Morris. And he reinforces the point in his review of *Looking Backward* the following year, when he remarks that the unmixed modern temperament 'makes its owner (if a Socialist) perfectly satisfied with modern civilization, if only the injustice, misery, and waste of class society could be got rid of' (pp. 420–21). Bellamy's fiction marks a return to the pragmatic utopianism of the prophet of 'True Socialism', Georg Kuhlmann. Marx chastised him because 'he transforms the real social movement which, in all civilised countries, already proclaims the approach of a terrible social upheaval into a process of *comfortable* and *peaceful conversion*, into a *still life*

---

[112] Morris 1994, pp. 99–100.
[113] Sorel 1916, pp. 137, 138n.
[114] Morris 1994, pp. 337–38.
[115] Marx and Engels 1976c, p. 513.

which will permit the owners and rulers of the world to slumber *peacefully*. The utopian's doctrine, like that of the prophet, is, in Marx's word, 'sedative'.[116]

The author of the first significant biography of Bellamy claimed in the 1940s that 'but for him there would have been a complete surrender in America to class warfare as the way to freedom from class dominance and exploitation'.[117] In Britain, so one literary historian has later insisted, 'Bellamy's presentation of a peaceful evolutionary achievement of the socialist state put to rest the spectre of mounting class warfare and hatred' that many people thought inseparable from socialism.[118] If these are exaggerations, they are at least suggestive of *Looking Backward*'s sedative effect. It is difficult to measure its success as a prophylactic; but it seems clear that, on both sides of the Atlantic, *Looking Backward* helped to fasten reformist connotations to the term 'socialism'. Linn Boyd Porter's *Speaking of Ellen* (1890), about a factory as it is and as it might be, provides evidence of this. Though not in formal terms a utopia, this Owenite fantasy, subsequently published in Britain as *Riverfall* (1903), is utopian in content. Towards the end of the narrative, the aristocratic hero Philip, backed by his wife Ellen, formerly a labour organiser and feminist in her husband's workforce, announces his intention to build 'an ideal community in which each will share in all work and the benefits to be derived therefrom'. In explicating this principle, Philip appends the following phrase: 'or, as it has been better put by our great Master, "From each according to his ability, to each according to his need"'.[119] A footnote clarifies that the 'Master' Porter has in mind is 'Edward Bellamy'. The authentic source of this quotation is of course the *Critique of the Gotha Programme* (1875), where Marx discusses 'a higher phase of communist society', quite distinct from the early phase in which socialist relations of production and consumption remain scarred by their foetal origins in capitalist society. It therefore seems ironic that one of the few references Marx made to the future socialist society – that is, to a qualitatively different world in which, finally, 'the narrow horizon of bourgeois right' can be crossed 'in its entirety'[120] – should be traduced in the context of Bellamy's practical-utopian doctrine.

[116] Marx and Engels 1976a, pp. 538–39.
[117] Morgan 1944, p. 244.
[118] Marshall 1962, p. 118.
[119] Porter 1903, p. 357.
[120] Marx 1989, p. 87.

Porter's mistake is symptomatic of the muddle over the meaning of socialism that prevailed at this time. Bellamy acknowledged this confusion when in his essay on the 'Clear Use of Terms' he differentiated between the Marxist motto, which he interprets in class-specific terms as 'from each labourer according to his ability or to each according to his earnings', and his own, 'Nationalist' motto, 'from each man and woman equally to each equally'.[121] To compound the confusion, the slogan of the *Nationalization News*, organ of Bellamy's British acolytes, was a gung-ho 'Each for All and All for Each!' – an individualistic as well as a collectivist battle-cry, perfectly consistent with a capitalist ethic. This confusion is intrinsic to his conscious effort to sanitise socialism for the middle classes. For, if Bellamy rejected the rhetoric of revolutionary socialism, then he also appropriated its power. The Nationalist maxim, as his plea for clarity makes apparent, is parasitic upon the Marxist one. Bellamy ghosted Marx's writing in order to exorcise its spirit from contemporary socialism. Utopian fiction 'apparitionalised' revolutionary politics, in an attempt to ensure that the spectre of communism remained merely spectral.

At the *fin de siècle*, utopian discourse often serves as a means of managing insurgent energies. I use this phrase in order to make a clear distinction between the reformist utopia, such as *Looking Backward*, and the utopia informed by revolutionary politics, of which *News from Nowhere* is the singular example in the late nineteenth-century. In the 'Postscript' to his seminal biography of Morris, E.P. Thompson claims that *News from Nowhere* announces the fact that 'Utopia's proper and new-found space [is] the education of desire'.[122] There can be no doubt that 'the education of desire' was central to Morris's socialist politics. He himself repeatedly said that, if the point of socialism is 'to obtain for the whole people, duly organized, the possession and controul [sic] of all the means of production & exchange', then 'the means whereby this is to be brought about is first, educating people into desiring it, next organizing them into claiming it effectually'.[123] But Thompson, who takes his cue from Miguel Abensour's claim that the education of desire is the organising function of Morris's utopia, treats the phrase like a magic formula for understanding Morris's relation to the Marxist tradition, and fails to define it in any detail.

---

[121] Quoted in Bowman 1962, p. 34.
[122] Thompson 1976, p. 791.
[123] Morris 1987, p. 307.

Abensour offers a more focused discussion of the education of desire, because he distinguishes between, on the one hand, Morris's utopia, which tries 'to awaken and energize desires so that they might rush towards their liberation', and, on the other, 'those utopias that are an imaginary projection of a new mode of social repression of impulses'.[124] But he misrepresents this other sort of utopia when he portrays it simply as a repressive force. Utopia must appeal to more or less radical hopes in the first place, even if it seeks to repress them. It is, therefore, an imaginary projection of contradictory tendencies. I characterise this other form of utopia in terms of its capacity for managing insurgent energies for two reasons: first, because (unlike Abensour) it accepts that even the most myopic vision of the future is compelled to shape potentially liberatory impulses; second, because it conveys the coercive or disciplinary function of 'education', which is occluded in Thompson's frankly abstract discussion of the term.

The late-nineteenth-century utopia is a compound of impulses. If 'utopia was always an ambiguous ideal', as Jameson affirms, 'urging some on to desperate and impossible realizations about which it reassured the others that they could never come into being in the first place', then this ambiguity is ultimately structural to its reformist manifestation.[125] The real paradox of the reformist utopia, of utopia-from-above, is that, even as it ferments a disaffected desire for an alternative future, it fosters a supine acceptance of either the predestination or the impossibility of change.

VI. Dialectics of utopia

Utopian thought performs both positive and negative roles. It contains 'critical' and 'ideological' dynamics. Polemical attempts to question and oppose contemporary social divisions, utopias are at the same time, like ideological representations, 'resourceful strategies for containing, managing and imaginarily resolving them'.[126] In a passage from The Prison Notebooks, Gramsci captures utopia's dialectical composition with some precision, when he argues that 'religion is the most gigantic utopia . . . that history has ever known, since it

---

[124] Abensour 1999, pp. 133, 145.
[125] Jameson 1994, pp. 52–3.
[126] Eagleton 1991, p. 135.

is the most grandiose attempt to reconcile, in mythological form, the real contradictions of historical life'.[127] Secular utopias are themselves redemptive narratives that use a fantastic form to resolve the conflicts characteristic of a post-lapsarian society. And like the vision of a heavenly city, the realm of freedom portrayed in utopian fiction at the *fin de siècle*, as an attempt to reconcile the real contradictions of historical life, is a consolation for them as well as a critique of them. A fragile negotiation of competing impulses, utopia inspires hope and displaces it.

This is the kind of contradiction with which Marx comes to terms in his remarks on religion, when he claims that '*religious* distress is at the same time the *expression* of real distress and also the *protest* against real distress', and that 'religion is the sigh of the oppressed creature, the heart of a heartless world, just as it is the spirit of spiritless conditions'.[128] Religion is a legitimation of existing conditions and a protest against them. Utopia describes the same dialectic of critical discontent and ideological acquiescence. This correlation of liberation and containment is not, however, static. The sense of helplessness with which the pious grasp the spiritual as opposed to material equality of humanity can be a source of comfort or frustration. Similarly, utopia's capacity to pacify or to provoke action depends upon contingent factors, the subjective and objective conditions of its production and reception. That is to say, the image of the future is there to be fought over. And, if the dominant version of the socialist ideal at the end of the nineteenth-century was instilled with evolutionism, then this was not inevitable, as Morris knew. The late-Victorian period witnessed a sustained debate about the extent to which utopian thought might act as an organ of historical awakening.

This debate turned on the competing claims of the 'practical' and the 'utopian', as I have already implied.[129] The latter, needless to say, tended to be used as a term of abuse. An article by Hyndman, on 'Revolution and Reform' (1884), mimics the characteristic logic of 'Social Reformers', of whom he disapproves, attacking 'Socialists', of whom he approves: '"We are Social Reformers, not Socialists: we can make the best omelette gourmet ever smacked lips over, without breaking a single egg. . . . In short, we are Social Reformers

---

[127] Gramsci 1971, p. 405.
[128] Marx 1975a, p. 175.
[129] For a discussion of this debate in relation to Oscar Wilde's 'The Soul of Man Under Socialism' (1891), see Beaumont 2004.

and Practical Politicians. You are Socialists and Dreamers"'.[130] The problem with Hyndman's underlying position is that it reproduces the social reformer's prejudice against utopianism. This is evident some six years later, in his review of *In Darkest England and the Way Out* (1890), a book by General Booth, the leader of the Salvation Army. In an aside on 'Socialist Utopianism', Booth had declared that, though he sympathised with the aspirations underlying 'Socialist Dreams', he himself was 'a practical man, dealing with the actualities of to-day': 'I am quite prepared to hail with open arms any Utopia that is offered me. But it must be within range of my finger-tips'.[131] Booth's comment amounts to the claim that he is prepared to accept a utopia if it is practical; in other words, if it is not a utopia at all. Hyndman's response fails to subject his opponent's false logic to critique: 'The Utopians are those who, like General Booth, imagine that the vast problems of our civilisation can be solved by ignorant beneficence from above'; the 'practical men', Hyndman asserts, are those who 'resolve that scientifically and surely they will teach even hungry John Jones how to grasp hands with his fellows on either side of him', and to substitute justice 'for the cruel charity of his masters'.[132] This kind of crude name-calling is typical of the pernicious circularity with which discussion of strategic questions was frequently conducted by socialists at the *fin de siècle*.

Morris stood outside the terms of this debate. In 1888, he complained of those self-appointed 'practical' socialists from across the spectrum of social reform who 'read the present into the future', and who are consequently inclined to imagine a socialist community in which 'people's ways of life and habits of thought will be pretty much as they are now'.[133] This is the pragmatic utopianism of the unmixed modern temperament. Morris himself enacted its dialectical inversion, in the form of a utopian praxis, when he proclaimed that he was one of those 'visionary or practical people'.[134] He tried to envisage an anti-capitalist society that, if it is germinated by the contradictions of present society, is nonetheless qualitatively different to it, and can inspire not deaden people's desire. In his fictional account of the Peasants' Revolt, Morris carefully probed the balance of forces between utopia's active and passive

[130] Hyndman 1884, pp. 181–82.
[131] Booth 1890, p. 79.
[132] Hyndman 1890, p. 16.
[133] Morris 1994, pp. 336–37.
[134] Morris 1973, p. 190.

impulses. *A Dream of John Ball* (1886) is about the capacity of past struggle to inspire socialists of the present day. But, at the end of the story, before the narrator returns to consciousness in the nineteenth-century, John Ball speculates as to the political value of a vision of future history: 'and scarce do I know whether to wish thee some dream of the days beyond thine to tell what shall be, as thou hast told me, for I know not if that shall help or hinder thee'.[135] Spoken as an aside, this is a surreptitious straw poll of the readers of *Commonweal*: it asks, would you be prepared to read a communist utopia in these pages?

It was, of course, the success of *Looking Backward* that convinced Morris that the utopian novel was a necessary site of struggle over meaning within the socialist movement. Morris, who had always had a densely textured understanding of what social relations of production might entail under communism, was not about to lose ground to someone whose conception of the concrete workings of socialism, once scrutinised, revealed an idealised version of capitalism. Just as he thought it 'necessary that the *Commonweal* should notice [*Looking Backward*]' (p. 420), so it became imperative to write a popular political romance, in order to capture utopia for revolutionary purposes. He finally wagered that, as Lafargue was to argue, the 'imaginary conception of the unknown, which cannot but be hypothetical, is one of the most powerful incentives to action, it is the very condition of every forward step'.[136]

News from Nowhere is an attempt to promote the ' "activating presence" of utopia in human action'.[137] In his reflections on utopian fantasy at the very end of the narrative, Morris seeks to overcome the contradictory nature of utopia as a merely ideological representation. Lying in his bed in his house in dingy Hammersmith, 'thinking about it all', William Guest tries to work out whether he is overwhelmed with despair at finding he has been 'dreaming a dream' (p. 210). For a moment, he resembles the idealist 'drained by the whore called "Once upon a time"' in Benjamin's sixteenth thesis on the philosophy of history.[138] But then he finds that he is 'not so despairing' (p. 210). And he reconfigures the message from the future traced out in 'Ellen's last mournful look':

---

[135] Morris 1912b, p. 286.
[136] Lafargue 1907b, p. 141.
[137] Bauman 1976, p. 17.
[138] Benjamin 1970, p. 264.

Go back again, then, and while you live you will see all round you people
engaged in making others live lives which are not their own, while they
themselves care nothing for their own real lives – men who hate life though
they fear death. Go back and be the happier for having seen us, for having
added a little hope to your struggle. Go on living while you may, striving,
with whatsoever pain and labour needs must be, to build up little by little
the new day of fellowship, and rest, and happiness. (pp. 210–11.)

This is News from Nowhere. 'Nowhere may be an imaginary country, but
News from Nowhere is real news', as Lewis Mumford emphasised.[139] The
import of this news is that the socialist future can only be the product of an
active struggle systematically to remould the social materials available in the
present. Unlike the hero of *Looking Backward*, who is confined to the future,
Guest is free to go out and transform his 'dream' into a 'vision'. 'He remains
in control of his powers, man enough to blast open the continuum of history'.[140]

'In wishing', says Bloch, 'there is not yet any element of work or activity,
whereas all wanting is wanting to do'.[141] Wanting forges an organic link
between the past and present and the future. In effect, Guest has already
started to make this connection, since the readership of *Commonweal* is a
repository of activists – '10 men sharing an idea begin to act, a hundred draw
attention as fanatics, a thousand and society begins to tremble, a hundred
thousand and there is war abroad, and the cause has victories tangible and
real'.[142] Hammond intimates as much when he muses, 'Who knows but I may
not have been talking to many people?' (p. 135). The task that Morris sets
before this socialist audience is that of building up 'the new day of fellowship'
from within an alienated world in which people 'live lives which are not their
own'. It is a question of wresting capitalism's negation from the conditions
of its reproduction. Perceiving the dialectical relationship between capitalism
and communism, such that the former creates the conditions of its supersession
by the latter, Morris detects the Not Yet, the unsettling and inspiriting presence
of a potentially different future in the present. It constitutes 'the standpoint
of redemption' interior to the present – from which the world is displaced

[139] Mumford 1923, p. 24.
[140] Benjamin 1970, p. 264.
[141] Bloch 1986, p. 46.
[142] Morris 1973, p. 85.

and estranged, '[revealed] to be, with its rifts and crevices, as indigent and distorted as it will appear one day in the messianic light'.[143]

From this perspective, the relationship between future and present in Morris's 'epoch of rest' is dialectical. The Nowherean future is haunted by the present; that is, communist society is stalked by the spectre of its capitalist pre-history. Hence, on his return to Victorian England, Guest wonders why, when he was in Nowhere, he continued to be conscious 'that [he] was really seeing all that new life from the outside, still wrapped up in the prejudices, the anxieties, the distrust of this time of doubt and struggle' (p. 210). But, in late-Victorian London, at the end of the novel, the present is haunted by the future. Their relationship is inverted. Guest thus occupies the point of overlap between the two worlds. And, in this respect, he is an allegorical figure for the dialectical function of concrete utopian fiction, which secretes the real into the utopian even as it also secretes the utopian into the real. In Walter Benjamin's terms, he marks out 'the strait gate through which the Messiah might enter'.[144] I will return to Morris's utopia, and to the radical importance of its portrayal of the utopian future, in Chapter 5. In Chapter 3, I focus on another variant of reformist utopianism that is prominent at the *fin de siècle*, the utopia of feminism.

---

[143] Adorno 1974, p. 247.
[144] Benjamin 1970, p. 266.

Chapter Three
Feminism and Utopia

I. Introduction

Here is one woman's description of her experience as a reader of utopian fiction in a period that appeared to promise political change:

> I bought and read all the utopian works I could get my hands on, and felt a powerful emotional response to most of them. These novels gave me a fictional representation of the unexpressed anger I felt at abuses I saw daily but felt powerless to stop. They also gave me models of female characters who were not helpless, who did in fact stop the abuses in one way or another, and who often along the way created worlds of real beauty. I could for a few hours imagine myself in these utopian worlds and come away with a modicum of hope that, despite the depressing evidence of my daily newspaper, we could in fact make a better world.

As its diction might indicate, this is in fact a recent account of the excitement that feminist political fantasy generated in the 1970s.[1] But it is also evocative of female readers' reactions to the first stirrings of this same literary form almost a century earlier – in

---

[1] Crowder 1993, p. 238.

the 1880s and 1890s, at the time of the ascendancy of the New Woman novel. Noting the intensity of emotion with which contemporary female readers discovered Olive Schreiner's *The Story of an African Farm* (1883), Kate Flint has convincingly argued that its popular appeal resided in its 'optimism that there is, somewhere, a reachable ideal which lies outside both domestic and political structures, and, moreover, that one's struggle to attain this is tied in, at a more microcosmic level, with the feminist cause'.[2]

Diane Crowder's description of encountering feminist utopian fiction, in the passage cited above, is suggestive because, as well as illuminating the basic workings of the utopian form under question, it casts speculative light on the reception of earlier instances of the genre. Leaving aside its compelling confession of the sheer appetite with which she consumed these publications, her narrative poses a revealing problematic. It unintentionally dramatises the conflictual relationship between the individualist and collectivist political impulses typical of utopianism. Crowder knows that it is only a collectivity that can 'make a better world'; but, significantly, she interprets the impact of feminist utopias along individualist lines, in terms of their capacity to encourage vicarious identification with powerful female characters capable of stopping sexist abuses while creating 'worlds of real beauty' along the way. So, if Crowder initially turned to utopian novels, as she says, out of anger over injustices she felt powerless to stop, then she is content to find within them a refracted image of her very isolation. Far from addressing the issue of collective social change, the utopian fantasies to which she refers would seem instead simply to inscribe the heroic inverse of that sense of personal impotence from which she initially recoiled.

The heroine of the feminist utopia, precisely in her capacity to act, thus appears as the fantastic obverse of – rather than a social alternative to – the atomised and inactive intellectual whose experience of suffering is ultimately restricted by her class position. In Crowder's paradigm, the anger aroused and aggravated by reading utopian fiction, once channelled into an empowering identification with its heroine, returns the reader, as in a circuit, to the lonely experience of encountering the 'depressing evidence' of women's oppression in the daily newspaper. Hence, despite Crowder's claim to be less desirous than angry, and despite the fact that her imaginary excursion to another world

---

[2] Flint 1993, p. 244.

leaves behind a residue of hope in some collective social transformation, utopia's escapist impulse seems uppermost here, and 'its very images of harmony threaten to hijack the radical impulses they hope to promote'.[3] This is telling, for the appeal that utopian fiction makes to a social collectivity is always inextricably tied to the individualist conditions in which it is produced and consumed, and its call for social and material change is always unavoidably supported by an idealist faith in the transformative power of individual consciousness. Utopian fiction necessarily remains anchored to the room in which it is written or read.

In the late-Victorian period, of course, even those middle-class women who had started to question their marginal social status remained more or less physically confined to the domestic sphere. The socialist-feminist novelist Margaret Harkness, who circulated uneasily amongst Engels's acolytes in the Social-Democratic Federation, searching vainly for a socialist model of friendship that could console her sense of alienation, tried to make a virtue of necessity: 'I read the papers and have a little political world of my own', she confided to her second cousin Beatrice Potter in a letter written in February 1880.[4] Harkness's reluctant solipsism is at once a retreat from the outside world from which she feels excluded, and a restless attempt to apprehend it (as in Crowder's account of the 1970s, the newspapers represent women's link to the everyday domain of politics, as well as their separation from it). In this sense, for all that her novels are realist, the personal and political conjuncture out of which Harkness's fiction emerges mirrors the conditions that engender utopian writing. Utopia, too, is a way of creating a little political world of one's own, in order simultaneously to elude and contend with a larger political world beyond one's control. In the end, the feminist utopian fiction of the late nineteenth-century returns the reader to a room of her own. If it is a site of production, this space is also a site of entrapment.

Elizabeth Corbett's *New Amazonia* (1889), a utopian novel to which in the last section of this chapter I return in detail, is in this sense typical of what Elaine Showalter calls 'the confused aspirations and dreams and the claustrophobic femaleness of the feminist aesthetic' at this time.[5] The narrator,

---

[3] Eagleton 1990, p. 371.
[4] Quoted in Hapgood 2000, p. 130.
[5] Showalter 1978, pp. 194–95.

a woman writer, enjoys a liberating dream of an ideal country run collectively by a far-distant feminist sisterhood, but finally awakes in the present to find herself alone in her study, 'surrounded by nineteenth-century magazines and newspapers, and shivering all over, for I had let the fire go out during my long nap'.[6] Her shiver is symptomatic of a social condition as well as a physical one – the isolation of the middle-class feminist forced by circumstances into a reliance on imaginary experience. Corbett's narrator's cold, dank study functioning only as a framing device, is nonetheless the novel's absent centre, the empty space at the core of her utopian society. To encapsulate the point we might risk an anachronism and say that the kernel of Charlotte Perkins Gilman's utopia *Herland* (1915) is the hallucinatory psychosis suffered by the female protagonist of her earlier short story 'The Yellow Wallpaper' (1891).

This contrast, between the fantasy of collective social harmony and (its all-too-real underside) the lonely individual consciousness of the woman writer, provides the basic structure of the feminist utopian novel. But to summarise this variant of the utopian form in terms of that particular opposition is to repress its hidden, dialectical dynamic – that is, the subtextual dream of reconciling the contradiction, and of transcending it, by positing an imaginary collectivity, apparently within the individual writer's grasp already, in the form of an ideal readership, whose function is to forge a bridge between a state of present isolation and one of future socialisation. If Olive Schreiner's utopian 'Dreams in the Desert' (1891) is implicitly premised on the claustrophobia explored in *From Man to Man* (written between 1875 and 1920), then this is not only because the heroine makes a refuge of the room in which she writes her journal, but also because she there imagines 'what it must be like to be one of a company of men and women in a room together, all sharing somewhat the same outlook on life'.[7] What interests me is the utopian subtext that runs through many New Women novels at the end of the last century, but which operates in a particularly telling, dialectical way in openly utopian feminist texts. The real import of late-Victorian feminists' utopian fiction lies less in its manifest content, its grand dreams of a future matriarchy or gynocracy, than in its latent content, its frankly more modest fantasy of a like-minded

---

[6] Corbett 1889, p. 146. Subsequent references are given after quotations in the text.
[7] Schreiner 1926, p. 174.

community of women in the present. It is not so much the abstract utopian hope for a perfect egalitarian society as the more concrete utopian hope invested in an ideal fellowship of women readers that conducts these novels' political charge. In this sense, the feminist utopia displays the unconscious aspiration of all utopian fiction, which is, as I explain in the Conclusion to this book, to be the foundation of a group of people capable of implementing or inspiring the necessary social transformation.

In what follows, I begin by offering a few general remarks on the New Woman and the climate out of which she grew. I then explore what I term the 'politics of fellowship', a utopian structure of feeling peculiar to the feminist and socialist-feminist movement in the late nineteenth-century. This part is intended to supply a context for my subsequent discussion, in Section IV, of the feminist utopian novel, the polemical premises of which are of particular interest to me. In Section V, I focus on the mechanics of the feminist utopian fiction, and especially on the way in which it is used to furnish 'proof' of the ideal future. I conclude the chapter with an account of *New Amazonia* in which I excavate the meta-utopian content of the feminist utopian form at the *fin de siècle*. Ironically, it turns out that analysing the New Woman in terms of her relation to the future may be the most effective way of historicising her.

II. The New Woman

In the late 1870s, the German Social-Democratic leader August Bebel urged women 'to take their share in the present contest for a better future'.[8] This sense of the present as a site of social experimentation, the laboratory of future history, had diffused and intensified into a widespread assumption by the turn of the century. In the 1890s, as Holbrook Jackson later testified, the future itself seemed up for grabs, and people 'were convinced that they were passing not only from one social system to another, but from one morality to another, from one culture to another, and from one religion to a dozen or none'. Not least among the 'thousand "movements"' that seemed to be making history at this time was the women's movement.[9] Its middle-class emissary, the

---

[8] Bebel 1885, p. 263.
[9] Jackson 1913, p. 34.

cigarette-smoking, cycle-straddling New Woman, was the *cause célèbre* of the late nineteenth-century.

One of the index entries to the apparatus of notes that accompanies Elizabeth Wolstenholme's poem *Woman Free* (1893) says, with symptomatic simplicity, 'Future of woman and humanity'.[10] The status of the New Woman, whose prominent public profile was premised on her class position as well as on her personal stridency, seemed at the time especially indicative of future trends. Women's changing economic and legal status encouraged a widespread conviction that it was their movement above all that embodied the values of modernity. The expansion of educational and employment opportunities for women from the 1860s onwards had led them, as it were, to assimilate Marx's dictum that 'the degree of emancipation of woman is the natural measure of general emancipation'.[11] Indeed, many of them also apparently understood their historical role in terms of Fourier's rather different claim (from which Marx had freely paraphrased), that '*the extension of the privileges of women is the basic principle of all social progress*'.[12] They tended to see signs of women's advance, in other words, as the cause rather than the symptom of change.

The narrator of Isabella Ford's *On the Threshold* (1895), for instance, tells us that her heroine, Kitty, who attends a meeting of middle-class radicals 'on the best way to reform the world, and on the ideal future we each longed for', 'believed that the awakening of women was the key to the problem'.[13] To a socialist such as Eleanor Marx, of course, this position was an inversion of the issues at stake, since 'the woman question is one of the organization of society as a whole'.[14] But howsoever the 'woman question' was answered at this time, it was framed in terms of the future as well as of the present. Feminists, as the 'rational dress' worn by the New Woman itself seemed to announce, stood at the Front of history.

This sense of being 'on the threshold' of the future was a contradictory experience, as I argued in Chapter 1 with reference to the wider movement for social reform in the late-Victorian period. Havelock Ellis tried to express that experience in his didactic novel, *The Nineteenth Century: A Dialogue in*

---

[10] Ethelmer 1893, p. x.
[11] Marx and Engels 1975b, p. 196.
[12] Fourier 1996, p. 132.
[13] Ford 1895, pp. 28–9. Subsequent references are given after quotations in the text.
[14] Marx Aveling 1886, p. 5.

Utopia (1900), which, set at a distant future date, still hinges on the turn of the twentieth-century. The student of Victoria's reign in Ellis's future makes the following claim: 'There is but a hair's-breadth between us and the nineteenth-century. If we had quite reached perfection, there would be nothing left but death; if they had not almost touched it, they could not have lived at all'.[15] These softly ventriloquised sentences, slightly wistful in tone, convey something of the curiously hesitant or halting optimism felt by energetic reformists and radicals like Ellis. The end of the century was stuck on the brink of a social alternative. 'We have looked through the door of freedom, and we cannot go back again, we cannot!' cries Kitty, in a kind of euphoria of frustration, halfway through Ford's novel (p. 108). The aspirations of reformers outstripped the concrete conditions necessary for their fulfilment. And the ultimate source of this uneasy faith in the future was their isolation from the mass movements necessary to realise their ideals. For it was not until the first years of the next century, after the formation of the Women's Social and Political Union in 1903, that the hopes of feminists rhymed with the development of history itself. At that point, 'the personal aspiration for freedom was accompanied by a militant suffrage movement and widespread social upheaval'.[16]

Until this moment, the legacy of the women's movement from the 1860s, the time at which Eliza Lynn Linton first identified a 'Shrieking Sisterhood', remained highly ambiguous. By the 1880s, some of the vocational aspirations of earlier middle-class feminists were fulfilled in the form of jobs in teaching, nursing and social work, as well as clerical and retail employment. Those fighting on the 'education front' also made considerable advances: women's colleges were established at Oxford and Cambridge, against the background of a general improvement in secondary education. So middle-class women's social mobility improved markedly. But, at the same time, the suffrage campaign suffered setbacks and delays, in spite of occasional victories like that of the campaign against the Contagious Diseases Acts in 1886. For, while the 1884 Reform Bill offered hope of female enfranchisement, this was first depressed by Gladstone's threat to withdraw the entire piece of legislation, and then dashed by the final result of the vote, in which one hundred and four Liberal MPs opposed the franchise. Sylvia Pankhurst subsequently described this as

[15] Ellis 1900, p. 158.
[16] Rowbotham 1997, p. 9.

a 'drift from the Suffrage Movement', in which 'the hopes of reformers were turned in other directions', and in which 'to secure enthusiasm for votes for women was therefore to work against the current of popular interest and desire, now flowing towards other objectives'. The 'other directions' that Pankhurst had in mind, apart from the incipient socialist discussion groups and parties, included both 'the women's organisations formed by the political parties to do their election canvassing' and the Theosophical Society.[17]

The New Woman should be situated in relation to this constellation of tendencies, since she emerged in the latter half of the 1880s, a few years before being christened in 1894, as a product of the very process of sundering and splintering that Pankhurst recounts. In a sense, the New Woman embodies feminism's impasse at the end of the century. 'Her hallmark was *personal freedom*', as Lucy Bland remarks, and this recourse to an individualist politics was the product of hope and despair.[18] It was the result, on the one hand, of women's new sense of social and intellectual confidence; and, on the other, of their loss of faith in a suffrage movement based on the joint efforts of men and women within the sphere of parliamentary politics.

For the anti-feminist press, which played such a significant role in fashioning her identity, the New Woman functioned as a floating signifier for any or all forms of feminism. Ultimately, in a misogynistic twist, she was made to stand in for the female sex itself. A subtle ideological strategy was at work here, one belied by the crude bombast with which newspapers, periodicals and other publications berated the 'Girl of the Period'. This strategy involved the promulgation of a minority of women as 'typical' of the majority of women. The sociological basis of the New Woman was the increasing surplus of 'odd' or unmarried middle-class women revealed by census figures from the 1860s (unmarried working-class women were not considered 'odd' because they were kept occupied in domestic or manufacturing employment). These women owed their single status, where it was not a matter of choice premised on principled hostility to men, both to the demographic fact that the excess of women over men precluded marriage for a minority, and to the difficulty of combining a 'career' in marriage with a professional occupation capable of securing financial independence. They posed an inherent threat to patriarchal

---

[17] Pankhurst 1931, pp. 91–2.
[18] Bland 1995, p. 144.

orthodoxy, since their very lives refuted the Victorian belief that domestic life was women's destiny. Consequently, they were demonised in the press, where their social position tended to be subsumed to a political attitude that many of them did not share.

The feminist minority of 'odd women' thus served as a sign for the entire social category. Meanwhile, in an analogous ideological manoeuvre, the most immiserated of all these single women, the prostitute ('a not unimportant type of the odd woman', as Gissing argued), could also be made to stand in for the rest of them.[19] The suffragist Lydia Becker expressed this point in 1889: 'Nothing shows more clearly the contempt which underlies some of the most specious professions by men of respect for women than the instinctive manner in which, when women lodgers are in question, men ignore the great body of the respectable women, and single out as a type of the class the unfortunate beings whom they maintain in a condition of degradation, and on whom they impose the reproach of their own sins'.[20] Becker here shows a clear understanding of a classic hegemonic operation – one that, historically, has been used against women in particular.

Slavoj Žižek has recently expounded this ideology of the typical, with reference to the US anti-abortion campaign's representation of women who terminate pregnancies. He demonstrates how, in this context, the 'atypical' is transformed into the 'typical': 'The "typical" case is the exact opposite: a sexually promiscuous professional woman who values her career over her "natural" assignment of motherhood – although this characterization is in blatant contradiction to the fact that the great majority of abortions occur in lower class families with a lot of children'. Thus 'the operation of hegemony "sutures" the empty Universal to a particular content'.[21] The late-nineteenth-century strategy of implicitly substituting both the prostitute and the feminist for the single woman, and, further, of substituting this composite 'odd woman' for a spurious universal Woman, as in much misogynist propaganda of the time, employs the same ideological mechanism. The result of this surreptitious stitching of identities is that the New Woman, the underside of whom, it is insinuated, is the prostitute, becomes associated with the female sex itself,

---

[19] Gissing 1893, p. 221.
[20] Becker 1889, p. 7.
[21] Žižek 1997, p. 29.

which is at once masculinised and denigrated to the status of a passive and parasitic puppet.

George Egerton, often considered one of the most important New Woman fiction writers of the 1890s, dramatises the effects of this process in her short story 'The Regeneration of Two' (1894) – though she pulls back from offering a critique of it, preferring instead to retain her reactionary, woman-worshipping hero as the agent of her female protagonist's salvation. The latter, an affluent 'odd woman', encounters the former, a peripatetic poet, in the Norwegian countryside, where he proceeds to paint a compelling picture of a world corrupted by brutalising social institutions. In search of solace and inspiration, he tells her, he sought out 'the advanced women – some on platforms, some in clubs, some buttonholing senators in the lobby of the senate, or cooing politics or social economy over afternoon tea'. He discovers instead that, amongst these women, wherein '"suppressed sex" was having its fling', the 'great mother heart' of his quest was nowhere to be seen. Dolefully, he writes off the female sex: 'I found her half-man or half-doll. No, it is women, not men, who are the greatest bar to progress the world holds'. Unfortunately, Egerton's heroine is profoundly influenced by this conclusion, so that, after a few turns of the plot, which traces her new career as the matriarchal manager of a women's hostel, she finally comes to fill in for the poet's fantasy, functioning, in their free union, as his fairy-tale surrogate mother. Lacking any sense of irony, this short story has to be read against its grain, so that it illustrates not only the reactionary association of the New Woman with Woman, here disguised as something far more radical, but also the extent to which the New Woman may secretly accept her maternal and moral destiny, internalising, as it were, the ideology of the typical. 'The Regeneration of Two' demonstrates the contradictory nature of the New Woman, and, because of the subtlety as well as the crudeness of her ideological construction in the press and elsewhere, the difficulty of pinning her down, despite, or rather because of, her very individuality.[22]

In an article of 1896 entitled 'Is the So-called "New Woman" a Modern Prodigy?' a member of the Pioneer Club, answering her question with a resounding negative, resists this very desire to taxonomise the phenomenon. She argues that 'the woman who is conscious of political instinct, of powers

---

[22] Egerton 1894, pp. 194, 197.

of organisation, of economic analysis, of possessing a message for humanity, is no new wonder, no unseemly oddity, but a perfectly natural genius begotten of Divine Intelligence'.[23] In the light of this elastic (not to say mystical) definition, it is perhaps safest to grasp the concept of the New Woman as an attempt to sustain a feminist politics in an age in which the mass movement for the emancipation of women is in partial retreat, or in a faltering state of suspension at least. In this context, that of the 1889 'Appeal Against Suffrage' as much as of the satirical attacks on 'Novissima' in the 1890s, the New Woman may simply amount to a conceptualisation of her own condition of possibility. That is to say, the New Woman is the impossible attempt, during a period of uncertain political expectation, to think the authentic new woman of a period capable of realising feminism's egalitarian ideals. And, as such, to appropriate Marx's distinction, she describes feminism's pre-historical dream of its history proper. The New Woman tries to apprehend her own coming-into-being. The article by 'Pioneer 363' describes this attempt to historicise her conditions of possibility. It proves the perennial status of the New Woman by referring back to a late eighteenth-century journal, *The Female Spectator*, from which it quotes the founding statements of a progressive women's club. The New Woman is a feminist in search of New Women.

Above all, feminist politics were fragmentary at this time: 'rather than a unified and cohesive body, feminists comprised a fractured collectivity of groups and webs of affiliation marked by disagreement as much as by consensus'.[24] Women's political demands or dreams differed widely, ranging easily across the family, the workplace and the public sphere. Thus, the term 'New Woman' covered independent women of all kinds, from suffragists to cyclists to socialists. For anti-feminists, as we have seen, it served to construct a monolithic ideological opponent. For feminists themselves, reversing the discourse, it superficially sealed up the fissures within the women's movement (as popular references to the continuity between some Primal Woman and the New Woman testify). The heterogeneity of this movement could not be resolved quite so easily, however. Its incoherence exerted a singular pressure to discover an alternative lifestyle based on shared experiences of female, and male-female, solidarity. In addition, the social isolation that many feminists

---

[23] 'Pioneer 363' 1896, p. 146.
[24] Felski 1995, p. 147.

felt, the consequence of their subordinate sexual position within the dominant class (which ensured that they were cut off from the daily experiences of the mass of women as well as from the working lives of their fathers, brothers and husbands), encouraged a quest for some alternative to the family structure. After all, the traditional refuge of the family was now more precarious and unsafe than ever, incapable of offering adequate protection against an increasingly godless society undermined by class conflict and unstable sexual roles.

In the face of this dystopian prospect, the utopian search for fellowship, for fragmentary evidence of a collectivist and egalitarian future, was a significant feature of feminism at this time. If the culture of early socialism 'had to provide a kind of home for people made spiritually homeless in capitalism', then so too did the overlapping culture of feminism.[25]

III. The politics of fellowship

The 'politics of fellowship' is the term I use to designate the specific structure of feeling characteristic of feminist and socialist-feminist utopianism in the late nineteenth-century. The New Woman is one of those 'radically new semantic figures' that appears in a period of social recomposition, 'when a formation appears to break away from its class norms, though it retains its substantial affiliation'.[26] Freeing herself from her family and from the Church, but frustrated with the male preserve of party politics, as well as with the fragmentary nature of the women's movement, she searched for communities that might embody alternative forms of life. These communities practised personal relations that, at a local level, were a prophetic symbol of the universal fraternalism of the future. They stood in for the inter-subjective solidarity of the ideal collective.

The classic instance of this politics was the Fellowship of New Life itself, a British society of so-called 'ethical' socialists, which set out its intentions as follows: 'THE FELLOWSHIP OF THE NEW LIFE aims to secure the intimate association of Men and Women desirous of living and of commending to others an honest, healthy and completely human life. That is, it proposes to

---

[25] Rowbotham 1977, p. 66.
[26] Williams 1977, pp. 133–35.

itself the task of working out the ideal of such a life, and determining the conditions of its realization; of attempting here and now to conform as thoroughly as possible to this ideal: and of rendering its full attainment desirable and possible to all'.[27] Male and female 'New Lifers' sought compensation in the present for the deferral of their longed-for future of social and personal freedom. The politics of fellowship were premised on the conviction that the embryonic image of the egalitarian society could be conceived, and gestated, in the individual choices and personal relations of its adherents and activists. The focus of its 'socialistic feeling', according to one contemporary commentator, was not 'the larger economic questions', but 'the practical problems of everyday life'. It tried to demonstrate, 'by discussions and printed matter and by cooperative experiments in home and domestic life', that the outcome of a principle of interdependence 'must be thoroughgoing social equality'.[28]

Self-consciously feminist organisations tended to offer less secure foundations for the future social life than socialist ones in the late nineteenth-century. In her forecast for feminism in the coming century, Enid Stacey wrote in 1897 that 'the movement in which the question of women's labour, women's chances of bettering their economic position, women's claims to a higher social status and political equality have been most sympathetically treated is the labour movement, especially in the purely Socialist section thereof'. The socialist movement was scarcely the perfect environment for feminists, however: as Stacey admitted, though socialists were 'believers in equality between men and women *at least in theory*', 'many traces of the old Adam might show themselves from time to time in their actual conduct'.[29] One literary historian has recently remarked that, while socialism in the 1880s and 1890s 'seemed to offer a "way out" for women, particularly the promise of equality in employment outside the home', at the same time it 'failed to offer women a way to actively transform the private sphere'.[30] Harkness's restlessness in the Social-Democratic Federation bears witness to this, as well as to the strain with which women tried to assimilate themselves to a movement that often suffered from stubbornly sexist attitudes in strict contradiction to its ideological

---

[27] See the notice facing the first full page of text in Davidson 1888.
[28] Woods 1892, pp. 50–1.
[29] Stacey 1897, p. 94.
[30] Sypher 1993, p. 128.

commitment to equality. But, despite this, it is true to say that socialism, and especially the socialism of fellowship, proved comparatively accommodating to feminists.

This was for a number of reasons. First, socialist organisations fostered an emergent counter-cultural sphere in which a few women were free to develop their skills as activists and commentators. Their emphasis on a personal style of politics, and on cultural concerns, made them appealing to women whose confidence was scarcely inspired by the public sphere of bourgeois politics. Second, socialist fellowships promised a far more systematic transformation of society, a transformation that, as some feminists perceived, might ultimately be required in order to overcome patriarchal relations. Third, the utopian aspect to the politics of ethical socialism, which flourished on the worn threshold between faith in the imminence of some sort of social revolution and despair of its ever occurring, was attractive to some women.

Like the New Woman, 'the ethical socialist was forever waiting in limbo'; as Rowbotham indicates, 'the ideal belonged to the long term' while 'in the short term there was the immediate compromise'.[31] Her assessment is broadly correct; but it underestimates the importance of the role played by the ideal in the 'immediate compromise' characteristic of the short term, as well as of the role played by reformist attitudes in the ethical socialist's conception of utopia. A more dialectical assessment of the politics of fellowship might emphasise not only the evolutionist assumptions of its vision of the future, but also that the values of this future were self-consciously lived or enacted in the present. Ethical socialists tried to infiltrate an ideal future into the present.

Edward Carpenter, pioneer of the New Life, best exemplifies this political trend, and not least because he argued so forcefully and consistently for '[woman's] right to speak, dress, think, act and above all use her sex as she deems best', in the effort to forge a free identity for the future: 'Let every woman whose heart bleeds for the sufferings of her sex, hasten to declare herself *and to constitute herself, as far as she possibly can*, a free woman'.[32] Precisely because of the strictly personal sphere of action that it invoked, this kind of call to action could not but be influential within the atomised women's

---

[31] Rowbotham 1977, p. 75.
[32] Carpenter 1896, p. 61 (emphasis mine).

movement of the time. Its impact was palpable, for example, in the feminist journal *Shafts*, a champion of Carpenter's books and pamphlets. There, the articles and correspondence made disciplinarian demands on its readers, persuading them, in Carpenterian tones, to cultivate vegetarian eating habits, or 'a less ardent love of their furniture', in order to lay the foundations for the future.[33] It was also felt in the discussions of the Men and Women's Club, an environment in which Carpenter's close friend Olive Schreiner argued with its founder Karl Pearson, and various other middle-class radicals of the later 1880s, on the subject of sex and sexuality. The club's guest-list, which included Annie Besant, Jane Clapperton, Eleanor Marx and the novelists Mona Caird and Emma Brooke, reads like a roll-call of celebrated New Women. Together, despite ultimately intolerable levels of internal disagreement (symptomatically, these tended to turn on the implicitly sexist attitudes of the male members, who treated sex, and even women, as a static object of pseudo-scientific study), these socialists and feminists tussled with the task of instituting 'a basic vocabulary of sexual desire'.[34]

According to Lucy Bland, the female members of the club, 'call[ing] into question the very legitimacy of [its] obsession with establishing objective, rational and politically neutral knowledge', struggled to articulate a language of social desire too: 'To many of the women, [club member] Annie Eastty's hope for a common ideal that would aid reform seems to have referred to a vision of an emancipated femininity and a moralized masculinity – a "new woman" and a "new man". The women hoped that the club would prove to be a site for the building of this common ideal'.[35] This hope was to be disappointed, principally because Pearson and his supporters regarded the female activists as inappropriately partisan. But despite the fact that the utopian aspirations of these women were suppressed, their commitment to the club as a microcosm of change, the seedbed of an alternative society, was typical of the way in which, at the *fin de siècle*, a politics of fellowship fought for the future about which it fantasised on the local terrain of inter-personal experimentation. Rowbotham has rightly insisted that this tendency among socialists and feminists of the time, the tendency 'to argue that cultural changes

---

[33] Grenfell 1895, p. 82.
[34] Walkowitz 1986, p. 47.
[35] Bland 1995, pp. 7, 27.

could only arise after the revolution, but then in practice to behave as if such changes were at once imperative and imminent', 'meant a favourable climate for understanding the interpenetration of private and public, psychological and material, characteristic of the "woman question"'.[36] They acted out utopian relations. Fellowship was a rehearsal, in full dress, for utopia itself.

The 'proto-utopia' of the politics of fellowship points to late-nineteenth-century feminism's uneasy absorption of its political precursors. In a sense, the sometimes muddied and meandering women's movement of the *fin de siècle* traces the confluence of two earlier traditions, the feminism of Owenite utopian socialism, which flourished in the first half of the century, and the feminist reformism that followed on from it in the second half. The former remained buried for much of the Victorian period, forced underground by the scandal and dissension that led to the collapse of the Owenite colonies, as well as by external factors such as the stabilisation of the economy and the rise of Chartism in the mid-century. But, in the 1880s and 1890s, having survived in the secularist movement, its warm current emerged again, influencing the politics of fellowship, while the cold current of pragmatic feminist reformism sank and slowed beneath it. Owenite socialism's continuity with 'ethical socialism', in which so many later feminists found uncomfortable refuge, is evident not only in the seriousness with which it associated women's rights and transformed social relations, and the earnestness with which it sought to popularise this association in lecture halls and discussion groups, but also in what Barbara Taylor identifies as its defining feature – that is, 'not the community strategy *per se*', but 'the commitment to constructing a New World inside the shell of the Old'.[37]

As at the *fin de siècle*, this commitment was the response to an uncertain economic and cultural conjuncture, one that raised hopes of the collapse of capitalism yet increasingly reasserted its apparent stability. If the utopianism of the late-Victorian period began to peter out towards the turn of the century, because the suspicion on which it was in part premised, that the present system was indestructible, appeared to have been fulfilled, then an approximately analogous situation can explain the entropic climate in which Owenite socialism languished at the mid point of the century. Taylor explains

---

[36] Rowbotham 1972, p. 88.
[37] Taylor 1983, p. 241.

that 'by the end of the 1840s it was becoming obvious to everyone, Owenites included, that the competitive system was by no means as impermanent as they had thought', and that 'capitalism itself had become the terrain on which the struggle for its own supersession would have to be fought'.[38] She is right to register this shift from a utopian perspective that sees 'outside' the boundaries of the capitalist system to a reformist one that recognises no 'outside' at all; but it needs, of course, to be added that, even in their ascendancy, the Owenite communities had only tucked themselves into a fold of the system, there keeping faith with fundamental reformist principles, notably an idealist confidence in the social diffusion of progressive beliefs. This idealism is every bit as evident in the assumptions of ethical socialism at the end of the century, when, despite the rise of working-class organisation in England, the politics of fellowship affirmed a programme of social change based on enlightened intellectual and social example. Engels's assessment in 1880, that 'the Utopians' mode of thought has for a long time governed the socialist ideas of the nineteenth-century, and still governs some of them', remained accurate for some twenty years.[39]

At the moment when Owenism entered its crisis, Marx and Engels were forging their critique of utopian socialism. It is this critique that offers the most insightful understanding of the utopian feminism of the *fin de siècle*, which, with its bifocal vision, its focus on personal change in the short term and social change in the long term, often overlooked the geography of the intervening country. Many of the radicals prosecuting the 'woman question' at this time, for all that they may have fulminated against capitalism, solved it independently from analysis of the economic structure of society. As Eleanor Marx and Edward Aveling said of the sentimental or professional ideas of the so-called 'advanced' women of their day, 'not one of them gets down through these to the bed-rock of the economic basis . . . of society itself'.[40] In the absence of an understanding of how women could emancipate themselves collectively, Marx himself wrote, 'future history resolve[d] itself, in their eyes, into the propaganda and the practical carrying out of their social plans'.[41]

---

[38] Taylor 1983, p. 262.
[39] Engels 1989, p. 297.
[40] Marx Aveling 1886, p. 5.
[41] Marx and Engels 1976c, p. 515.

It was precisely as a propagandist history of the future, designed to resolve the central contradiction of their politics of fellowship – the failure to formulate a transitional society – that feminists turned to utopian fiction. Preliminarily, this claim can be explained with reference to the socialist feminist Jane Hume Clapperton. According to her book on *Scientific Meliorism* (1885), the utopia of the state socialists influenced by Edward Bellamy was '"the baseless fabric of a vision"'.[42] The point of her utopian account of *A Socialist Home* (1888) – which depicts a 'small communal group' or fellowship 'as a unit in the great order or system of the future' – was to build in the present just such a foundation for her own social dream.[43] The problem with this scheme was that it did not get down to the underlying bedrock of the economy. Utopias tend to be dreams of the transformation of the superstructure. It is in this sense that, as Marx and Aveling implicitly perceived, the utopias of the *fin de siècle* feminists 'make no suggestion that is outside the limits of the society of to-day'.[44] They are simultaneously too utopian and not utopian enough. In the terms that I formulated in my account of the state socialists, they are pragmatic utopians. They try to invent new forms of social relations before the conditions for their existence have been challenged or abolished.

Like liberal feminism itself, therefore, the New Woman's utopia only 'questions the traditional status and role of woman from within the ideology that insists on it'.[45] This individualist and idealist ideology, which insists that social change must percolate down through society, underpins the politics of the New Woman, whose assumption is that the heroic effort of individuals is enough. 'The personal is the political!' is a slogan that might have been invented by the New Woman.

IV. Feminist utopianism

If the feminist-utopian fiction of the *fin de siècle*, like the New Woman novel in general, confined its appeal for change to the middle class, and thus radically curtailed its subversive impact, its discourse on social and sexual relations

---

[42] Clapperton 1885, p. 395.
[43] Clapperton 1888, p. 73. Subsequent references are given after quotations in the text.
[44] Marx Aveling 1886, p. 6.
[45] Goode 1976, p. 238.

was neither lifeless nor anaemic. Feminist utopias contributed directly and with a lively combativeness to contemporary debates about women in the past, present and future. They derived their popular appeal in part from their practical intervention in this polemical context. They addressed the desires of many women for some glimpse of a society not premised on the oppression of their sex; but they also functioned as an initiation to the task of building communities of sympathetic men and women, fellowships for the future.

Especially for feminists, therefore, the 'prophetic romance' of the late nineteenth-century was also the 'propagandist romance'. In the hands of the New Women, who saw themselves 'as disciples of a social, not a literary, movement', the novel functioned as a political tool. This politicisation of women's fiction was partly the cause, partly the consequence of the intensely ideological struggle over the status of the so-called New-Realist novel at this time. The trend towards realism in the late 1880s and early 1890s, as well as an attempt to save the novel from censorship, represented 'a movement to reclaim it for male readers and free it from literary conventions and restrictions that had come to be identified as feminine'.[46] This campaign backfired in the sense that, as censorship mechanisms were eased and social stereotypes consequently became eroded, especially in the face of the collapse of the circulating library system and the rise of a generation of newly educated women, women's issues came to dominate literary discourse to an unprecedented extent. Women thus reinforced their control over the realist novel, reclaiming it for polemical purposes, at the very time that realism was being used to 'masculinise' the genre. As Hubert Crackanthorpe complained, 'the society lady, dazzled by the brilliancy of her own conversation, and the serious-minded spinster, bitten by some sociological theory, still decide . . . that fiction is the obvious medium through which to astonish or improve the world'.[47]

The absence of a unified feminist movement at the *fin de siècle*, and the resulting attention paid by feminists to the politics of interpersonal relations, made the novel seem especially attractive to the New Women. As Gail Cunningham argues: 'It was the novel which could investigate in detail the clash between radical principles and the actualities of contemporary life,

[46] Miller 1994, pp. 11, 18.
[47] Crackanthorpe 1894, p. 269.

which could portray most convincingly the shifting social conventions from which the New Woman was trying to break free, and which could present arguments for new standards of morality, new codes of behaviour, in the context of an easily recognisable social world'.[48] The problem with this realist format, though, was that it tended to encode a pessimistic politics. In order to appeal to its female readership as realistic, feminist heroines had to struggle unsuccessfully against patriarchal institutions like marriage. Utopian fiction described an attempt to escape this constraint. If the stylistic conventions of the 'grosser realism', according to the literary critic Arthur Waugh, encoded an injunction to the writer to 'repeople Eden with creatures imagined from a study of the serpent's head', then the feminist utopian novelist would instead re-people Eden with creatures dreamed up from a study of Eve's imagination.[49]

This search for the New Woman's new world incorporated realism and romance, proclaiming an optimistic commitment to women's capacity to live an alternative existence, at the same time that it implicitly exposed the inadequacy of escapism as a response to the conditions of women's oppression. In her preface to *Gloriana; or, The Revolution of 1900* (1890), the travel-writer and war correspondent Lady Florence Dixie, an exemplary New Woman, insists that the purpose of her feminist utopia 'is to speak of evils which DO exist, to study facts which it is a crime to neglect'.[50] Its purpose is also to oppose to these evils the redemptive values that, suppressed and perverted in the present, will in the end define a free society: 'Gloriana [*sic*] may be a romance, a dream; but . . . it is inextricably interwoven with truth' (p. viii).

Until the late-Victorian period, the utopian genre remained the almost exclusive preserve of male authors. Despite Mary Wollstonecraft's affirmation of 'Utopian dreams' in *A Vindication of the Rights of Woman* (1792), feminists made few forays into utopian territory over the course of the nineteenth-century.[51] It seems plausible to suggest that this was because the political discourse that had shaped utopian fiction since Thomas More's *Utopia* (1516), defining the genre as a form of social dreaming, had necessarily rendered it

---

[48] Cunningham 1978, pp. 16–7.
[49] Waugh 1894, p. 217.
[50] Dixie 1890, p. vii. Subsequent references are given after quotations in the text.
[51] Wollstonecraft 1792, p. 72.

inaccessible to those sealed off from the public sphere. The turning point, as I have intimated, was the late 1860s and early 1870s, when the hopes raised by the possibility of a partial enfranchisement of middle-class women, which inspired such an energetic upsurge in feminist political activity, foundered in the defeat of Mill's amendment to the second Reform Bill. For if the prospect of women's suffrage receded after this event, it left a utopian residue that pointed to women's political potential. Women's hitherto privatised fantasies were stretched into social dreams by an expanding political vocabulary that, in a painful paradox, it was impossible to implement.

The origins of a distinctly feminist appropriation of the utopian genre lie in the very mixture of hope and disappointment that I have described as characteristic of the dialectical conjuncture out of which the late-Victorian women's movement emerged. So Nan Bowman Albinski is inaccurate when she stresses that '*although* a time of feminist aspiration rather than achievement, [this] was a period of intense activity in the history of the utopian genre'.[52] The upsurge in utopias by women at this time occurred *because of* and not in spite of this excess of aspiration over achievement. It was precisely this climate that clustered together the concerns of this chapter – utopian fiction, the politics of fellowship, and the New Woman. By 1900, the utopian focus of feminist fiction had faded, as the New Woman fiction, and the socialism of the New Life, entered into decline.

The first stirrings of a feminist utopian fiction in the 1870s are hesitant and fitful, and in this sense they reflect the contradictory character of the feminist movement. To assert that women suddenly wrested the conventions of the utopian genre from its male practitioners at this time, successfully twisting them in feminist directions, is to lend an illusionary and tendentious linearity to literary history. It is incorrect to claim, as Darby Lewes has done, that, while women had begun to employ utopias 'to articulate their own philosophies and agendas' before the end of the nineteenth-century, 'in 1870, this gynotopic impulse finally emerged full-blown, as women commandeered a historically male genre and used it to blend feminist and historical perspectives into entirely new forms of social interaction and gender relationships'.[53] Annie

---

[52] Albinski 1988, p. 19 (emphasis mine).
[53] Lewes 1995, p. 42.

Denton Cridge's *Man's Rights; or, How Would You Like It?*, a Swiftean satire on patriarchal gender relations, did appear in the United States in 1870, but it scarcely signalled the triumphant emergence of a distinct genre.

In England, it was not until the second half of the 1870s that feminists started to write polemical fiction in the future perfect tense. Millicent Garrett Fawcett had published her *Tales in Political Economy* in 1874; but, apart from its narrative strategy of using a story-line to sweeten its political message, 'of hiding the powder, Political Economy, in the raspberry jam of a story' as she put it, this sustained allegorical advertisement for the benefits of free trade bore little resemblance to subsequent feminist attempts to imagine future relations between the sexes.[54] And these attempts did not at first embody a full-blown 'gynotopic impulse'. For example, the feminist journalist Frances Power Cobbe's early excursion into a fictional future, *The Age of Science: A Newspaper of the Twentieth Century* (1877), only incidentally addresses the issue of sexual politics.

It might be possible to interpret this Erewhonean satire, which depicts a world in which scientific values have been raised into a religious creed, as a coded attack on the phallocentric thrust of technology in the late nineteenth-century; it is however scarcely evidence of a confident utopian treatment of feminist subject matter. Its dystopian format, which bespeaks a certain pessimism from the start, indicates that Cobbe is answering the anti-feminists on their own terrain. This terrain had been staked out during the previous year in a novel called *Caxtonia's Cabinet* (1876), by William Soleman, in which the male author recounted his female narrator's nightmare of being elected prime minister of a country that consequently descends into social anarchy. Cobbe's book, with its awful image of a streamlined society dominated by male technocrats – the result of a backlash against women's educational advances – reads like a reversal of Soleman's anti-feminist scenario. These anti-utopias, as G.K. Chesterton might have said, prophesy 'in the hope that their prophec[ies] may not come true'.[55] If *The Age of Science* inaugurates women's appropriation of utopian fictional techniques in England at the *fin de siècle*, then, symptomatically, it seems uncertain how to affirm a feminist future.

---

[54] Fawcett 1874, p. v.
[55] Chesterton 1917, p. 1.

The rise of the socialist movement over the course of the 1880s, with the limited opportunities that this provided for feminists, as well as the partial renewal of the suffrage campaign, evident in the institution of the Women's Franchise League in 1889, created the conditions in which, from the end of that decade, the feminist utopia began to flourish. But if this climate was a little more optimistic than that of the later 1870s, feminist figurations of the future still developed, out of necessity, in embattled opposition to the anti-feminism that dominated the portrayal of women in the press and in popular fiction. It is not, to repeat, a question of women simply 'commandeering' the utopian form. Feminists turned to it because of a strategic imperative to offer positive images of the future.

The New Woman, as we have seen, was frequently identified with the future at the *fin de siècle*. 'She talks of the future of women, of coming generations and women's influence thereon', as one 'Character Note' in the contemporary press put it.[56] And, if she talked about the shape of things to come, she also appeared to embody it. So anti-feminists, trading anti-utopian images of 'advanced women', fought assiduously over her historical status, her role in the future development of society. Feminists were forced to compete with their opponents, and produce alternative myths. In the remainder of this section, I want to sketch the anti-feminist dystopian form that helped to create the preconditions for a feminist appropriation of utopian fiction, and outline Florence Dixie's feminist response to it.

James McGrigor Allan's essay *Woman Suffrage Wrong* (1890) is a classic piece of dystopian anti-feminism. Denouncing the archetypal women's rights activist as 'Miss Amazon', Allan argues that her chief use 'is to show what women ought not to be'; 'she poses and proses on a platform', he writes, 'as an exemplar or fugleman of what she wants her sex to be in the future, quite unconscious that by her dress and undress, she offers the strongest warning against that very emancipation which she demands for women, and takes personally to such a ridiculous extent'. Attacking women's suffrage, he enjoins the reader to picture a dystopian political scenario:

> Only imagine a strong-minded, strong-bodied, duly elected lady, forcing her way into the House [of Commons]. . . . Even were the 'resources of

---

[56] Anonymous 1894b, p. 368.

civilisation' competent to eject the intruder, could the House pass calmly to
the order of the day? Would not legislators be harassed by painful memories,
and by still more painful forebodings – to say nothing of imminent danger[.]
Imagine Trafalgar Square filled with women in revolt! Imagine the incomplete
lady member weeping, with dishevelled hair, making political capital out
of her sufferings, exhibiting marks of personal violence; appealing to an
Amazonian army awfully arrayed, ready and willing to copy the excesses
of Parisian women at Versailles 6th October, 1789.[57]

The fantastical content of this passage, it is obvious enough, worked especially
well in fiction, where the form could be used to elaborate a detailed
dramatisation of the reader's fears of feminism.

It was in the novel, above all, that the New Woman's transitional status
was explored. A dystopian snapshot of this feminist transition to the future
is included in Miles L'Estrange's *What We Are Coming To* (1892), a conservative
satire on the Americanisation of British culture, set some time in the twentieth-
century. At one point in the plot, the narrator attends a dinner with 'Mrs
Cumming Freedom'. Mrs Freedom, we are informed, 'carries the "claims of
women" theory to great lengths, and describes herself as always in the van
of reform, and an enemy to those traditional trammels which so block the
path of modern progress'. The pseudonymous author of the book has his
revenge on this distasteful representative of the 'female brigade' when the
narrator asks his hosts 'about the Woman Suffrage they were nibbling at [in
the late nineteenth-century]', since it turns out that, mainly thanks to 'the
intuitive good sense of womankind', the suffrage has scarcely progressed
from that time. The New Woman is here caught in a comic state of arrested
historical development, destined to remain permanently out of kilter with
the prevailing status quo, just as the 'rational dress' fashions prescribed by
what L'Estrange calls the 'Sensible Costume Association' are destined always
to remain aesthetically incongruous.[58]

In other dystopian novels about the 'woman question', horrified anti-
feminists pushed beyond this projected impasse to depict the historical
implications of what Havelock Ellis hailed triumphantly as 'the rise of
women – who form the majority of the race in most civilized countries – to

---

[57] Allan 1890, pp. 60, 68, 48, 185–86.
[58] L'Estrange 1892, pp. 61, 98, 99.

supreme power in the near future'.[59] The purpose of these anti-utopias, like that of the 'Appeal against Suffrage', was to prove that women are congenitally unsuited to taking responsibility for life outside the domestic sphere. Walter Besant, who wrote *The Rebel Queen* (1893) just as the New Woman was starting to make her scandalous presence felt, provides a relatively early example of the anti-feminist fantasy in *The Revolt of Man* (1882), which was partly inspired by contempt for his campaigning sister-in-law Annie. He narrates the process by which a cabal of male aristocrats, secretly discontented with the despotic feminist régime under which they live, plot a vast and finally successful conspiracy to overthrow it and restore the king. In this way, the doctrine of the 'Perfect Woman', the dominant ideology of the 'oligarchical and maternal government', is overthrown by the spreading faith of 'the PERFECT MAN', and women are as a result returned to their 'true place' as wives and mothers.[60] Remarkably, Besant appears to be unconscious that the oppressive matriarchal culture that he depicts replicates the oppressive patriarchal culture of Britain at the *fin de siècle*, and that, in consequence, the basis of his own critique is fatally weakened. *The Revolt of Man* celebrates the social structure that it simultaneously attacks, and is therefore a curiously contradictory attack on feminism. Like all misogynistic arguments, it is utterly tautological: it announces that matriarchies are dystopian because they are governed by women, and that patriarchies are utopian because they are governed by men. In this context, ironically, Besant's dream of a conspiracy of aristocratic men restoring patriarchal order looks structurally identical to the feminist fantasy of a vanguard of women overcoming patriarchy in the first place.

'Masculinist dystopias fuel feminist utopias', argue Gilbert and Gubar; 'for if woman is dispossessed, a nobody, in the somewhere of patriarchy, it may be that she can only become somebody in the nowhere of utopia'.[61] They claim convincingly that Gilman's *Herland* is a feminist revision of H. Rider Haggard's novel *She* (1887). From this perspective, Florence Dixie's *Gloriana* can be read, indirectly at least, as a revisionist version of *The Revolt of Man*. In spite of its conservative emphasis on parliament as the preserve of aristocratic politics, the novel is contemptuous of 'men who think the world must be

---

[59] Ellis 1890, p. 10.
[60] Besant 1882, pp. 79, 168.
[61] Gilbert and Gubar 1989, p. 72.

coming to an end if women are to be acknowledged as their equals' (p. 51). It imagines exactly the kind of society that Besant excoriates.

The 'Revolution of 1900' that *Gloriana* narrates is engineered by an élite army of suffragists, which instigates female suffrage and successfully agitates for England's first female prime minister. Dixie's eponymous heroine, as her mother predicts when she is a young girl, is 'the messenger that shall awake the world to woman's wrongs' (p. 9). Impersonating a boy, she is educated at Eton, where, under the pseudonym Hector D'Estrange, she distinguishes herself by writing an influential article for the *Free Review,* in which she argues that women must be granted access to Whitehall and Westminster. Subsequently, after a stellar career at Oxford, she establishes educational institutions throughout Great Britain and Ireland, in which women can receive intellectual schooling and physical training. In addition, she introduces so-called 'foot clubs', 'the members of which she is forming into volunteer companies, who are drilled by the hand of discipline into smartness and efficiency'. She calculates that she 'will be able to bring into the field quite 100,000 well-drilled troops' when the revolution comes (pp. 50–1). The 'Woman's Volunteer Corps', which soon consists of some 200,000 militant suffragists, is Gloriana's revolutionary vanguard.

Still disguised as Hector D'Estrange, and now a Member of Parliament, she uses her connections with the more progressive sections of the aristocracy to pass a women's suffrage bill. She celebrates this triumph, in a formal display of regimental power, by opening a Hall of Liberty for women. At this point, Dixie's plot starts to accelerate. In the guise of D'Estrange, Gloriana is elected prime minister; but she quickly becomes embroiled in personal and political controversy. Sentenced to death for a murder she has not committed, she reveals that she is a woman. A cavalry troop from the Volunteer Corps rides to her rescue, and in the battle that ensues hundreds are killed. A social revolution commences. The Corps is made illegal, and Gloriana is forced underground, but she manages to escape police detection, and at numerous political meetings recruits people to her cause. Conveniently enough, the reactionary government finally collapses of its own accord, and, to slightly anti-climactic effect, a liberal successor is appointed to implement reform: 'the light of a pure and noble life has penetrated the darkness of opposition and prejudice', comments the narrator (p. 318). Gloriana, 'a free woman, a victorious general who has conquered the demon armies of Monopoly and

Selfishness, and thrown open to the people the free gates of happiness and reform', is welcomed back from exile (p. 333). This time in her own name, Gloriana takes up the post of prime minister again. As in Besant's novel, a conspiracy, one at least partly composed of aristocrats, has acted as the historical force capable of implementing the requisite reform. *Gloriana* in this sense recounts 'The Revolt of Woman'. It plays out the dream of the end of patriarchy from which *The Revolt of Man* had secretly derived its anti-utopian plot.

The last chapter of Dixie's novel is a utopian postscript to the narrative. In 1999, a hot-air balloon circles over England, 'a scene of peaceful villages and well-tilled fields, a scene of busy towns and happy working people, a scene of peace and prosperity, comfort and contentment, which only a righteous Government could produce and maintain' (p. 345). The balloon's tour-guide tells a tourist that Gloriana lived long enough to oversee the creation of an imperial Assembly, consisting of England, Ireland, Scotland and Wales, and containing 'representative men and women from all parts of our glorious Empire, working hand in hand to spread its influence amongst the nations of the world' (p. 348). In the form of this vision of utopia, which the narrator declares is the direct outcome of the late-Victorian suffragist campaign, Dixie's feminist fantasy finally offers counter-factual 'proof' of the possibility of an alternative future. It is to this feminist epistemology of the future that I turn in the next section.

V. Utopian epistemology

Reviewing a reissue of Olive Schreiner's *Dreams* in 1912, Rebecca West revealingly wrote that 'the worst of being a feminist is that one has no evidence'.[62] The 'evidence' that she sought was a female 'genius', in particular a literary prodigy, whose very biography or life's work might point towards the human possibilities that the abolition of patriarchy would realise in the future – like Diane Crowder's 'models of female characters who were not helpless'. The difficulties confronting female writers in this period are triumphantly flaunted in one particularly unpleasant anti-utopian parody,

---

[62] West 1982, p. 70.

Harold Gorst's mysogynistic short story, 'The Struggle Against Woman' (1898)
Here, the wife of a novelist returns home from an afternoon lecture at 'some
women's club' and announces that, from now on, she will write novels herself
while he cleans their rooms and prepares their meals. 'She didn't intend to
sit down, she said, and look on while other women advanced the sex'. The
man punishes her by making her pregnant; so she is in a dual sense confined
and consequently fails to finish her novel: 'The struggle between husband
and wife was over. The fittest had survived; and Dick was master of the field
But the baby had won his battle'.[63]

West wanted to assemble an alternative, feminist epistemology, an
epistemology of the future, to set against the 'common-sense' assumption of
the anti-suffragists that 'the emancipating process has now reached the limits
fixed by the physical constitution of women'.[64] She was petitioning for
anticipatory 'proof' of the indispensability and practicability of female
emancipation. Gilbert and Gubar make a comparable point about a utopian
epistemology when, in their discussion of *Herland*, they remark that 'Gilman's
project to decenter definitions of the real woman requires an imaginative leap
beyond empirical data to postulate the possibility of female primacy'.[65] Utopia
represents a heuristic exercise; it is a counter-factual thought experiment
Tracking West's search for 'evidence' back to the period in which Schreiner's
book was published, the years of her association with the New Woman, it
can be used to illuminate the quest for liberated inter-personal relations
initiated by utopian feminists.

In the absence of a mass political movement that supplied women with
concrete expectations of systemic social change, many middle-class feminists
promoted themselves as living evidence of the golden age to come. The New
Woman proclaimed herself an emissary from Nowhere. In the late 1880s, for
instance, Schreiner herself was convinced that she and a select number of
friends and fellow progressives were striding so far in advance of the stumbling
gait of history that they risked outstripping it entirely. As she exclaimed in
a letter to Pearson, 'our danger is that we will reach the goal and sweep
wildly past it into space! We can get *any*where; but the question is whether

---

[63] Gorst 1898, pp. 121, 124, 128.
[64] See the 'Appeal against Female' 1889, p. 782.
[65] Gilbert and Gubar 1989, p. 74.

we can stop there when we get there!'.[66] The truth was that, in a dual sense, they could get *nowhere*: on the one hand, they were stranded where they were, ultimately immured within the late nineteenth-century social relations against which they strained; on the other hand, they were exploring new relations in the non-space emplotted by their utopian dreams of an alternative to these relations. But, if they straddled present and far-future somewhat uncomfortably, it was their politics of fellowship that constituted the attempt to found a firm association between the two.

Fellowship amongst feminists and their male followers was an inchoate form of the utopian future. It is something like this perception, of the need to import the redemptive perspective of the future into the present, and to construct inter-personal relations in the present that might do justice to the feminist vision of the future, which underpins the first example of the feminist utopia in the later nineteenth-century, the American writer Elizabeth T. Corbett's 'My Visit to Utopia' (1869). Her short story is a lightly allegorical argument for a tolerant attitude towards 'all those reformers, as they are too often derisively called, who are fighting, with too much violence and too little grace, perhaps, in the cause of progress, on the side of liberality'. Utopia itself, which the narrator reaches by train, is simply a town to which a friend of hers has moved, a town where men and women marry for love, and fathers rather than mothers rear their children. But, despite the banal romanticism of this treatment of utopian space, and despite her disappointing resolution not to return to Utopia (on the grounds that 'the effect even of my brief stay was to make me (at least so my husband said) "very unreasonable and exacting"'), Corbett's narrator concludes the piece with an interesting defence of social reformers. I support them, she intimates, 'because I see that they too have been in Utopia, and that they are striving to reproduce even a dim outline of that symmetry and beauty which have led their souls, as mine, captive'.[67] This rather lonely expression of solidarity perfectly captures the sense in which alternative communities appealed to middle-class women suffering from social alienation. News from Nowhere is real news.

---

[66] Schreiner 1988, p. 98.
[67] Corbett 1995, p. 73. Note that *The Feminist Companion to Literature in English* falsely claims that Elizabeth Burgoyne (Mrs George) Corbett, author of *New Amazonia* (1889), the novel that I discuss in Section VI below, 'must be the Elizabeth T. Corbett' who wrote 'My Visit to Utopia' (1869), Blain, Clements and Grundy 1990, p. 237.

In his influential underground best-seller, *What Is to Be Done?*, a fictional utopia published in Russia in 1863, and first translated into English two decades later, Nikolai Tchernuishevsky had used the device of the dream to formulate a manifesto promoting the importance of utopian 'evidence' in the feminist quest for universal fellowship. The heroine Viéra Pavlovna's fourth dream centres on her encounter with a character representing 'Equal Rights', who announces that 'when a man recognizes the equal rights of a woman with himself, he ceases to regard her as his personal property'. Equal Rights concludes as follows:

> What you have been shown here will not soon reach its full development as you have just seen it. A good many generations will pass before your presentiment of it will be realized. No, not many generations: my work is now advancing rapidly, more rapidly with every year; but still you will never see the full sway of my sister, at least you have seen it [*sic*]; *you know the future.* It is bright, it is beautiful. Tell everybody. *Here is what is to be!* The future is bright and beautiful. Love it! seek to reach it! work for it! bring it nearer to men! *transfer from it into the present whatever you may be able to transfer.* Your life will be bright, beautiful, rich with happiness and enjoyment, in proportion as you are able to transfer into it the things of the future.[68]

Here is what is to be! Viéra is a redemptive version of the archetypal, not to say stereotypical, woman constructed by Havelock Ellis in *Man and Woman* (1894), his 'Study of Human Secondary Sexual Characters', at the height of the New Woman's ascendancy, for she is simultaneously a utopian ('women are greater dreamers than men', says Ellis) and a realist (women, adds Ellis, 'are, in a sense, more close to the social facts of life than men').[69] She sees and yet does not see the egalitarian future. It is the dialectic of these fantastic and realist impulses – and the interaction of present and future – that defines the feminist search for fellowship.

So, if dreams of universal fellowship and equal rights between the sexes at this time were small-scale experiments with egalitarian social relations, there was nothing irrationally subversive or anarchic about them. After all, a commune like the one under fragile construction in Clapperton's *Margaret*

---

[68] Tchernuishevsky 1886, pp. 387–88 (emphasis mine).
[69] Ellis 1894, pp. 265, 324.

Dunmore could not afford to be linked with incendiary associations – 'petroleum! dynamite!' (p. 42). It is necessary, then, to correct a consistent tendency in studies of feminist utopianism of the Victorian period, particularly studies that consign this phenomenon to the pre-history of the sexual politics of the 1970s – the tendency to celebrate women's utopias as carnivalesque attacks on phallogocentric rationality. The utopian form was not simply deployed by women because their marginal social status meant that they were 'drawn to the irrational realm of social dreaming to develop a model of empowered womanhood', as Lewes claims.[70] The social dream was a broadly rational medium. It afforded an opportunity, from within the realist discourse of contemporary fiction, to explore the conditions of possibility of as-yet non-existent inter-personal relations. If the New Women were constructed by conservatives as anarchic, then their utopias were 'much more concerned with practical matters, with the division of labour and the care of children, than with anarchy, revolt, or matriarchal rule'.[71]

Feminist utopias, and especially proto-utopias, those novels set on the threshold between present and future, testify to the rationality of the utopian project. *Margaret Dunmore*, to take Clapperton's book as an example, is a novel whose central axiom is encapsulated by a passage in which one character exhorts her sceptical comrade 'to show yourself not a theorist – a dreamer only, but a practical socialist, willing and able to cope with the dry details of a homely but important economic experiment' (p. 23). Clapperton promotes this pragmatic imperative in less sloganistic ways too. She introduces a young artist called Rose, who is so intensely interested in poverty and other 'pressing questions of the day' that she is 'in danger of falling victim to hysteria, or some other morbid action of the nervous system' (pp. 17, 18). Hysteria is, in this context, the product of patriarchal society's failure to provide her with a practical outlet for her reforming spirit. Her subsequent involvement in the utopian project to build a sexually egalitarian 'Socialist Home' signals an attempt not to displace her hysterical impulses but to channel them in the expression of political energies. This lends credence to Showalter's argument that 'hysteria and feminism exist on a kind of continuum': 'the availability of a woman's movement in which the "protofeminism" of hysterical protest could be articulated and put to work, offered a potent alternative to the self-destructive and self-enclosed strategies of hysteria, and a genuine form of resistance to the patriarchal order'.[72]

The Image-Breakers (1900), by Gertrude Dix, explores this continuum too, but from its opposite end. Far more pessimistically, it portrays the retreat from political rebellion to hysterical protest. One character, Justin, a frail and effeminate Christ-figure, falls into a feverish illness after the collapse of his attempt to create a utopian farm colony, 'a little heaven of perfection on the edge of hell'. Another character, a New Woman called Rosalind, who leaves her husband and cohabits with Justin, breaks down and suffers a serious illness, because her ideals have been fatally corroded by the difficulty of successfully living in opposition to middle-class opinion. In the book's concluding chapter, she is forced to take mechanical work in a stained-glass factory, and in her disillusionment turns from socialist feminism to the consolations of Christianity. Justin, from whom she is tragically estranged, has become 'a hireling of the capitalist press', and he too turns to mysticism, in the form of Christian science and occultism.[73] The collapse of their utopian aspirations has precipitated a personal crisis. The lives of Justin and Rosalind testify to the appalling challenge faced by those engaged in the attempt, prematurely, to transform their dreams into visions that can be rationally implemented; but they also celebrate the doomed heroism of the attempt itself.

Dix's powerful and troubling book, published on the cusp of the new century, is scored with an impending sense of the demise of a utopian politics, of its proximity to a more properly psychological escapism. But she refuses to collapse the former into the latter, and insists instead on the importance of founding social relationships that prefigure some more auspicious future. Both *Margaret Dunmore* and *The Image Breakers* situate their action just inside the social system of the late nineteenth-century, on the uncertain edge of present and future, and this is because it is there that 'evidence' of the ideal society can best be assembled. Jean Pfaelzer, in her account of American women's utopias in the 1880s and 1890s, has written suggestively that 'utopia is "nowhere" not because it is not real, but because it contains more truth,

---

[72] Showalter 1987, p. 161.
[73] Dix 1900, pp. 115, 271.

more information – hence more political possibility – than does everyday reality, in which truth, information, and political possibility are often tucked away, hidden in institutions, personal relations and cultural traditions'.[74]

Ford's *On the Threshold*, like the novels by Clapperton and Dix, concerns this attempt to piece together fragmentary information or truth about the realm of freedom. Its narrator, and her heroine Kitty, two 'odd women' in their twenties who move to London and there encounter a group of socialists and feminists, suddenly and stirringly find themselves, as they subsequently say, 'stepp[ing] over the threshold of life', and experiencing their 'first glimpse of freedom' (p. 202). Their politics, and Ford's own feminist socialism, are signalled by Kitty's assertion that she 'regards men and women as equals, as co-workers, as each other's helpers and friends' (p. 31), as well as by her corollary conviction that women's awakening is the key to the problem (p. 29). The narrative, which tracks its female characters to the point at which they ultimately become isolated from any collective political association of the kind described by Kitty, betrays a certain critical nostalgia for the utopian idealism of youth (Ford, who joined the Independent Labour Party in 1893, had met Edward Carpenter when she was herself only nineteen or twenty). The novel's most compelling scene occurs in the third chapter: narrator and protagonist together attend the first meeting of 'an entirely new society, that will have as its object the reformation of the world on quite new lines' (p. 29); and they align themselves with a young man, Estcourt, whose desire for a 'spiritual society', 'something that will bind everybody together as comrades', accords most closely with Kitty's ideals (p. 34). Thereafter, thwarted by numerous practical obstacles, their fellowship flounders, so that they remain arrested in a state of frustrated anticipation, freeze-framed on the threshold of the new world of which they dream. And thus the book describes an *impasse*. The prophetic 'information' that they gather up from where it is pleated into 'institutions, personal relations, and cultural traditions' remains fragmentary. As the plot trails off at the end, where it is revealed that Kitty is affianced to Estcourt, the rather solitary narrator reports in a tone of wistful irony that her friend's favoured reading is Mazzini's 'Faith and the Future' (p. 202).

---

[74] Pfaelzer 1984, p. 158.

If *On the Threshold* seems melancholy, its optimism ultimately undermined by the narrator's isolation, then this is because its realist format, its present setting, dictates the impossibility of fitting together the fragments of some future fellowship and thereby fashioning them into a total picture of utopia. In the feminist proto-utopia, in other words, the fragments of 'information' or 'evidence' are as much shored against a sense of ruin as they are established as the building blocks of a new society. Any utopian experiment under the existing conditions of capitalism, if at first simply embattled, is at last bound to fail.

VI. *New Amazonia*

The full-blown feminist utopia, of which *New Amazonia*, by Elizabeth Corbett, a journalist for the *Newcastle Daily Chronicle* and a popular novelist specialising in the commissioned serial writing of adventure and society stories, is the most comprehensive and compelling example in the late nineteenth-century attempts to overcome this problem by treating the utopian society as an historical fact. It is effectively written in the future perfect tense, so that a teleological link can be forged between the fragmentary struggle for fellowship in the present and the entire society successfully founded on fellowship in the future. Historicised after this fashion, the 'evidence' to which I have been referring is transformed. It now aspires, within the conventions of utopian fiction, to a sociological and anthropological status. Indeed, as is hinted by its 'Amazonian' setting, Corbett's utopia plays with the common Victorian anthropological belief both that a Golden Age of primitive communism or matriarchal social relations once existed, and that 'myths and legends could be used as historical evidence to prove the existence of this era'.[75] It uses a myth about the future as a form of 'truth' intended to expand the political possibility of the present. *New Amazonia* tries to forge a path between faith and the future.

It was written at white heat in response to the 'Appeal Against Female Suffrage', which Corbett described as 'the most despicable piece of treachery ever perpetrated towards women by women' (p. 1). The 'Appeal', published in the *Nineteenth Century* in June 1889, was the brainchild of Mrs Humphry

---

[75] Rowbotham 1977, p. 102.

Ward, who was instrumental in establishing Somerville College at Oxford. On hearing that a private members' bill on female enfranchisement might gain government support, she concocted what, in a letter to Thomas Arnold, she called 'a women's manifesto against women's suffrage'.[76] One hundred and four 'ladies' – including women who subsequently fought for the suffrage (Louise Creighton, Charlotte Green and Beatrice Potter) as well as ones who continued to oppose it (Mrs Matthew Arnold, Mrs Walter Bagehot, Mrs Leslie Stephen, Eliza Linton and Christina Rossetti) – signed a statement which argued that women's influence should remain restricted to a moral role within the domestic sphere.

A patriarchal seal of approval was appended to this statement by J.T. Knowles, the editor of the *Nineteenth Century*: it assumed the form of a postscript urging female readers of the periodical that 'in order to save the quiet of Home life from total disappearance, they should do violence to their natural reticence, and signify publicly and unmistakably their condemnation of the scheme now threatened'.[77] Knowles was apparently unaware of the irony underscoring this 'Appeal', that a movement determined to maintain women's enforced political silence by an ideological insistence on their 'natural reticence' should nonetheless be forced to entreat them to contradict their nature and break that silence.

Angry defences of the suffrage campaign followed in the *Nineteenth Century* and other periodicals and pamphlets, most of them insisting that the signatories of the 'Appeal', in Fawcett's arch phrase, were those 'to whom the lines of life have fallen in pleasant places'.[78] The *Fortnightly Review*, Knowles's main competitor in the liberal periodical press, retorted swiftly and efficiently: in July 1889, it published the more prominent names to have signed a pro-suffrage petition comprising at least two thousand signatures.[79] Corbett's polemical Preface to *New Amazonia*, which cites this petition as well as Fawcett's response, deliberately inserts itself into the debate. It mounts a coruscating attack on the class affiliations of the anti-feminists: 'The principal signatories are in comfortable circumstances; have no great cares upon their shoulders;

---

[76] Quoted in Sutherland 1991, p. 198.
[77] 'Appeal Against Female Suffrage' 1889, p. 788.
[78] Fawcett 1889, p. 89.
[79] Anonymous 1889, pp. 123–39.

they plume themselves upon occupying important positions in society; it is to their interest to uphold the political principles of the men whose privilege it is to support them; they do not see that life may be made any brighter for them, therefore they conspire to prevent every other woman from emerging from the ditch in which she grovels' (p. 6). The Preface alone constitutes a powerful indictment of the anti-suffrage campaign.

The utopian framework within which Corbett formulated her rebuttal of the 'Appeal' can be traced back to the debate about the future of women that lies buried in the arguments for and against suffrage in the 1880s and 1890s. The 'Appeal' itself rests its case on the assumption that 'the emancipating process has now reached the limits fixed by the physical constitution of women, and by the fundamental difference which must always exist between their main occupations and those of men'.[80] And this thesis, for the end of women's history, was underlined by Louise Creighton's contribution to the debate, which appeared in the August 1889 issue of the *Nineteenth Century*:

> The vote is supposed to have a certain magical power. . . . The attitude of many of the advocates of female suffrage seems to suppose an ideal woman, working side by side with an ideal man in an ideal system of politics. But we have to do with realities; there is a great deal of work to be done, and the practical question is how to do it. It has yet to be proved that giving women the vote will enable them to do better in the future the work which they have neglected in the past.[81]

Creighton accuses her opponents of being credulous utopians only in order to advertise the impossibility of altering the status quo. She is incorrect to assert that advocates of suffrage supposed an ideal woman; on the contrary, they dreamed of an ideal woman, and supposed only that her realisation would involve a personal struggle of which enfranchisement was a preliminary, political part. This is the import of the verse 'Introduction' to Dixie's *Gloriana*, in which a mythical Everywoman's dream of emancipation 'is stern reality, / Mingled with visions of a future day' (p. 4).

The vote was not an end in itself but a means to an end for many of the

---

[80] 'Appeal Against Female Suffrage' 1889, p. 782.
[81] Creighton 1889, p. 350.

feminists of the late nineteenth-century. As M.M. Dilke testified: 'It is useful as a lever to lift a weight, or as a key to open a door, but has in itself no intrinsic value. Women do not imagine that the Millennium will have been attained when some or indeed all of them have votes; but as long as they have no votes they risk the loss of all those improvements in the position of their sex for which they have toiled so unremittingly'.[82] Or as Caroline Biggs commented in a piece published by the Central Committee of the National Society for Women's Suffrage at this time, 'if women respect themselves, they will make the acquisition of the suffrage the foundation stone of their political building'.[83] In the face of claims that women had reached the limits of their political development, nothing less than the historical representation of the present, and, consequently, the narrative of the near future, were at stake in this controversy.

It is for this reason that Corbett responded to the appeal in the format of a utopian fiction, one that figures women's struggle for freedom in the nineteenth-century as the force that, in the future, will finally inaugurate 'Universal Suffrage!' (p. 37). At the end of her Preface, encouraged by the protests directed at the 'Appeal Against Suffrage' by Fawcett and Dilke, Corbett indulges in a daydream: 'I find myself stringing together all sorts of fancies in which women's achievements form conspicuous features, and I am just noticing how pleasant Mrs. Weldon looks in the Speaker's chair, listening to Mrs. Besant's first Prime Ministerial speech, when my senses become entirely "obfuscated" . . . and I sink into a slumber as profound as that which overcame the fabled enchanted guardians' (p. 8). She awakes in a mysteriously beautiful garden, beside a young man of aristocratic appearance who recalls only that he has been smoking hasheesh in Soho. The two of them are approached by a monumentally tall woman wearing clothes that embody 'health, comfort and beauty': 'a magnified Venus, a glorified Hebe, a smiling Juno, were here all united in one perfect human being' (p. 11). Mistaken for children at first, they are taken to a refectory to eat a vegetarian meal, and there informed that they are in New Amazonia, formerly Ireland, in the year 2472.

---

[82] Dilke 1889, p. 99.
[83] Biggs [n.d.], [p. 3].

It was in Ireland at the end of Queen Victoria's reign, it transpires, that 'the incidents which ultimately resulted in the disruption of the British Empire' took place. Ireland had lapsed into a state of anarchy, after a failed attempt to achieve national self-determination, at a time when Germany and France threatened the supremacy of the empire. So after the victory of the suffragists, 'one of the greatest political events the world has ever seen', it was resolved that the 'odd women' who so outnumbered men in mainland Britain should colonize Ireland (p. 38). A powerful state, known as 'the Mother', became the basis of the new nation, which was semi-autonomous from Britain. Recalling Victorian England in conversation with a denizen of Amazonia, Corbett's narrative persona notes that 'a true and tender interest will never be felt in the units of the nation until our Constitution becomes less that of rulers and ruled, and more like that of mothers and children' (p. 130).

The colony is a eugenicist fantasy as well as a feminist one. Amazonians are selected on the basis of their physical and moral fitness, and Malthusian doctrines are strictly enforced (malformed children are destroyed). 'Health of body, the highest technical and intellectual knowledge, and purity of morals have ever been the goal aimed at in New Amazonia', the narrator's Ciceronian interlocutor tells her, 'and it can to-day boast of being the most perfect, the most prosperous, and the most moral community in existence' (p. 47). Corbett's utopia is not gynocratic, however; and it does not have recourse to parthenogenic reproduction. It has a male as well as a female population. For the most part, in fact, 'the sexes stand on an equal footing'; but women occupy the most important legislative posts, because 'the world's experience goes to prove that masculine government has always held openings for the free admission of corruption, injustice, immorality, and narrow-minded, self-glorifying bigotry' (p. 80). Corbett's creative fantasy of a realm of freedom for women is, regrettably, built on a dilapidated essentialist conception of racial and sexual identities.

Corbett is quite clear about the function of the utopian experience that she outlines in New Amazonia. Her narrator, who, while staying in Amazonia, expresses her hope of returning to nineteenth-century England, intends to use the knowledge she has acquired about equal sexual relations in order to advance what she calls 'the "Onward" portion' of her sex: 'I hope to win an immense number of recruits when I get home again, and describe all I have seen here' (p. 133). The narrative's motto might have been that of the first

German women's magazine ever to be published, the masthead of which read, 'I recruit female citizens for the realm of freedom'.[84] For the late-nineteenth-century feminist utopia interpellated an imaginary community of men and women who, in the here and now, might start to realise the promise of utopia. Felski has argued that, like the political essay, the literary utopia offered a 'framework for inspiratory and programmatic writing' at the *fin de siècle*, adding that 'feminist discourse here acquired a performative and prophetic function, seeking to bring into existence through its own writing that political community to which it aspired'.[85] If it sought to create and consolidate this community by furnishing 'evidence' of the looked-for future, then it also implicitly posited this very community as concrete 'proof' of that future. In other words, the feminist utopia encodes a kind of meta-utopia, the dream of an ideal readership that, in some embryonic form, is already fulfilling the desires of the writer. This readership, a fellowship of like-minded men and women, is an imaginary community that, for the writer, represents the basis and beginning of the future society.

Corbett's novel is instructive in this context because of its persistent preoccupation with the act of writing, which is ultimately translated into a species of activism. Her narrator is a professional writer, and remains one in Amazonia. This emphasis has to be understood within the context of the growth of both the new journalism and the cheap book trade in the 1880s, which opened up unprecedented opportunities for women writers.[86] Discussing her own century with one utopian interlocutor, she informs him that she writes for a living. In a sentence that recalls the proliferation of mass-produced publications in her own time, she adds excitedly that 'I could probably find employment on one of your numerous journals' (p. 113). In Corbett's far-distant future, the state's Literary Bureau publishes every book and journal: authors pay their own costs, sometimes with the assistance of state credits, and, apart from a 5% tax, receive all the profits from sales. 'The long-suffering author had triumphed at last', the narrator declares with relief, 'and his erstwhile oppressor was shorn of his glory' (p. 127). The description of the New Amazonian book trade therefore underlines the impression that the

---

[84] Bloch 1986, p. 591.
[85] Felski 1995, pp. 146–47.
[86] See Kranidis 1995, Chapter 2.

novel's utopian subtext centres on a literary and political freedom, licensed by a marketplace in which 'no grasping publisher [is] allowed to step in and reap the profits of an author's brain toil' (p. 128). Corbett's social fantasy is also a professional one.

It is in some respects comparable to the petty-bourgeois utopia, sketched by William Morris, 'of the industrious *professional* middle-class men of to-day purified from their crime of complicity with the monopolist class, and become independent instead of being, as they now are, parasitical'.[87] Corbett's narrator dreams of the fulfilment of the promise represented by the new journalism, a promise to bypass the circulating libraries and so secure a literary realm of political autonomy, beyond which an unmediated relationship with some ideal readership is imaginable. This is underlined when the New Amazonian state commissions her to write a book about nineteenth-century England – an attractive prospect precisely because its utopian audience will read the work from the standpoint of redemption. The description of her experiences in Amazonia – which throughout her stay there the narrator has wanted to write up for a Victorian readership – is the flipside of this historiographical exercise. Instead of inscribing themselves as the narrative *telos* of her history of the past, the narrator's Victorian readers must see themselves as the point of origin of her history of the future.

New Amazonia doubles back on itself, merging narrative with meta-narrative, since it recounts the conditions in which a history of utopia might be written, whilst at the same time positing itself as that history. The narrative traces Corbett's narrator's attempt to collect information on Amazonia prior to her return, even as it represents that information itself. Corbett shadows her narrator and protagonist at every turn of the plot. In this way, the reader is constantly reminded both of the historicity of utopia, its status as a type of anti-empirical proof, and of the political import of the act of writing. Penny Boumelha's assessment of the way in which the New Woman novel blurs the boundaries between author and character proves particularly pertinent to *New Amazonia*: 'it is as if at moments there is no mediating narrator; the writing of the fiction becomes for a time its own action, its own plot, enacting as well as articulating the protest of the text'.[88]

---

[87] Morris 1994, p. 421.
[88] Boumelha 1982, p. 66.

It is in this sense that writing utopia represents for the New Woman a species of activism as well as a displacement of it. The utopian impulse that underpins Corbett's romance is captured by H.R. Haweis's announcement in 1894, that 'in women's hands – women's writers' hands – lies the regeneration of the world'.[89] Like other feminist utopias at the *fin de siècle*, it is the product of a period in which 'women were exhilarated by the prospect of a new age in which female ability would have more scope', and 'wherein writers were the anointed priestesses of their sex, and their creed was influence'.[90] The conclusion to Corbett's later novel about female prostitution, *Mrs. Grundy's Victims* (1893), exemplifies this missionary confidence. There, she addresses her audience directly as 'my sisters', before going on to say that she hopes that, at best, her story will have moved people 'to an attempt to remove some of the evils that reign rampant in our midst', and that, at the very least, it will have altered the opinion of its readership.[91] *New Amazonia* had pushed these principles one step further, by using the utopian form both to estrange its readers' judgement and to move people to build an alternative world, in which the kind of evils to which she refers no longer reign rampant.

If New Woman fiction, in Kate Flint's words, 'may be said to have created and consolidated a community of woman readers, who could refer to these works as proof of their psychological, social, and ideological difference from men', then feminist utopias at the *fin de siècle* may be said to have interpellated this same female readership, so that they might refer to it as heuristic 'proof' of a possible future opposed to the patriarchal present, 'proof' to be put to political purpose in the struggle for women's rights.[92] The final image of *New Amazonia*, as I pointed out at the start of this chapter, is of the narrator's discovery that she has been sleeping in her study 'surrounded by nineteenth-century magazines and newspapers' (p. 146). The heroic confidence of Haweis's female writer here shades into something far lonelier. Corbett's dream is of overcoming her sense of political isolation through writing. The feminist utopia dramatises a dream of social fellowship whose embryonic form is expressed in the bonds forged between writer, reader and a wider audience. It tries to suture those 'two fields of action', the writer's and the reader's,

---

[89] Haweis 1900, p. 71.
[90] Showalter 1978, pp. 182–83.
[91] Corbett 1893, pp. 250, 252.
[92] Flint 1993, p. 205.

that Charles Dickens, addressing the conditions of industrial society in the mid-nineteenth-century, and demanding whether 'similar things shall be or not', left mutually distinct, but undefined, in the final paragraph of *Hard Times*.[93]

In the absence of a homogeneous, mass women's movement, this attempt is finally a poignant failure. The politics of fellowship, the specific structure of feeling on which, in the late-Victorian period, feminist-utopian fiction is premised, cannot compensate for the fact that, under capitalist relations of production and consumption, a readership is in effect a *public introuvable*. The social dream projected by the New Women is implicitly an appeal to a pre-capitalist past in which 'the relationship between artist and public was still in one way or another a social institution and a concrete and interpersonal relationship with its own validation and specificity'.[94] As I explain in the Conclusion to this book, utopian fiction at the *fin de siècle* is a literary form that identifies its readership in the present as the germ of an organic community in the future. Feminist-utopian fiction exhibits this fact with particular clarity.

[handwritten marginal notes: "utopian fiction = fin de siècle = a literary form that identifies its readership in the present as the germ of an organic community in the future"]

---

[93] Dickens 1854, p. 352.
[94] Jameson 1992a, p. 18.

Chapter Four

Anti-Communism and the Cacotopia

I. Introduction

'A spectre is haunting Europe – the spectre of
Communism'. By the time the opening salvo of
the *Communist Manifesto* appeared in print, in
February 1848 the series of revolutions that heralded
the nineteenth-century's 'springtime of peoples'
had already exploded throughout Europe. This
'momentary realisation of the dreams of the left, the
nightmares of the right', as Eric Hobsbawm puts it,
was succeeded by a period of spectacular global
growth for the capitalist system. It was not until 1871,
the year of the Paris Commune, that 'the spectre of
social revolution once again irrupted into a confident
capitalist world' – in the form of a proletarian
government that, until its brutal suppression by
the Versailles troops, presided over the capital of
the nineteenth-century for some two months. In the
aftermath of this event, the European bourgeoisie
was beset by the social and economic anxieties
associated with the Great Depression. As a result, 'it
was a little less self-confident than before, and its
assertions of self-confidence therefore a little shriller,
perhaps a little more worried about its future'.[1]

---

[1] Hobsbawm 1962, pp. 248, 308.

Marx's explicit intention in publishing the views, aims and tendencies of the communists in the *Manifesto* had been 'to meet this nursery tale of the Spectre of Communism' – that is, to refute the infantile propaganda of the bourgeoisie in the form of a compressed historical epic.[2] After the Paris Commune, however, the anti-communists' cautionary tale – in which Marx, presiding over the International, appeared as the political equivalent of Strüwelpeter – was enriched with colourful illustrations of the grotesque antics of the French working class. The expedience of this *'spectre-rouge* trick', as Paul Lafargue styled it, was proved by the conjurations of the French state: 'Thiers found in the massacres of the commune, instigated by himself, the bloody rags for a new red-spectre, in order to overrule the unruly Assembly of Versailles'. In general, Lafargue argued, 'political men who value their places' invoke the red spectre in order to persuade 'the shopkeepers, the millowners, [and] the moneylenders' of two facts: first, 'that the *bourgeois* will be robbed of his life which is barely worth living and of his purse which is well worth fighting for'; and second, 'that, there they are, at the helm of the State, ready to save France and the world along with it from wreck and ruin'.[3]

'But what is the secret of the red bogey', wrote Marx and Engels in a letter to Bebel and others in 1879, 'if not the dread the bourgeoisie has of the inevitable life-and-death struggle between it and the proletariat?'[4] For the anti-communist imagination, the Paris Commune forced a confrontation with the primal scene of the 1790s, or with its repetition in the 1840s. The European bourgeoisie was terrified by the prospect of a working-class movement motivated by socialist ideas and mobilized by socialist organizations. Its traumatic encounter with the Communards had the impact of the return of the repressed. And journalists and political commentators lost no time in importing the nursery tale to England too in 1871. Correspondents of the London newspapers, drawing on the influential rhetoric of Burke's *Reflections on the Revolution in France* (1790), and on conservative reaction to the insurrections of 1848, developed a nightmarish demonology of the so-called 'Fourth French Revolution' – a demonology that acquired popular currency at the very moment when establishment journals in France were being suppressed by the Communards.

[2] Marx and Engels 1976c, p. 481.
[3] Lafargue 1883, p. 103.
[4] Marx and Engels 1984, p. 260.

It is thus because of, rather than despite, the fact that the English experienced the Commune vicariously, through the thick and densely metaphorical description of daily newspaper reports, that it had such a huge impact on the gothic fantasy of the domestic anti-communist imagination. In a sense, if the Commune was the first revolution to be recorded by the camera, then for the English, bombarded as they were by hallucinatory images of cataclysmic social change, it was also an early example of history's 'hyperrealisation'. Staging it as 'a theatrical representation of a sensational melodramatic kind', as one *Times* correspondent put it during the May fighting, the capitalist media ensured an ideological production of the revolution that, in representing real events, also derealised them.[5] Analysing the analogical device employed by French commentators on the Commune, who described workers in terms of bestial imagery, Paul Lidsky explains that 'the comparative image, at first simply juxtaposed with the real fact, completely invades it and stands in for the representation of the real, ending up by eliminating it'.[6] In this way, contemporary historians superimposed the spectre of communism on the substance of the Commune, employing the rhetoric of fantasy both to unleash and to tame the horrors imputed to the Parisian working class. In the late-Victorian period, in Britain as well as in France, the Commune shaped the social imaginary of an entire generation.

If the mythopoeic English press actively moulded the literary ballistics of anti-socialist rhetoric in the 1870s, they were also forged in a different discursive context. A fictional form – what I call the 'cacotopia' – nurtured the anti-revolutionary animus at this time. Coined by Jeremy Bentham in 1818, the word 'cacotopia' (from the Greek *kakos* meaning 'bad') was used by John Stuart Mill in 1868, only three years before the Commune, during a debate in parliament on the state of Ireland. Mill accused the Conservative government not of being 'Utopians' in their policy-making – for that, he said, would be too complimentary – but of being 'dys-topians, or cacotopians': 'What is commonly called Utopian is something too good to be practicable; but what they appear to favour is too bad to be practicable'.[7] I use the term 'cacotopian',

---

[5] *The Times* 27 May 1871, p. 5.
[6] Lidsky 1970, pp. 153–54: 'L'image de la comparaison, d'abord simplement mise en rapport avec le fait réel, en vient à tout envahir et a se donner pour la représentation du réel, qu'à la limite on finit par éliminer' (my translation).
[7] *Hansard* 12 March 1868, p. 1517.

in a slightly different sense, to specify a particular manifestation of the anti-utopian, or dystopian, imagination. The dominant current of anti-utopianism in the late-Victorian period proceeds by satirising the utopian form itself. 'Cacotopianism' is concerned less with repudiating the literary expression of utopianism than with combating its practical embodiment in the proletariat. Cacotopia implies not simply the opposite of utopia but something pernicious in its own right (as Anthony Burgess said, it 'sounds worse than dystopia').[8] It depicts the working class, *in corpore*, as dystopian. So its grisly fascination is with chthonic insurrection rather than with the corrupt power structures of the putative socialist state. According to Krishan Kumar, the anti-utopia can be understood 'as an invention to combat socialism, in so far as socialism was seen to be the fullest and most sophisticated expression of the modern worship of science, technology and organization'.[9] The cacotopia can be understood, by contradistinction, as an invention to combat communism, in so far as communism (so Engels claimed) was seen to be the 'very opposite' of a 'respectable' middle-class movement.[10] A fiction of social catastrophe, cacotopianism portrays revolution as a sexual and political apocalypse. It is not so much satire as shatire. I deploy the term 'cacotopia' in an attempt to reproduce the sheer pungency of the form's anti-communist politics.

In novels and fictional pamphlets, up until the end of the century, the fantastic image of an 'English Commune', which one correspondent for *The Times* rightly regarded as 'no sort of danger', was nevertheless fostered.[11] The cacotopia, which mapped the menacing figure of an insurgent working class onto the political geography of London, was the offspring of the Great Depression as well as of the Commune. An imaginary history of the present, in the form of a 'prospective history', it reflected the intensifying class struggle of the final decades of the nineteenth-century. The 1880s and 1890s mark an important moment in the formation of the English working class. It now seemed alarmingly homogeneous. And the emerging socialist movement promised to glue it together all the more securely. What in the aftermath of the Hyde Park riots of 1866 Matthew Arnold called the 'Populace' – 'that vast portion . . . of the working class which, raw and half-developed, has long lain

---

[8] Burgess 1978, p. 52.
[9] Kumar 1987, p. 49.
[10] Engels 1990, p. 517.
[11] *The Times* 10 April 1871, p. 8.

half-hidden amidst its poverty and squalor, and is now issuing from its hiding-place to assert an Englishman's heaven-born privilege of doing as he likes, and is beginning to perplex us by marching where it likes, meeting where it likes, bawling what it likes, breaking what it likes' – was far from unformed some twenty years later.[12]

The nursery tale of the spectre of communism consequently came to underpin what Morris acidly called 'contemporary history as written by the daily press'. After the riots of February 1887, he commented on 'the very rapidly growing myth of the *Wicked Socialist and the Heroic Butcher*'.[13] This myth had evolved from accounts of the Terror in the 1790s. Ten or fifteen years after the Paris Commune, the nightmare of an insurrectionary capital city was reanimated in London. It is no accident that Émile de Laveleye's survey of *Le socialisme contemporain* (1881) – which warned that 'we may see our capitals ravaged by dynamite and petroleum in a more ruthless and systematic manner than even that which Paris experienced at the hands of the Commune' – was translated into English in the mid-1880s.[14] Domestic anxieties about social crisis and class conflict reinforced the imaginative impact left by events in Paris. And this fear of revolution continued to define reformist as well as conservative politics at the *fin de siècle*. The secularist and freethinker Charles Bradlaugh made this exemplary statement in 1884: 'I desire to avoid encouragement of revolution in this country. The memories of 1870–1 in France are too close and too terrible, and the echoes of 1848 on the Continent have scarcely died away. I desire to avoid a revolution which in some of our overcrowded cities might awaken monstrous passions, and involve shocking consequences'.[15] For Bradlaugh, the Paris Commune supplied a crucial pretext for the prophylactic programme of reform that I explored in Chapter 2.

In this chapter, I anatomise the anti-communist, and more specifically, anti-insurrectionary imagination that is identifiable in England after the Commune; and show how it shaped the body of literary texts that I designate cacotopian. Its second section examines the cacotopia's conditions of possibility from the late 1860s and early 1870s, with reference to seminal imaginary histories by Frederick Gale, George Chesney and Samuel Bracebridge Hemyng. Section

---

[12] Arnold 1965, p. 143.
[13] Morris 1996, p. 195.
[14] De Laveleye 1884, p. xliv.
[15] Bradlaugh 1884, pp. 6–7.

III explores the impact on the English imagination of the Commune itself, and outlines its shaping influence on the propagandist function of cacotopian fiction. In the fourth section, I propose a rough typology for the anti-communist imaginary, focussing in particular on its fear of political conspiracy, its xenophobia and racism, and its sexism. In Section V, on the Paris Commune and metropolitan experience, I map the characteristic topos of the cacotopia, sketching a number of fictional narratives from the 1880s and 1890s that contribute to the gothic geography of a city corroded by class conflict. Finally, I return to the cacotopia's propagandist function and conclude that, in depicting revolution as a traumatic encounter with the Real, the form represents a surreptitious utopian appeal to its imagined community of readers, an appeal for a new bourgeois consciousness centred on the need for defence against the class enemy. *When All Men Starve* (1898), a striking cacotopia by Charles Gleig, published in the final years of the century, illustrates the derelict condition of the ideological barricades mounted by the middle classes at this time.

II. The emergence of the cacotopian genre

The cacotopia's emergence as a genre or sub-genre coincided with the sudden resurgence of utopian fiction in the early 1870s. 'The last four or five years', wrote James Presley, the director of the Cheltenham Library, in 1873, 'have been remarkably fruitful in works of a Utopian character'. As I pointed out in Chapter 1, 1871 was something like the founding moment of turn-of-the-century utopian fiction. The year of the Prussian siege and the Paris Commune, 1871 passed in a mood of military and political apprehension in Europe – a fitting climate for the publication of cacotopian fantasy too. *The Battle of Dorking* (1871), Colonel Chesney's forecast of a Prussian invasion of England, offered a template for such fiction. Published in *Blackwood's Magazine*, it was rapidly reprinted to appease the swelling appetite of its middle-class readership. Its popularity lent credence to Presley's claim that the turn to utopian fiction was caused, in part, by 'the new political influences resulting from the late Franco-German war'.[16] The bibliographer's coy allusion to the Paris Commune,

---

[16] Presley 1873, p. 22.

which pressed hard on the heels of the Prussian siege, occludes the scene of insurrection even as it manifests an implicit awareness of its influence on the collective imagination.

As a propagandist romance, the cacotopia constitutes the missing link between the new utopianism and future-war fiction of the early 1870s on the one hand, and the 'anti-utopianism' of the end of the century on the other hand. In the 1890s, a number of critics, including William Morris of course, rebutted Bellamy's vision of 'State Socialism', and in *The Time Machine* H.G. Wells started to problematise the more optimistic prophecies of much early science fiction. But the cacotopias grew out of a slightly earlier climate of pessimism. The first stirrings of a cacotopian impulse were responses not to literary events, nor to the scientistic fantasies that fretted Samuel Butler, but to the 'visionary ideas' taking hold of the working class, bred in what Lord Salisbury called the 'seething imaginations of the foreign conspirators' who implemented them in the Commune.[17] *The Times* referred to 'the Utopia which the Commune of Paris have undertaken to introduce into the domain of practical ideas' [sic].[18] The momentary materialisation of utopia in the spectre of Parisian communism helps to explain the traumatic impact of the Commune. The Commune ruptured the bourgeoisie's faith in progress. Arnold's diagnosis, that 'the Paris convulsion [was] an explosion of that fixed resolve of the working class to count for something and *live*, which [was] destined to make itself so much felt in the coming time, and to disturb so much which dreamed it would last forever', was a perspicacious one.[19] The reactionary propaganda that proliferated in England from 1871, and throughout the troubled years that followed, tried to suture that ruptured dream.

In the early 1870s, when the politics of the labour movement were largely defined by the Liberals' agenda, there was not the remotest chance of working-class revolution in England. We must look beyond the scant signs of socialist organisation at the time in order to understand the disproportionate perturbation of the dominant class. Its causes lie in the fact that, from the Reform Act of 1867, the Liberal and Tory parties found themselves compelled to compete on the terrain of mass politics. A recomposition of the political

---

[17] Salisbury 1871, pp. 568, 555.
[18] *The Times* 29 March 1871, p. 5.
[19] Arnold 1895, p. 57 (letter to his mother, 31 May 1871).

settlement consequently took place, and a widespread sense of insecurity attended it. Forced in part from below, as the unsettling impact of the riots in Hyde Park implies, the Act was a very limited extension of the franchise, largely to skilled workers. It embodied a dual strategy: it attempted to harness the voting power of a portion of the working class in order to preserve the status quo; and it sought to retard the political growth of the labour movement and forestall the potential revolutionary force of the proletariat. But, despite its pre-emptive intention, it actually compounded ruling-class suspicions of a link between suffrage and revolution. Even Macaulay had been against democratisation, on the grounds that it 'sooner or later' led to the destruction of 'liberty, or civilization, or both'.[20] Thus, the bourgeoisie's relationship with the working class was acutely contradictory. Pushed into closer proximity with the propertied class, the working class seemed more incomprehensible and unknowable to its rulers than ever before, and this 'alienation from the people', in Lukács's useful formulation, 'constantly change[d] into hostility towards the people'.[21]

The 'peak of religious and philanthropic energy' that Gareth Stedman Jones identifies between 1866 and 1872, a time of epidemic disease as well as social crisis, is symptomatic of this contradiction. Octavia Hill, Edward Denison and Dr. Barnardo, among others, tried in piecemeal ways to address the material needs of the urban poor. But, confronting failure even on a local scale, and facing the systemic scale of poverty, especially in London, for the first time, their philanthropic and educationalist efforts also comprised a consolatory attempt to erode the sheer abstraction of the masses and interpellate the people. Stedman Jones suggestively includes John Ruskin's *Fors Clavigera* in the same category of 'reforming concern'; and his 'Letters to the Working Men of England' were indeed a kind of wish-fulfilment identification with, as well as of, the working class.[22] One letter, 'Charitas', records the consternation Ruskin's politics of reform ran into when confronted with the Parisian uprising of 1871.[23] As we shall see, the Commune was to mark the limits of this accommodating reformism, and to re-cement the class unity of the bourgeoisie, be it liberal or conservative.

---

[20] Macaulay 1982, p. 284 (letter to H.S. Randall, 23 May 1857).
[21] Lukács 1989, p. 238.
[22] Stedman Jones 1983, p. 190.
[23] See Ruskin 1907, p. 115.

This fragile negotiation of social relations in the atmosphere generated by the Reform Bill is played out to its utopian consummation, of class harmony, in one important forerunner of the cacotopian texts of the post-Commune period, an imaginary history by Frederick Gale, *The History of the English Revolution of 1867* (1867). A decade earlier, the anonymous *Imaginary History of the Next Thirty Years* (1857), had predicted the ratification of a new Reform Act, since 'the country had outgrown the settlement of 1832'.[24] Gale builds on the imaginary history by 'looking backward'. His fantastical nightmare of the consequences of 'the memorable Reform Bill of 1867' is narrated in the form of a lost manuscript. This manuscript is unearthed in the year 3867, by an itinerant editor who has been commissioned by 'His Majesty Albert Edward 100th, King of the World' to discover whether it is wise to extend the franchise to 'the gorilla and Darwinian tribes'. It reveals that England enjoyed a Golden Age until 1867, at which juncture a parliamentary coup, commandeered by a demagogic Quaker called Buster, led to the abolition of church, state and standing army. The newly enfranchised working class jubilantly greets the spontaneous 'vision of a hatful of guineas and oceans of beer for a single vote; but their day dream [is] as quickly dispelled'. Beset by infighting and bureaucratic disorganisation, their Cockayne rapidly vanishing, the workers demand the reinstitution of the monarchy, to the relief not only of the former prime minister, but of Buster, who turns out to be 'a good chap' unhappily carried before the mob. 'And so England was England once more'.[25]

As the last sentence indicates, the polemical point of Gale's farcical satire is that, beyond a biased deal between rulers and decent but deluded middle-class reformists, working-class control leads to anarchy; and that, consequently, there is no alternative to the status quo. The narrative is a fantasy of friendship between the classes, but its sentimental solution is undermined by violent prejudice, typified by its pervasive association of workers with primates and savages. These themes, social-Darwinist as well as anti-socialist, will crop up in the 'future histories' of the 1880s and 1890s, where they are inflected with the imagery of open class war furnished by the Paris Commune. In the meantime, in addition to the anxiety generated by the Reform Bill, but not unconnected to it, a fear of foreign invasion served to reinforce the middle

---

[24] Anonymous 1857, p. 15.
[25] Gale 1867, pp. iii, 24, 29, 31.

class's fear of insurrection. As the *Annual Register* of 1871 put it in its report on the Franco-Prussian war: 'The foreign enemy pacified, Government became aware that an enemy more formidable, because more fatal to all patriotic bonds of sympathy, existed in the heart of Paris'.[26] In Britain, the dual dread of the enemy within and the enemy without obtruded into middle-class consciousness during the Franco-Prussian War, and became implacable as the first siege of Paris culminated in the Commune.

The Battle of Dorking, Chesney's portentous polemic against national complacency and the myopia of contemporary military planning, exploited more than just a widespread fear of conflict with the strong Germany that Britain had provisionally supported against France. It also capitalised on the sense of social disquiet that I have been discussing, by locating the causes of the imaginary Prussian invasion in the fact that 'power was then passing away from the class which had been used to rule, and to face political dangers, and which had brought the nation with honour unsullied through former struggles, into the hands of the lower classes, uneducated, untrained to the use of political rights, and swayed by demagogues'.[27] Chesney's reference to a post-war France subject to 'foolish communism' implicitly points to a similar fate for Britain unless the necessary action is taken (p. 5), confirming Darko Suvin's speculation, in his account of Victorian science fiction, that 'in some subterranean ways ... much of the force of this text comes from an unacknowledged equation between fear of foreign invasion and of revolutionary uprising'.[28]

The author of *The Battle of Dorking* is in addition troubled by the prospect of impending economic decline, and this fear, fulfilled especially in the mid-1880s, is also symptomatic of the state of social flux characteristic of the late 1860s and early 1870s. For Chesney, England's wealth is the result of free trade, which 'had been working for more than a quarter of a century', such that 'there seemed to be no end to the riches it was bringing us' (p. 3). But Britain is merely 'a big workshop' dependent on the needs of other nations, and it is the failure to build some kind of safety mechanism into the economy, in order 'to insure our prosperity', that precipitates the collapse of the City

---

[26] Annual Register 1872, p. 175.
[27] Chesney 1871, pp. 63–4. Subsequent references are given after quotations in the text.
[28] Suvin 1983, p. 342.

when the threat of invasion arises (pp. 4–5). 'We thought we were living in a commercial millennium, which must last for a thousand years at least', the narrator ruefully observes (p. 63).

Further warnings against commercial complacency are encoded in the scattering of other future histories published at the onset of agricultural recession in 1873. 'Glimpses of the Future', printed anonymously in *Blackwood's* in 1872, explores the crisis in the North Riding mill-owning community. It centres on a debate between the narrator, Collins, and his wealthy friends, who, 'reduced to one servant-of-all-work', are convinced that 'evil times [are] at hand'. Despite his own confidence in the *status quo*, Collins is 'tormented with queer sights and revelations' of a future in which prices become as uncontrollable as the working class – the workers strike incessantly, torch mills, and eventually clash with the army in a riot that leaves thirty one dead and ninety injured.[29] *Little Hodge* (1873), another wry tale of rural instability, asks whether 'the country [will] lie listless and dead to the crack of doom?'. Its author, John Edward Jenkins, who published the bestseller *Ginx's Baby* in 1870, argues for an economy controlled discreetly by the State, so that 'the holy brotherhood of Capital and Labour' can be allowed to get on and secure lasting financial stability.[30] He is committed to a social solution that maximises profits with the minimum of working-class agitation. Both these stories share the concerns of Charlotte Brontë's *Shirley* (1849), which, especially in its riot scenes, exerts a palpable literary influence on them: all three are 'much preoccupied with middle-class solidarity in the face of the proletarian enemy'.[31]

The first fiction directly to register the impact of the Commune, a pamphlet entitled *The Commune in London* (1871), a 'Chapter of Anticipated History' by Samuel Bracebridge Hemyng, an aristocratic writer of adventure novels, is a repository for these fears. The threats of a working class stirred into sedition by the cumulative impact of the Reform Bill, a German invasion and an imminent economic depression are all played out in its pages. Its nightmare vision of an English revolution inspired by the Commune locates the causes of social upheaval in a labouring population 'intoxicated by their successes in obtaining the suffrage and the ballot', in a Prussian invasion at Harwich

[29] Anonymous 1872, pp. 283–84, 293.
[30] Jenkins 1873, pp. 24, 43.
[31] Eagleton 1976, p. 80.

and Dorking in 1871, and in 'a decreasing trade'.[32] Set in the imaginary aftermath of Victoria's reign, it looks back with nostalgia to the 'Victorian Era' – if not quite a 'commercial millennium', still a time of flourishing trade and peace (p. 4). This order is shattered by the uprising of a bloodthirsty working-class mob that, led by cosmopolitan demagogues and backed by demonic female insurgents, sets up a despotic state only overthrown by the Prince of Wales's counter-offensive. Although formally unoriginal (in fact, parasitic on *The Battle of Dorking*), this text signals the repopulation of a distinct literary topos, the class war as living nightmare. As a financially and politically opportunistic narrative which, as Suvin says, 'threw together an "Anticipated History" . . . and *the* red-hot theme of the day in a hasty concoction mixing gory Paris-style street carnage with muddled political disquisitions', it is the prototype of those cacotopian texts of the 1880s and 1890s which, in one way or another, recast the nursery tale of the spectre of communism for the late-Victorian middle classes.[33]

If Chesney furnished the Victorian bourgeoisie with a new mythology of imaginary wars that played out the fantasies of Western nationalism, then Hemyng traced out a fantasy of revolution in order to dramatise dreams of a ruling-class hegemony secured by disciplined class oppression. In effect, he advocates conservative reform of the status quo. 'What suffices it that the insurrection was put down, that the gutters ran blood, and that the Communists were hunted down and destroyed like rats?' his narrator asks, concluding that 'there must have been something radically wrong in the government of the nation to make the establishment of a Commune possible' (p. 42). This fantastical rhetoric is instrumental to the propagandist function of the narrative. 'It seemed as if the end of the world was come, and the whole of London toppling down in one common ruin', he intones with vengeful satisfaction (p. 40).

III. The impact of the Paris Commune

At the time of the Commune, Prime Minister Gladstone, keen not to involve the British in French affairs, had refused to accept the possibility that the

---

[32] Hemyng 1871, p. 4. Subsequent references are given after quotations in the text.
[33] Suvin 1983, p. 328.

germs of socialism might spread. Reluctantly responding to Robert Peel's petition for support of the Versailles government, he referred evasively to 'events so entirely, I think, without precedent in history'.[34] More energetic ideologues suspected that the spectre of communism could not simply be wished away, and that at the very least a propaganda effort was required to rebuild Britain's internal class defences. Just as both the Left and the Right conducted a 'graphic warfare' through cartoons and caricatures in the Parisian daily press in 1871, so the Right led a literary offensive by fashioning a tropology of anti-communism.[35] The French bourgeoisie 'built images and representations to justify launching its own pre-emptive terror'; the British bourgeoisie, glancing askance at the Commune, might be said to have developed an equivalent tactic.[36] This was intended to prevent the Paris insurrection from radicalising the British working class, and, additionally, to deter dissenting members of the middle class from leading the urban poor astray. In general terms, it was a strategy motivated by the need to cement bourgeois ideological hegemony, to ensure that the ideas of the ruling class remained the ruling ideas in society.

A transparent example of this propaganda effort is *The Communists in Paris* (1871), a litany of 'Types, Physiognomies, Characters' of the Commune, published in Paris as a series of forty caricatures in the summer of 1871 and reprinted with an extensive English commentary in London in the autumn of 1873. Its creator and cartoonist, Charles d'Arnoux, who had edited the Paris edition of *Soir* (suppressed under the Commune), pretended impartiality in the first edition, which claimed to be no more than a 'just and truthful' visual account of the 'little Episodes of the History of the Days we live in'. Two years later, in a second preface, the pretence slips: acknowledging that the 'strange and disastrous Masquerade' of the Commune has started to recede into the past, he insists nonetheless that 'there is reason to believe, that the Actors have but retired behind the Scenes, demanding to reappear on the Stage hereafter'.[37] The book is reissued on the conspiratorial assumption that it is of persistent political relevance. Of course, its republication is also a commercial manoeuvre; but it is one that would scarcely have proved viable

---

[34] *Hansard* 25 May 1871, p. 1265.
[35] See Leith 1978, p. 101.
[36] Harvey 1985, p. 185.
[37] Bertall 1874, Prefaces of 1871 and 1873 [no page numbers].

had there not been pervasive and palpable fears of another uprising on which to play.

In England, these fears may have been more prevalent in the years after the Commune than in France: in the latter, as Edmond de Goncourt recorded with relief, the blood-letting of late May had 'defer[red] the next revolution by a whole generation'; whereas in the former, the working class was to an increasing extent disquieting bourgeois consciousness.[38] The introduction to the English edition of Bertall's caricatures, signed simply 'J.E.', is cleverly conscious of the need to wed the commercial venture to the ideological one. It starts out by anticipating criticism of this republication – accepting first that, even after a lapse of only two years, the work and its subject may seem out of date and of little interest to the general public; and second that, 'from a mercantile point [of view], the Title may prove its own worst Enemy', since 'the word COMMUNE is now only known with reprobation, and execration for the special doctrines and actions the Name revives'. It ends up by directly addressing 'those who are of opinion that this Reproduction is late in the day', and urging that 'since Oblivion will not wipe away the Communist Stains from our modern Civilisation, nor prevent their reappearance or imitation, it were yet better and wiser to paint them as they have been, before a renewal or resuscitation is attempted'. 'Signs are not wanting indeed', it concludes, 'of the gathering of Clouds in the far distance' (see the 'Introduction').

Implicitly, the purpose of J.E.'s detailed comments on each of the forty illustrations in this 'visual Text-book' of the Commune is to anchor the ideological cargo of these figures in an analogy with the social situation in England. By explaining all the 'peculiar, uncouth, and even improbable' characteristics of the Communard 'types', every 'descriptive Notice' ensures that their moral meaning is wholly unambiguous to the English reader. Indeed, the reader is subliminally persuaded to superimpose Bertall's physiognomic taxonomy on the population of the poor creeping about in England's metropolitan cities – a mass that seemed at the same time too homogenous and too diverse to comprehend. It thus serves, in a secondary sense, as a guidebook not only to the exiled Communards now supposed to be 'safely housed in London – *or elsewhere*' (see the 'Introduction'), but to the domestic working class itself. Just as a tourist manual simultaneously exoticises and

---

[38] Goncourt 1969, p. 312.

domesticates the features of a foreign country, so this book estranges and familiarises the middle class's social other, making the second of Disraeli's legendary 'two nations' seem both utterly alien and uncomfortably close to home.

A similar, if less systematic, classificatory system is at work in a vitriolic article on 'The Moral of the Paris Catastrophe' published in *Fraser's Magazine* soon after the Commune. Its anatomy of 'the France of to-day' deliberately sets up echoes across contemporary Britain, as is especially clear in one composite description of 'the vast urban population which forms the substratum of society, where life is congregated into masses':

> [It is] where honest artisans in toilsome yet noble poverty; ignorant idealists, maddened by wild dreams of which they feel the fascination but are unable to detect the falsity; men furious with privation, men demoralised by idleness, men steeped in crime; socialist aspirers after a model government and an ideal community; desperadoes, the irreconcilable foes of every government and of any social system; fools who would live on visions, wretches who would live by pillage – lie seething together in one heterogeneous, perilous, and fermenting mass.[39]

The author of this frenzied piece has stared into the social abyss, and, to his horror – like the contemporaneous hero of *The Coming Race*, as he penetrates the subterranean world and encounters, 'emerging from a dark fissure in the rock[,] a vast and terrible head, with open jaws and dull, ghastly, hungry eyes'[40] – the abyss stares back.

An essay on 'The English Working Classes and the Paris Commune', by a 'Journeyman Engineer', voiced this anxiety on behalf of the bourgeoisie when it argued, in the same issue of *Fraser's*, that 'the Commune has only been scotched, not killed', and furthermore that 'its essential elements are left alive, and they will breed and brood, and under that name, or some other, break forth again'. Written by the Liverpool blacksmith Thomas Wright, who effectively acts as the bourgeoisie's friendly go-between in the abyss, it tries to defuse the middle-class fear that the Channel is no inoculation against contamination of the native working class by revolutionary insurrectionism. As a labour aristocrat, Wright describes a classic contradiction in this article

[39] W.R.G. 1871, p. 116.
[40] Bulwer-Lytton 1871, p. 10.

(the product of his own sense of class dislocation): on the one hand, he appeals to his readers' fear of revolution and announces, apparently from the position of an insider, that 'the Communist war [is] staring the world in the face'; and on the other, he gratifies their desire for reassurance, by revising an essentialist argument about national difference and pointing out that English workmen are less political than their French counterparts. His conclusion is confused. The working class that he purports to represent is not 'en rapport with the Paris Communists as Communists', he says. Yet 'the spirit that in France took the name of Communism' is 'stalking abroad', and 'if not exorcised, will mean social disturbance, and may come to mean social destruction', since 'it has entered into the minds of the English working classes, and is sinking deeper, and becoming more dangerous as it sinks'. His advice to 'those in power' is not to ignore the opinion of the poor, and not to neglect the need for exorcism – a plea both for reform and for a pedagogic propaganda effort against those ideas 'still spreading among the working classes'.[41]

By the mid-1880s, these recommendations, scarcely new to the ruling class, had been partially implemented. The Reform Act of 1884 extended the male vote from the boroughs to the counties and increased the electorate by 76 percent; and primary education increased throughout the last three decades of the century, introducing the values as well as the privileges of the middle class into the working class. But the Reform Act merely placed a formal barrier between the propertied and the threat of revolution; and the expansion of primary education facilitated the spread of socialist ideas at a time of trade-union growth and escalating class struggle, culminating in the Dock Strike of 1889. The years after the third Reform Act were dominated by the Conservative government of Lord Salisbury, who was notoriously suspicious of populist politics and especially antipathetic to socialism. At the time of the Commune itself, he had emphasised the susceptibility of the British proletariat to radical influence – especially the 'great moral power' of the International Working Men's Association, which, despite its doubtful political potential, has already proved 'able to efface the natural instincts of Englishmen on the subject of assassination'.[42] It is during his subsequent terms of office (1885–6, 1886–92 and 1895–1902) that the anti-communist imagination, creating the

---

[41] 'The Journeyman Engineer' 1871, pp. 62, 66–8.
[42] Salisbury 1871, p. 554.

climate in which the cacotopia flourished, is consolidated in its central defensive role in the ideological armoury of the ruling class.

If, in 1871, there was 'no matter of more vital moment to England at the present time than the right understanding of the Communal insurrection in Paris', as the editor of *Fraser's* put it, then this remained the case in the following decades, as economic crisis deepened and the labour movement grew.[43] In 1884, one reviewer of Lissagaray's *L'Histoire de la Commune de 1871* (1876) demonstrated that he had understood the implications of the Paris uprising: 'The war of the Commune was the war of elements that are not extinct, that are present to-day as really as they were present in 1871; they exist in every country, they are not to be localized on the banks of the Seine'.[44] This threatening claim is effective as propaganda to the extent that it inscribes a prophetic warning into its analogy between revolutionary France and non-revolutionary, or perhaps pre-revolutionary Britain. Like Lytton's narrator, it enacts an assumed duty to its fellow-men 'to place on record these forewarnings of The Coming Race'.[45]

The cacotopian form, nascent in the climate of the Commune's reception, and of the publication of *The Coming Race*, takes up an equivalent vatic duty, and discharges it within the context of contemporary social developments. It tries to historicise the social turmoil that lies dormant in the present – partly awakened by the riots in central London of 1885–87, and by the militant industrial activity associated with the ascendancy of the New Unionism. The crises that it imagines are recognisably the outcome of hitherto unstable elements in society. Its time-scale is commonly the next five, ten or twenty years, as a glance at some of their titles reveals, and this sense of immediacy, of imminence, is intended to maximise the audience's incentive to contribute actively to the conservation of the status quo. *A Radical Nightmare* (1885), for example, envisages a bloody civil war that is the consequence of the rise of a Radical government. On its final page, it warns the reader that this 'nightmare will come true' – unless you 'take care for whom you vote in the coming Election'.[46]

---

[43] Editorial comment at the head of an article by 'A Vicar of the Church of England' 1871, p. 230.
[44] Anonymous 1884, p. 83.
[45] Bulwer-Lytton 1871, p. 292.
[46] 'An Ex-M.P.' 1885, p. 62.

The first formulation of the propagandist function of this 'historico-prophetic' technique is the *Imaginary History of the Next Thirty Years*, which, in 1857, had recommended 'writing history before [rather] than after the facts' in order to 'throw a light forward into the darkness and *prevent danger*'.[47] This narrative's appeal to preventative action was diligently obeyed by the anti-radicals of the late-Victorian period. Typically, a later cacotopia, *'England's Downfall': or, the Last Great Revolution* (1893), addresses itself to 'the rising generation', upon which 'everything depends'. Its message is a predictably conservative and paternalistic one: 'The destinies of England are in your hands. Show the world what you can do. Think of what England was once and what it is now, and remember that it is never too late to mend'.[48] Paradoxically, cacotopias construct themselves as false prophecies. Their status as false prophecies depends on the hopeful assumption that their readers have the power and the will to execute the political responsibility ascribed to them.

This cannot, of course, be guaranteed. So the anti-socialist prophecies of the late nineteenth-century are scored with insecurity about their own efficacy. The naïve optimism of the *Imaginary History* – which announces that 'Histories of the Future could hardly fail to influence the future, for the mere proclamation of oracles often ensures their fulfilment' – is qualified as the narrative form matures under altered domestic circumstances in the later cacotopias.[49] The final polemical appeal of Edgar Welch's *Monster Municipality* (1882) – 'May the recital of the horrors I suffered prove sufficiently deterrent to prevent their ultimate realization!' – is plaintive by comparison.[50] Writing a book is a gesture uncomfortably similar to sending a message in a bottle: it is not always possible to predict who will read it and how it will be interpreted. E.H. Berens and I. Singer, joint authors of *The Story of My Dictatorship* (1894), seem to be aware of the difficulty that they face when, in a contradictory conclusion to their vision of a political future ruined by populism and pluralism, they invite each reader to 'put on it his own interpretation', and then insist that, in fact, it 'has but one meaning and one moral'.[51]

---

[47] Anonymous 1857, p. 5.
[48] 'An Ex-Revolutionist' 1893, pp. 174–75.
[49] Anonymous 1857, p. 6.
[50] Welch 1882, p. 128.
[51] Berens and Singer 1894, pp. 220–21.

These cacotopian writers tend to displace their own sense of political helplessness onto their readers. The narrator of *The Commune in London*, after describing the insurrection, exclaims: 'Would to heaven it could be torn out of the book, but there it stands, red and forbidding, a warning for all time to come' (p. 42). He betrays Hemnyng's sense of isolation as a writer. Only the text's readership, he implies, is in a position to tear the leaf from the book, to efface the traumatic image of a future revolution, by taking political action in the present. But it is just this implicit notion of a readership that compounds the problem, for it is based on a false, wish-fulfilment identification of the fiction's audience as a politically effective collectivity. Hemyng's book dreams of a kind of Primrose League of utopian readers. Symptomatic of all cacotopias, this is an embattled response to the advance of a mass politics in Britain, to a nightmare peopled with ignorant voters at the ballot box and insurgent workers taking concerted action in the streets, the world of the second and third Reform Acts and of the Paris Commune. The authors of these novels and pamphlets waged a fictional offensive by forging the rhetorical tools of an anti-revolutionism that, by filling their readers' imaginations with the spectral symbols of a fictional socialist menace, sought expressly to influence bourgeois class consciousness.

IV. The anti-communist imaginary

As far as the Right was concerned, communism and socialism, if they were separable at all, formed part of the same conspiracy of the 'masses' against the 'classes'. Analysing the 'multitude of projects . . . threatening society with convulsions' in the 1880s, Goldwin Smith was less interested in distinguishing between 'Communists or Socialists' than in identifying their most sensational manifestation, 'political Satanism', which 'seeks, not to reconstruct, but to destroy, and to destroy not only existing institutions, but established morality – social, domestic, and personal – putting evil in place of good'. Political Satanism included 'Nihilism, Intransigentism, Petrolean Communism, [and] the Dynamite wing of Fenianism', and so conveniently elided all revolutionary tendencies, real or imagined, under a single demonological sign.[52] Less obscurely, and more typically, Henry James – whose

[52] Smith 1886, pp. 7, 9.

allusions to anarchism and socialism in *The Princess Casamassima* (1886) 'are positively Gothic in their elusive and spectral mysteriousness' – 'was as little concerned as *The Times* to make any serious political distinction between socialism, communism, anarchism and terrorist violence'. Instead, as Graham Holderness indicates, the militant socialism figured in James's novel assumes 'the curiously unrecognizable form of a vast international underground conspiracy dedicated in some unspecified way to the destruction of civilisation as Henry James knew it'.[53]

This conspiracy was not entirely unrecognisable, however. The International Working Men's Association, dominated by Marx and Engels from its inception in 1864 to its crisis in 1872, had already become the fantastic repository of the bourgeoisie's fears of revolution. Founded through the spontaneous efforts of London and Paris workers expressing solidarity with the 1863 Polish national uprising, this pan-European labour organisation, consisting of substantial Proudhonist and Bakuninist sections as well as a Marxist one, developed an increasingly communistic character in the late 1860s. After the Commune, which it indirectly helped to produce, and with which it was widely identified, it came to represent the ultimate embodiment of the spectre of communism. Thus anathematised, it occupied a key position in the cluster of symptoms that characterised late-Victorian anti-socialism. The International 'was in reality immeasurably weaker than most governments and industrialists realized'.[54] But it was widely believed to be responsible for a 'Great Plot', first perceived during the trial of its members in June 1870, and subsequently scrutinised by the French parliamentary enquiry into the origins of the Paris insurrection. Little proof of the International's involvement in the Commune was found. This was virtually irrelevant, however, since its shadowy presence furnished the bourgeois press throughout Europe with a scapegoat that it ritualistically sacrificed in its coverage of every social upheaval. Furthermore, the press became accustomed to identifying the International as the sinister underbelly of its own working class: it was seen as 'a sort of Janus figure with a fair, honest workman's smile on one of its faces, and on the other a murderous conspirator's scowl', as one journalist described it in an interview with Marx.[55]

---

[53] Holderness 1987, p. 134.
[54] Schulkind 1972, p. 33.
[55] Marx and Engels 1971, p. 254.

Predictably, Hemyng's *The Commune in London* of 1871 subscribes to this conspiracy theory. There, the organ of 'the International', known as the *Age*, plays an important part in persuading the mass of people, including those 'tolerably well-governed and pretty well-off', to join an explosive battle in Hyde Park. 'Spoil, burn, slay', it enjoins in a religious ecstasy: 'in the Commune and the practice of its doctrines we shall find our salvation. Amen' (p. 35). Later anti-communist tracts also conjure up the spectre of a trans-continental conspiracy. *The Universal Strike of 1899* (1891), a Christian-Socialist fiction that mobilises cacotopian imagery in order to press its moderate proposals for reform, presents the strike referred to in its title as a drunken riot conducted through an 'international amalgam of labour' which has been conceived in Paris by the 'International Working Men's Society'.[56]

The Angel of the Revolution (1893), George Griffith's highly popular socialist scientific romance, in which a group of anarchists acquire the power of flight, may represent a parodic reappropriation of this trope. In this novel, a shadowy 'Inner Circle' of the 'Brotherhood of Freedom', which ultimately secures an international *pax aeronautica*, eradicating social conflict, dons shrouds in order to convene. 'Known to the outside world as the Terror', this fraternity 'is an international secret society underlying and directing the operations of the various bodies known as Nihilists, Anarchists, Socialists – in fact, all those organisations which have for their object the reform or destruction, by peaceful or violent means, of Society as it is presently constituted'.[57] Its leader, 'Natas the Jew', is a red Fagin, the ultimate, satanic incarnation of anti-socialist fears ored out of the creeping consciousness of an underclass that, swelled by the large-scale immigration of the mid 1880s, was thought to be swarming in the East End of London and the poor districts of other metropolitan cities.

'The police-tinged bourgeois mind', Marx wrote in *The Civil War in France* in 1871, 'naturally figures to itself the International Working Men's Association as acting in the manner of a secret conspiracy, its central body ordering, from time to time, explosions in different countries'.[58] Naturally, that is, because the bourgeoisie, well-nigh structurally resistant to the notion that the proletariat might emancipate itself, sought a pseudo-rational explanation for the revolutionary uprising of that year, in order to avoid having to inspect the

---

[56] Oakehurst 1891, p. 10.
[57] Griffith 1893, p. 32.
[58] Marx 1986, p. 354.

social conditions that had inspired it. In *'England's Downfall'*, a 'Revolutionary League' furnishes proof that 'labour was controlled by a few men who cared nothing really for the operatives, but used the power with which they had been entrusted to advance their own individual aims'.[59] In this sense, the demonisation of the International was, in part, the expression of straightforward xenophobia, that perennial reflex of a ruling class desperate to secure the support of an unsettled working class on the basis of a false rationale, through the identification of a fictitious common enemy to the nation. But this strategy actually only ever reveals the extent to which the domestic working class has itself become alien to its rulers. Hippolyte Taine's preposterous estimate that, in late May 1871, Paris contained 'about one hundred thousand insurgents, fifty thousand of whom are foreigners', is merely an admission of class isolation.[60]

The British bourgeoisie betrayed the same insecurity about its own working class, on two inter-linked fronts. First, on the foreign front, there were fears that English workers had been involved in the Paris uprising, and that they would import socialist ideas, as well as experiences, on returning home. The government was incensed by 'reports in Clubland that thousands, hundreds, scores of Englishmen had fought on the side of the Commune and had been captured by the Versaillais' – though, in reality, only about twenty Englishmen were imprisoned during and after the Commune.[61] Second, on the domestic front, there were even more acute worries that the Communard refugees fleeing Thiers's army for England – none of whom needed passports as a result of the Anglo-French rapprochement of the 1860s – would stir up insurrection in London. One commentator wrote: 'We do not wish England to be a *rendezvous* for the desperadoes of Europe, for the cosmopolitan professors of revolution, who, without any special or personal interest in the conflict, or right to intervene, rush, like the vulture to the carcass, wherever there is an incipient disturbance, to fan insurrection into rebellion and civil war, and who offer their swords to all insurgents, provided only that an established Government is the object of their animosity'.[62] The cryptic, perhaps accidental

---

[59] 'An Ex-Revolutionist' 1893, p. 9.
[60] Quoted in Lidsky 1970, p. 66: 'Environ cent mille insurgés, dont cinquante mille étrangers' (my translation).
[61] Smith 1972, p. 67.
[62] W.R.G. 1871, p. 132.

reference to 'the conflict' here is a telling indication of the middle class's sense of social volatility, for it reveals just how easily open class war could be envisaged in Britain even in the early 1870s.

It is scarcely surprising then that, by the mid-1880s, this precise scenario was being dramatised in cacotopian narratives. Of these, despite its uncharacteristic satirical flourish, *The Socialist Revolution of 1888* (1884) can stand as representative. Narrating scenes of insurgency in London, it refers to a report that 'many desperate characters, including thousands of foreign anarchists, were abroad, and that the latter were preaching the duty of personal vengeance upon the middle and upper classes, and the nationalisation of woman as well as of land'. The allusion here to the anarchists' vision of women as communal property deliberately hints at the underlying primitivism of communism. The narrator confirms his implicit claim that tribal barbarism is the obverse of internationalism when he later suggests that, if the aspiring socialist government had ultimately had its way, the population 'should have been reduced to the condition of the Bushmen of the Drakensberg'.[63] Anti-communism's xenophobic rhetoric is thus linked to a racist discourse that, at its most explicit, identifies the working class as latent savages, and so serves to underscore its radical dislocation from the middle classes. In the late-nineteenth-century cacotopias, as in the contemporary commentaries on the Commune, there is a systematic attempt to excommunicate workers as animals, savages and criminals. One anonymous writer called the Commune that 'yell from the lower man'.[64] The rhetorics of class and race are indissociably cemented into the discourse of social Darwinism.

The positivist Frederic Harrison diagnosed this tendency when he noted that, in the early 1870s, the cultured and wealthy class 'developed a hatred as horrible and as blind as the hatred of race – the hatred of a dominant race in a panic'.[65] He only failed to point out that the political vocabulary of the period after the Commune – a veritable dustbin of late-Victorian bigotry – was compounded by virulent anti-feminism. Marianne, the familiar Republican symbol of a red-capped and partially naked woman fighting for freedom, was violently troped by the Right, who invented the *petroleuse*, the female

[63] Fairfield 1884, pp. 8, 32.
[64] Anonymous 1894a, p. 14.
[65] Harrison 1871, p. 576.

incendiary. Although there was no empirical proof that *petroleuses* existed during the Commune, thousands of women were blamed for the destruction of Paris at the end of the 'second siege', and consequently lost their lives in the trials that followed Thiers's victory. The myth of the aggressive female Communard acting as the secret weapon of the working class – which grew out of an awareness of the important role that women played at the barricades – influenced almost every bourgeois account of the May fighting. Patriarchal anxieties about women's political mobilisation are invariably displaced onto sexual anxieties in these documents of class neurosis. Bertall's English collaborator provides a classic instance: blandly complaining that 'feminine liberty and activity, so useful at ordinary times, becomes troublesome when diverted from more private Concerns', he goes on to describe the type of the female military leader as 'completely unsexed . . . in her assumption of Manhood' (see 'Type 19').

In other historical accounts and journalistic sketches, and in later cacotopias, such as *Woman Unsexed* (1892), by the Staffordshire lock manufacturer H. Herman Chilton, this stress on the unsettling masculinity of militant working-class women is elaborated in images of rapacious female beasts with an orgiastic appetite for blood. As these gothic overtones suggest, however, peculiarly sexual insinuations end up undermining the construction of women as sexless masculine pretenders to traditionally male political and economic roles. A split attitude is displayed to women: like the working class, which is at once a degenerate race and a sort of superpower *in potentia*, they are, at the same time, vulgar and excessively attractive, subhuman and sexually seductive. This is especially apparent in the anti-communist novels of the 1890s, the decade in which the New Woman became an object of unsettling erotic fascination in male discourse.

A stark example of this dual sexual and social anxiety is G.A. Henty's *A Woman of the Commune* (1895), an upper-class adventure novel that, in one cacotopian *mise en scène*, mounts a sustained attack on 'the orgie of the Commune', particularly women's part in it. The woman referred to in the title of the first edition is not in fact the heroine, Mary, a wealthy English girl with 'all sorts of Utopian notions about women's rights', but the villain, Minette, a poor Parisian who acts as an artist's model for the narrator-hero, an aspiring painter as well as an accomplished military officer. Mary's feminism is rapidly undermined by her traumatic encounters with partially emancipated women during the Commune, and she is, in consequence, easily domesticated (the description of her marriage in the book's final pages celebrates her social subordination). Minette's politics, on the contrary, are activated by the events of the siege. So is her sexuality, which, initially restrained, now finds its full animal expression. 'She is like a panther', one male character says, 'as graceful and as supple, a charming beast when it purrs and rubs itself against the legs of its keeper, terrible when in passion it hurls itself upon him'. At the climax of the Commune, Minette joins with the other vampiric 'female fiends' in plundering Paris, a spectacle witnessed by the hero, who finds it 'too fascinating and terrible to be abandoned'. Her death, which follows with predictable swiftness, is a punishment for her political and sexual independence; but it is also, at the level of the text's unconscious, a revenge for her hidden role as Mary's dark other, for her status as the novel's sexual secret. The object of the narrator's reactionary political invective, Minette is also, as a working-class character, the object of his repressed fantasies of a woman who is simultaneously domineering and dispensable, sexual and unsexed.[66]

'Strange Emblem of Civilisation!' is the legend beneath Bertall's physiognomy of the woman at the barricade ('Type 36'). In the hand of the female insurgent during the Commune, 'the torch of Enlightenment ha[d] become the brand that set Paris alight'.[67] The bourgeoisie was certainly shocked by the Commune's assault on the advanced culture of Western Europe, as it perceived it. For Marx, the social crisis of 1871 laid bare the 'undisguised savagery' of the civilisation and justice of bourgeois order, but for the ideologues of this order it confirmed the bestial nature of those whom this culture was intended to curb.[68] Far from 'consecrating their lives to the cause of truth, of justice, of civilisation, of humanity, as against the cause of ignorance, of retrogression, of barbarism, and inhumanity', as the Radical *Reynolds's Newspaper* claimed of the Communards, they were seen as the very embodiment of savage barbarity.[69]

[66] Henty 1895, pp. 19, 275, 282, 285, 290.
[67] Agulhon 1981, p. 159.
[68] Marx 1986, p. 348.
[69] See Harrison 1971, p. 154.

The culture of the Commune – a kind of anti-culture – consequently posed a danger to other 'civilised' countries. British readers of *The Place Vendôme and La Roquette: The First and Last Acts of the Commune* (1871), by L'Abbé Lamazou, which was translated into English in 1872, would have had little trouble appreciating the contrast he makes between the 'imposing architecture' of Paris and the 'hideous groups' of 'dark and sallow' insurrectionaries that swarmed before them.[70] William Gibson, a Methodist minister living in Paris in the early 1870s, rendered the analogy quite unambiguous in his letters to his English congregation about the humiliation of 'the centre of civilization': applying the apocalyptic images of 'Revelations' to images of the French capital, he inferred that they alluded 'with far greater probability to a city such as London!'.[71]

V. The crisis of metropolitan experience

The irruption of the Paris insurrection into middle-class consciousness at the end of the century, and its indelible impact on the incipient anti-communist imaginary, was to a critical degree conditioned by what Raymond Williams called the 'crisis of metropolitan experience' at the end of the nineteenth-century.[72] Salisbury diagnosed something like this when he made this statement in his article on the Commune: 'It is the destiny of France to exhibit, for the benefit of others, the special dangers of modern civilisation in their most aggravated form. Among these, not the least serious is the obstacle to peaceable government which the growth of large cities has created'.[73] The population of London increased from 2.5 to 3.9 million between 1851 and 1881, leading directly to chronic overcrowding and slum conditions, but the social effects of this urban concentration were exacerbated by the displacement of the metropolitan population as a result of the commercial expansion and demolition of the city. In the second half of the century, the labour force was brutally evicted from the central districts, still the source of work, in a reorganisation of urban space which, as the arbitrary consequence of railway and dock development, warehouse-building and street clearance, led to dishousing

---

[70] Lamazou 1872, p. 27.
[71] Gibson 1872, pp. 44, 170.
[72] Williams 1973, p. 272.
[73] Salisbury 1871, p. 566.

comparable to the more systematic Haussmannisation of mid-century Paris. According to Stedman Jones, by the early 1870s the English capital 'was haunted by the spectre of Parisian barricades', conjured up by a housing problem that 'comprised a direct threat to social stability'.[74] The realisation of urban space as the space of revolution in Paris placed the city at the centre of the cacotopian project.

An open letter printed in *The Republican* of 1 May 1871, entitled 'Paris Today – London Tomorrow', underlined the point. 'Is not London seething with the same spirit of discontent?', it demanded, insisting that 'it only wants a combination of circumstances – say a bad harvest, and a run for gold to bring the battle between property and labour to the same issue in this country'.[75] Little more than a decade later, this collision of circumstances occurred. The severe economic depression of the mid-1880s, compounded by industrial decline and acute housing shortages, led, on the one hand, to the demoralisation and impoverishment of the artisans at the respectable end of the working class, and, more dramatically, on the other, to the expansion of the so-called 'residuum', the mass of desperately poor unemployed or sporadically employed people. The latter stratum, closely associated with criminal corruption and socialist agitation in the imagination of the middle classes, found its most famous literary expression in the *lumpen*, animalised Morlocks of Wells's dystopia, *The Time Machine*. By the mid-1890s, it was already established as the collective villain of cacotopian fiction, especially after the unemployed riots in central London of 1886 and 1887. Like the Paris Commune, imported memories of which were now pressed into service again, this rioting was significant for the British bourgeoisie less because of what happened than because of 'the strength of middle-class reaction to it and the extent of the fear of the casual residuum that it revealed'.[76]

The cacotopian texts of this time form a part of this defensive response in the face of the revelation of a potentially imminent social crisis. Their capacity to propagandise in this way was primarily dependent on the skill with which, conjoining realist and anti-realist literary devices, they gothicised the socio-politically charged topography of the capital, in order to impart a ghoulish immediacy to the prospect of revolution. *The Times* pioneered a fantastical

---

[74] Stedman Jones 1971, p. 178.
[75] Reprinted in Harrison 1971, p. 160.
[76] Stedman Jones 1971, p. 292.

naturalism in 1871, when, in a passage reminiscent of *Barnaby Rudge* (1841), it mapped 'the political geography of the Revolution' directly onto London: 'The Reds are at the Mansion-house; their army is in ruined forts about Clapham; the other army is about Sydenham and Wimbledon; the other Government is at Richmond; and the invaders are at Highgate and Harrow, and all over the north'.[77] Cacotopian fiction sophisticated this technique, depicting a faceless urban mass flattening central London in an offensive against imperial and ruling-class culture. In *The Commune in London*, the unruly mob mimics the destruction of the Vendôme Column during the Commune in Paris when it demolishes the Albert Memorial (p. 27). In *The Decline and Fall of the British Empire* (1890), to take a typical later cacotopia, 'a dirty unwashed crowd', demonstrating in Trafalgar Square, proceeds to burn down Buckingham Palace, Kensington Palace and all the gentlemen's clubs, ultimately reducing London to a post-revolutionary wasteland of poverty, incomparably worse than that of the nineteenth-century.[78]

Two cacotopian novels that allegorise the impact of an English revolution, although they are not overtly concerned with an insurrectionary urban working class, portray the capital in a state of particularly eerie gothic devastation. *The Last Man in London* (1887) tells the story of a man who, for one feverish week, experiences London as 'a City of the Dead'. In a revealing passage at the centre of the narrative, he runs amok in the empty streets, smashing the symbols of capitalist civilisation – windows of shops like Liberty's, busts of the great poets – and proclaiming himself monarch. He has been infected with a virulent strain of revolutionism.[79] *The Year of Miracle* (1891) sensationally relates the impact of a plague that, germinated in the squalid recesses of Whitechapel, wreaks havoc among the population, until Trafalgar Square, the scene of a later riot, looks 'like one vast charnel house'.[80] Such imagery served to convince its middle-class readers that the social chaos of the city was the creation of the urban poor, and that this degenerate class stratum was alone responsible for the barbaric prospect of revolution. Catastrophic images conduct the cacotopia's polemical charge.

---

[77] *The Times* 10 April 1871, p. 8.
[78] Watson 1890, pp. 220, 270.
[79] North 1887, p. 63.
[80] Hume 1891, p. 79.

If the physical business of building barricades, as Kristin Ross suggests, is a species of *bricolage*, since it entails wrenching everyday objects from their habitual context in order to use them for radically different ends, then something analogous to this process is at work in the late-Victorian cacotopias, which re-deploy familiar literary tropes, like natural and biblical metaphors, and use them as blocks to build the anti-socialist imagination and so shore up bourgeois ideology.[81] They help to construct the political myth that working-class action is inherently destructive, to the point of being apocalyptic. And as with the political myths that proliferated on the Right at the time of the Commune, they are composed not so much of theories and doctrines as of 'bundles of images and evocations', which exercise 'a cumulative and collective power to sway emotions'.[82]

The middle class' incomprehension of the amoebic 'Populace' is typically imaged in terms of a dangerous natural or infernal force over which supposedly rational human agents, like the state, have no control. This metaphoric strategy is indebted to the rhetoric of fictional and non-fictional accounts of the French Revolution, like Carlyle's *French Revolution* (1837) and Dickens's *A Tale of Two Cities* (1859). It is also mediated through the experiences of the last uprising of the masses in living memory, the Commune. Volcanic imagery, to take one example, is particularly popular. A distempered Francis Kilvert wrote in March 1871 that 'those Parisians are the scum of the earth, and Paris is the crater of the volcano, France, and a bottomless pit of revolution and anarchy'.[83] One author of a 'Journey through France and Spain in 1871' entitled it *Over Volcanoes*.[84] But if English residents of Paris felt themselves 'to be living on the side of a volcano' in the days leading up to the insurrection at Montmartre, as the Methodist Gibson put it, then the experience of respectable Londoners during and after the extreme social tension of the mid 1880s was a comparable one.[85] Chilton dramatises this comparison in *Woman Unsexed*, mocking British complacency. The narrator's premature declaration that 'here in England, eruptions of the substratum have been few and short, owing chiefly to the triumphant commonsense of the middle classes' is later ironically overturned

[81] Ross 1988, p. 36.
[82] Roberts 1973, p. 5.
[83] Kilvert 1944, p. 113.
[84] Kingsman 1872.
[85] Gibson 1872, p. 25.

by the spectacle of revolution in Central London: 'That mass of seething humanity surged away towards the West-End as lava, after labouring in the bowels of the earth, boils over its crater'.[86]

These images are freighted with infernal associations. And revolution itself, specifically the actual moment of insurrection, is frequently figured as a vision of hell in the cacotopias. The Commune once more provides the most recent and compelling precedent. Pope Pius IX's description of the Communards as 'devils risen up from hell bringing the inferno to the streets of Paris' was echoed by historians and journalists fascinated by the dramatic incendiary destruction of the city.[87] These impressions of 'a hell, with death for a girdle', as John Leighton put it, were still being invoked two decades later in Britain.[88] In an article on 'Recollections of the Commune in Paris', published in *Blackwood's* in 1894, the anonymous author, a friend of Laurence Oliphant, remembered the French capital as 'the universal furnace', and recalled that the 'lurid, lowering, looming awfulness' of the burning buildings created an effect 'that could only be called hellish'.[89]

The dominant experience of anarchy in the last days of May 1871, in fact, comes to substitute for the events of two months earlier, when the Parisian working class took power in a spirit of comparative calm. In the subsequent fictional representations of revolutionary uprisings in England, it is the working class who, in a cruelly ironic reversal, are blamed for the bloody saturnalia that should have been associated with the Versailles army. Condensing and displacing the history of the Commune, the author of *The Doom of the County Council of London* (1892), for example, describes the regimented ranks of ten thousand constables defending the nation's honour in Trafalgar Square, which is peopled by 'a shrieking, plundering mob of demons incarnate, rushing frantically hither and thither, as though the very gates of Hell had been broken down and its occupants let loose'.[90] These bloody scenes of plunder and destruction, most of them set in the West End, restage the middle-class melodrama of the Commune, even as they play out and repress the chthonic forces of contemporary London.

---

[86] Chilton 1892, pp. 99, 279.
[87] Quoted in Harvey 1985, p. 237.
[88] Leighton 1871, p. 331.
[89] Anonymous 1894a, p. 9.
[90] Anonymous 1892, p. 10.

Miasmic imagery, dense with moral meaning, links these two *topoi*. If, during the May fighting, 'Paris scarcely knew day from night', and a 'thick, black cloud of smoke . . . obscured and intensified the horrors of an awful drama', then this revolutionary cityscape was to resonate with the 'pre-revolutionary' experience of middle-class Londoners, for whom the infamous industrial smog concealed and revealed the lurking presence of the residuum.[91] William Delisle Hay, author of the social-Darwinist utopia *Three Hundred Years Hence* (1881), explored the allegorical potential of pollution a year earlier in a short cacotopian fiction expressing bourgeois fear of the urban masses. *The Doom of the Great City* (1880) is ostensibly about the destruction of London's entire population by fog, a natural phenomenon (though, as the opening passage of *Bleak House* (1853) reminds us, urban fog tended to obscure the difference between the natural and the social). In fact, it is about the poisonous influence of 'the black enormity of London sin', the crucible of which, of course, is the impoverished classes.[92] The real subject of this grimly gothic tale is glimpsed in a number of narrative and descriptive devices. Its very format is telling, for the narrative is presented as a letter from a survivor of this holocaust to his grandchildren, which immediately positions it within the formal tradition of *The Battle of Dorking* and *The Commune in London*. Also, it is set at a time of bad harvests, economic depression and 'continual strife between capital and labour' (p. 15).

It is an important aside on class, however, that makes the polemical purpose of the piece quite clear. Hay's narrator hymns the middle class as the 'real life' of the city, but warns that this life is threatened, because, on the one hand, degenerate aristocratic habits have filtered down to it, and, on the other, 'up from the lowest depths there [have] constantly ar[isen] a stream of grosser, fouler moral putrescence' (p. 15). The splenetic references to republicanism and socialism following this passage leave no doubt that it is the latter who are truly to blame for the impending cataclysm. This is further confirmed by the plot that unfolds once the initial scene-setting has ended in an analysis of the industrial causes and social effects of a fog that afflicts London in February 1882. This fog originates in the East End, where it chokes to death its first victims, before spreading to the suburbs. The first casualty encountered

---

[91] March 1896, p. 309.
[92] Hay 1880, p. 10. Subsequent references are given after quotations in the text.

by the narrator as he walks into an apparently deserted city-centre from Dulwich, where he happens to be staying, is (scarcely accidentally) a policeman. And 'the very heart and home of Horror itself' (p. 46), he finally discovers, is the West End – a scene of genocide.

The post-apocalyptic landscape of London imaged here evokes descriptions of Paris after the Commune, which *All the Year Round* likened to a desert, and which occasioned the *Fortnightly Review*'s declaration that the sheer lifelessness of the city proved 'that Paris has outlived its prime'.[93] By chance, it also anticipates the choking smog of February 1886, in which the unemployment riots took place, at the height of the depression. The 'wild phantasmagoria of frightful dreams' that afflict the narrator of *The Doom of the Great City* (p. 31) are fulfilled not only in the ensuing narrative but in the class conflict of the following years, and in the descriptions of revolution in later cacotopian fictions.

From this perspective, even *After London* (1885), Richard Jefferies's novel of ecological catastrophe, with its image of the English capital submerged under poisonous marshes, surrounded by a society that has relapsed into barbarism, could be interpreted as a covert meditation on the prospect of a fragile bourgeois order overturned by a degenerate working class: in a revealing use of language, Jefferies refers to London being 'overthrown' by natural processes.[94] After all, in Henry Watson's *The Decline and Fall of the British Empire* (1890), the narrator, who travels to England from Australia in the year 2990, finds that, after the revolution of the late nineteenth-century, London is no more than 'a small town, badly built', bordering the 'swampy land' where Whitechapel was once situated.[95] The image of the 'swift liquefaction of the social body' is central to Wells's *War of the Worlds* (1898), in which a 'red weed' spread by the Martian invaders reduces the Home Counties to a 'red swamp'.[96] It is perhaps not wholly speculative to interpret this process of decomposition as genetically related to the political epidemics imagined by contemporary writers of cacotopian fiction.

---

[93] Anonymous 1871a, p. 390; Dicey 1871, p. 494.
[94] Jefferies 1885, pp. 67–9.
[95] Watson 1890, pp. 54, 69.
[96] Wells 1898, pp. 150, 241–42.

VI. Cacotopia and the utopian impulse

Gustave Flaubert found it difficult to recover from what he called the 'Gothicity' of the Commune.[97] To the English middle classes, too, it seemed to have realised a nightmare. Its haunting power added a feverish intensity to fears of a domestic uprising throughout the remainder of the century. A contemporary article in the *Leisure Hour* identified it as 'an ugly dream of the past – a nightmare of terror as to what discontented democrats would bring about in this country if they were only given the time and opportunity to work out their crude schemes'.[98]

This trope, common in pseudo-objective accounts of the Commune, proved even more influential in fictional representations: their discursive register licensed them to subjectify the impact of the insurrection, fleshing out its proportions to the point of surreal grotesqueness. In *A Young Girl's Adventures in Paris During the Commune* (1881), Mrs John Waters's heroine sums up the months of the Commune 'as a troubled and horrible dream', the climax of which is the implausible murder of members of her family by a group of Communards.[99] And, in another adventure story on the same subject, Herbert Hayens's *Paris at Bay* (1897), the hero has a dream about the deaths of the French military officers Lecomte and Thomas, who were executed during the Commune: as their corpses stir uneasily, he ascertains with horror that their faces have his own and his fellow adventurer's features.[100] The cacotopias themselves, many of which, in addition to depicting revolution in some detail, systematically set out the terrible democratic reforms of their demonic socialist anti-heroes, are governed by the (il)logic of the nightmare at a molar as well as a molecular level of the text. Some merely characterise their image of the socialist state in terms of 'the hideous horrors of a prolonged nightmare'.[101] Others, like *The Monster Municipality* (1882), use the narrative device of a dream to imagine the 'dreadful nightmare' of 'London under the process of a certain reform'.[102] Just as utopia is the organised expression of a social dream, cacotopia has its own unconscious, the social nightmare.

[97] Quoted in Jellinek 1937, p. 417.
[98] Anonymous 1871b, p. 621.
[99] Waters 1881, p. 224.
[100] Hayens 1897, p. 232.
[101] Anonymous 1892, p. 38.
[102] Welch 1882, p. 6.

English commentators reached for something like this connection between cacotopianism and the bad dream of the Commune in 1871. A piece in the *Times* of 29 May 1871, entitled 'The Horrors of Civil War', described the atmosphere of Paris in the preceding days as a paranoid one, in which the correspondent is 'oppressed ever by the scenes of destruction and desolation' that surround him. It produces, he says, 'a sensation more nearly allied to nightmare than to any psychological experience with which I am familiar, but yet requiring some new word to define it'.[103] The new word for which he grasps, I propose hypothetically, is 'cacotopian'.

The historical precedence of the Commune was, for the bourgeoisie, who deemed it both impracticable and appalling in its implications, cacotopian *par excellence*. The philanthropist James Tuke, lecturing on the events of 18 March at the time, admitted as much. Imagining a recent riot in Hyde Park being played out to its Communal conclusion – London usurped by workers with 'little respect for anybody's life', troops fraternising with them, 'judges and all persons in authority' exiled or imprisoned – he concluded that 'that would be an analogous position to Paris on that day – a state about as dreadful as could be'.[104] It is this symptomatic response, the anxious introjection of the Commune by the English middle classes, and its fantastic projection, that explains the presence of the cacotopia as a literary form at this juncture, contemporaneous as it is with the origins of that more inclusive genre, the imaginary history.

The late-nineteenth-century cacotopia is a perverse expression of what Bloch calls the 'Novum'. This concept is used to signify a new consciousness engendered by 'the mandate of the time' – here, the ascendancy of the working class at the time of an incipient crisis of confidence in the advance of capitalism. As we have seen, anxiety and fear characterise the bourgeois response to the Novum, this collective apprehension of a new historical possibility, proletarian revolution in the metropolitan centre. And Bloch classifies these reactions as 'expectant emotions'. Like all manifestations of fear, the late-Victorian fear of revolution is an expectant emotion that 'extends beyond its "founding" idea-content; the expectant content shows a greater "depth" than the given idea-content'. The terrified imagination, in other words, elaborates the object of

---

[103] *The Times* 29 May 1871, p. 5.
[104] Tuke 1871, pp. 25–6.

its fear as it projects it into the future. 'Every fear implies, as a fulfilment correlate, total destruction such as there has not yet been before, hell let loose', Bloch writes.[105] The 'fulfilment correlate' of the fear of revolution in the late nineteenth-century is the socialist society raised on the dead bodies of the bourgeoisie: in *Caesar's Column* (1890), by the American Populist senator Ignatius Donnelly, the eponymous monument to the civilisation ushered in by insurrection is a pyramid built by pouring cement onto a vast pile of pestilential corpses.[106] If the reactionary myth of the Paris Commune, for the English middle classes, is the '"founding" idea-content' of the fear of revolution, then, stimulated by domestic turmoil, the cacotopian imagination extends this object to its apocalyptic conclusion.

'The only crime of the Commune', the Communard Barrère remarked, 'was to have anticipated the future'.[107] For the English middle classes, its comminatory power outstripped its material impact. In England in the 1870s, the proleptic impact of the revolution in Paris represented what Benjamin might have called the bourgeoisie's 'moment of awakening', which 'would be identical with the "now of recognizability", in which things put on their true – surrealist – face'.[108] The drama of the Commune seemed to be the phantasmagoria of a more or less imminent future. The indeterminacy of the spectre of communism imported to England from France, its undated prediction of social disaster, inspired, not despair, which for Bloch is 'expectation of something negative about which there is no longer any doubt', but, as I have indicated, fear and anxiety, which are 'still questioning, hovering, still determined by mood and by the undetermined, unresolved element of its Object'. The Commune, and the events of the 1880s that reactivated its memory in England, provoked an 'anticipatory' response. The cacotopia, in fact, incorporates a 'utopian function'.[109]

The cacotopian text of the late nineteenth-century, depicting revolution as an infernal state of social flux, conscripts reactionary political instincts in support of a utopian model of capitalism supposedly implicit in the present. At the end of *The Commune in London*, Hemyng's narrator, after briefly

[105] Bloch 1986, pp. 124, 108.
[106] Donnelly 1891, Chapters 36 and 37.
[107] Barrère 1871, p. 33.
[108] Benjamin 1999, pp. 463–4.
[109] Bloch 1986, pp. 111, 113.

recounting the Commune's defeat, concludes that now England can finally 'begin to look forward with hope to the future' (p. 45). The future to which he refers, a dimly luminous image of a triumphant capitalist system, might itself be termed Utopia Ltd. Like the 'progressive' utopian function, this conservative one is conditioned by what Jean Pfaelzer calls 'the incentives of utopia'. But Pfaelzer understates the dialectic of incentives that typifies the form. The 'incentives' of the late-Victorian utopia do not 'represent *either* a stimulus to *or* a digression from praxis'.[110] They simultaneously stimulate and dampen the impulse to act politically. Partly because of the irreducibly contradictory nature of the bourgeois notion of progress – its vision of a capitalist society emancipated from class conflict – the cacotopia, like the state-socialist utopia that I explored in Chapter 2, both encourages and discourages practical activity. Between the nightmare of proletarian dictatorship and the dream of a perfect, peaceful social hierarchy, these futurist fictions can only gesture, tentatively, towards a world freed from immediate class antagonisms.

This gesture, as I argued in the third section of this chapter, is inscribed into the form's almost structural appeal to the interpellated readership that these cacotopias project as a political collective. At the end of 'England's Downfall', the narrator makes a plea that is typical of the form. I now want to quote it in full:

> Let us go back to our old ways. Equality and fraternity may be all very well to talk about; but they won't do in practice, and the sooner we admit this the better. But everything depends on you, the rising generation. The destinies of England are in your hands. Show the world what you can do. Think of what England was once and of what it is now, and remember that it is never too late to mend.[111]

The appeal of this 'Ex-Revolutionist' is a utopian one in the sense that, as Jameson claims, any manifestation of class consciousness that figures to itself the unity of a collectivity is utopian. But this utopian impulse must be premised on a prior moment of class consciousness, that of the oppressed classes grasping their own solidarity. In the late nineteenth-century, this prior moment is embodied in the uprising in Paris of 1871. The Commune provided the

---

[110] Pfaelzer 1984, pp. 4–5 (emphasis mine).
[111] 'An Ex-Revolutionist' 1893, p. 174.

crucial glimpse of the danger of the 'unification of the laboring population', so necessary to the formation of that 'mirror image of class solidarity among the ruling groups'. In this way, it not only shaped the anti-communist imagination of the time, but also marked its most elaborate and sensationalistic mode of expression. The cacotopia describes the dialectical indissociability of an ideological function and a utopian one. By depicting the horrifying consequences of working-class power, it operates as 'a hegemonic work whose formal categories as well as its content secure the legitimation . . . of class domination'. And by insidiously promoting the ideal of a capitalist order exempt from internal contradictions, it attempts 'to resonate a universal value inconsistent with the narrower limits of class privilege which inform its more immediate ideological vocation'.[112]

The ideological force of these cacotopian texts depends on their belief that capitalism can abolish class conflict, and that the working class can be rendered quiescent. So long as they subscribe to this conviction, they are only subject to anxiety and fear, expectant emotions that enable their polemical strategy. W.A. Watlock concludes his account of the Terror of an English revolution, *The Next 'Ninety-Three* (1886), with a comforting moral: 'This revolution has caused infinite sorrow, suffering and mischief; but it has not been entirely without good effect in proving the abject folly of those mad schemes, which, for their own self-seeking purposes, the canting crew has advocated'. 'This being so', he announces, 'there yet seems hope for England'.[113]

At the point at which this potentially happy ending no longer seems feasible, the propagandist agenda of the cacotopian form is undermined by its own narrative structure. Charles Gleig's novel *When All Men Starve* (1898), written in the tradition of *The Battle of Dorking* and *The Commune in London*, ends abruptly, during a revolution set in London at the turn of the twentieth-century. The novel purports to be a 'brief sketch of the political and social events of the last months of the English monarchy', the downfall of which follows swiftly from the decline of Britain's economic and military supremacy, in the face of a famine on the one hand, and a hopeless naval conflict against the combined forces of Russia, Germany and France on the other.[114] In these

---

[112] Jameson 1981, pp. 290–91, 288.
[113] Watlock 1886, p. 36.
[114] Gleig 1898, p. 97. Subsequent references are given after quotations.

inauspicious conditions, after riots over bread shortages, a revolutionary force of some 30,000 rebels is assembled. It marches on London, and in 'the Wimbledon massacre', in which 6,000 policemen are butchered, it secures its first significant victory: 'the last bulwark of Capital was shattered; Society and the sacred rights of property were no longer protected by so much as a single truncheon' (pp. 177–79). In a 'carnival of license', the rebels sweep on through Wandsworth, Clapham, Battersea and Vauxhall, before crossing the river and conquering Westminster, Mayfair, the West End and, finally, 'the city of gold' (pp. 182–83).

Like a number of cacotopian fictions, including *The Doom of the Great City*, the author's vengeful invective has two specific targets. The first of these is the working class, which assumes the form of a 'great surging mob of yelling devils' (p. 183). Gleig does manifest some sympathy for the poor, so long as they are deserving and duly passive; but he reserves a visceral hatred for them when they take matters into their own hands. Describing the morning after a night of looting, he notes with gleeful disgust that, 'gorged with plunder, the scum of the great city retreat[ed] to its foul lairs, leaving the dead to taint the air and strike terror to the heart of trembling women' (p. 172). The second of the book's targets is the aristocracy and the plutocracy, the dereliction of whose social responsibility is a contributing cause of the revolutionary uprising. Gleig blames them for being decadent and parasitic. He berates them for their refusal to offer proof of a capacity for reform, and for compromise, after the massacre at Wimbledon Common:

> Even at this desperate crisis, Respectability might have restrained the advancing tide of anarchy had there been any cohesion between the upper and middle classes of society. . . . [But] society – using the term in the broader sense – had been based upon a rotten edifice of money-bags, it had too long been content to hire troops and police to enforce its selfish laws upon the workers. . . . The luxury of an effete civilisation had emasculated the moneyed classes and left them defenceless against the thews and sinews of sturdy Labour. (p. 181.)

The crime of the capitalist class is to have failed to forge an alliance with the middle class in the face of their common enemy. The crime of the proletariat is to have made history on its own terms.

The narrative's concluding scene, of the nocturnal burning and looting of Buckingham Palace, depicts an 'Eldorado of drink and plunder' that revises the myth of the carnivalesque destruction of the Tuileries at the end of the Commune (p. 184). 'From all corners', the narrator reports with cold contempt, 'come men and women and slatternly, drunken girls, until thousands are gathered round the glowing building, shouting, cursing, dancing a mad can-can in the flicker of the leaping flames'. The final sentence of the novel conjures up an image of the mob dancing 'till the grey dawn steals up from the east and the burnt palace looms black and haggard in the cold light of morning' (p. 192). There is no restoration of bourgeois order. The book does not contain a postscript in which this dystopian prospect is redeemed. The ruling class, Gleig's book aggressively argues, has destroyed civilisation itself by failing to make any concession to the working class that, bent and brutalised, has acted as its grave-diggers. The middle class, its property plundered, is a victim both of the plutocracy and the insurrectionary poor. It has absconded from its heroic, restorative role in this epic clash between classes, between these Eloi and Morlocks of the *fin de siècle*.

'Is this reality, or is it all a hideous nightmare?' the protagonist of *'England's Downfall'* had asked, mesmerised by the sight of Londoners looting and burning.[115] The response offered by most utopian fiction and by most cacotopian fiction is to proclaim that this experience of social anarchy, prefigurations of which can be glimpsed in the battles between capital and labour that mark the late nineteenth-century, is a nightmare from which we will awake to reality in the future. In the last and most powerful chapter of Bellamy's *Looking Backward*, West fears that twentieth-century Boston is merely a mesmeric fantasy, because, unaccountably, he finds himself wandering through the streets of nineteenth-century Boston once more, horrified by 'the festering mass of human wretchedness'. In fact, this return to West's past present is a hideous nightmare, and, to his relief, he wakes up in the future present: 'As with an escaped convict who dreams that he has been re-captured and brought back to his dark and reeking dungeon, and opens his eyes to see the heaven's vault spread above him, so it was with me, as I realized that my return to the 19th century had been the dream, and my presence in the 20th was the reality'.[116] In the late nineteenth-century, history is truly a nightmare from which West, and the more conservative authors of social dreams, are trying to awake.

---

[115] 'An Ex-Revolutionist' 1893, p. 111.
[116] Bellamy 1888, pp. 457–58, 467–68.

Gleig's answer to the 'Ex-Revolutionist's' question is less slippery and ambiguous: the social cataclysm is not a hideous nightmare from which there can ultimately be a reprieve, but an imminent future from which it is impossible to escape, an historical reality. In spite its rhetorical energy, *When All Men Starve* is an utterly spiritless cacotopia, because it commemorates the critical failure of prophylactic reform from above. It inscribes a vengeful warning of the dangers courted by the ruling class, but without much confidence in its own propagandist function. In its imaginary realisation of the spectre of communism, it buries the utopian impulse that formerly characterised even the cacotopian form.

By the turn of the twentieth-century, the certainties of capitalist society are in a state of deep corrosion – not least because of the insurrection in Paris in 1871 and the domestic disturbances of the end of the following decades. It is no longer self-evident that, as one commentator put it with desperate optimism in 1885, 'the English people have arrived at the highest known pitch of social happiness and national prosperity hitherto realized in the world's history'.[117] The cataclysmic final image of *When All Men Starve*, frozen for futurity, testifies to this fact. 'To the privileged classes', Old Hammond records with grim satisfaction in his account of 'How the Change Came' in *News from Nowhere*, 'it seemed as if the end of the world were come'.[118] It is to the post-revolutionary present pictured in Morris's utopian romance – a novel that perceives a redemptive future in the very conflicts of the *fin de siècle* – that I finally turn in the next chapter.

---

[117] Falkiner 1885, p. 14.
[118] Morris 1912a, p. 109.

Chapter Five

Utopia and the Present in *News from Nowhere*

I. Introduction

The rise of utopianism from the 1870s, as we have
seen, was a response to the socio-political impact of
the Great Depression, which evoked alternatives to
capitalist society that it was impossible to implement
at the time. It was also, concomitantly, a response to
the frenetic conditions of modern life that, at bottom
because of the concentration and acceleration of
European capital in its imperial and monopolistic
phase, defined the culture of the *fin de siècle*.
Technological developments in transport and
telecommunications, simultaneously opening up
geographical space and intensifying the experience
of social space, created an effect of 'time-space
compression'. According to Stephen Kern, 'the big
news of the age was that the present moment could
be filled with many distant events'.[1] In 'the vertigo
and whirl of our frenzied life', as Nordau identified
it, the present moment could in addition be crowded
with immediate events. And this created a crisis
of representation. Utopian fiction was, in part, a
symptomatic expression of this crisis. As I proposed
in Chapter 1, in the uncertain climate of the end
of the century, the discourse of utopia marked an

---

[1] Kern 1983, p. 81.

attempt not only to sketch the future, but also to perceive the present from the anamorphic perspective that this discourse afforded.

Under the economic and social conditions of capitalist modernity, the present becomes almost impenetrable. The accelerated metabolism of commodity culture, and of everyday life, makes any attempt to grasp the present in its objective form, as a moment in history, seem hopeless. This temporal phenomenon can perhaps be clarified, metaphorically, if it is compared to the spatial experience of the nineteenth-century railway passenger. In a lecture of 1872, on 'The Relation to Art of the Science of Light', John Ruskin contrasted the piercing sight of an eagle circling in its gyre with the blurred vision of a train traveller being shuttled along a track: 'When next you are travelling by express sixty miles an hour, past a grass bank, try to see a grasshopper, and you will get some idea of an eagle's optical business'.[2] This was not the first time that Ruskin had alluded to the difficulty of focusing on the world outside a railway-carriage window in order to illustrate the fact that, under the conditions of industrial modernisation, an unprecedented problem with perception serves to dissolve reality itself. Writing from Italy in 1846, he had complained that, when travelling by train, 'it matters not whether you have eyes or are asleep or blind, intelligent or dull, all that you can know, at best, of the country you pass is its geological structure and general clothing'.[3]

Ruskin's point is that, under the impact of express speed, immediate perceptual experience acquires an impressionistic quality. A train's motion 'causes the *foreground* to disappear', as Wolfgang Schivelbusch argues; 'it detaches the subject from the space that immediately surrounds him, that is, it intrudes itself as an "almost unreal barrier" between object and subject'.[4] In other words, it induces a species of presbyopia, a condition of the eyes 'in which the power of accommodation to near objects is lost or impaired, and only distant objects are seen distinctly' (OED). And this condition can serve as a metaphor for the crisis of representation induced by the contemporaneous disappearance of the present. The blurred space onto which the late-Victorian train traveller trains his presbyopic vision is analogous to the opacity of immediate experience encountered by anyone hoping to grasp the present moment as a distinct temporality. Ernst Bloch called this problem 'the darkness

---

[2] Ruskin 1906, p. 201.
[3] Ruskin 1909, p. 62.
[4] Schivelbusch 1980, p. 183.

of the lived moment', which one recent commentator has paraphrased as 'the inadequate relationship between subject and object that manifests itself in the greater availability of experience to foresight or recollection than to immediate consciousness'.[5]

In *The Principle of Hope*, Bloch provides a sketch of this concept:

> The Here and Now stands too close to us. Raw experience transposes us
> from the drifting dream into another state: into that of immediate nearness.
> The moment just lived dims as such, it has too dark a warmth, and its
> nearness makes things formless. The Here and Now lacks the distance which
> does indeed alienate us, but makes things distinct and surveyable.[6]

The 'darkness of the lived moment' is at the centre of a crisis of representation with which utopianism grapples in the late-Victorian period.

Utopian fiction describes an attempt to impose a narrative structure on the present in order roughly to decipher its contours. In the early twentieth-century, modernist writing will find a formal solution to the recalcitrance of the historical here-and-now, immersing itself in the fetishised details of everyday life. In the later nineteenth-century, utopian writing projects a fictional future from which the present, for all its emptiness, can be anamorphically perceived in the approximate shape afforded by an imaginary historical perspective. The utopian novel is a view from the 'roof-top' that I outlined in relation to Grant Allen's hill-top. It tries to totalise a fragmentary and reified society by seeing it from the standpoint of an alternative future. 'For without distance, right within, you cannot even experience something; not to speak of representing it, to present it in a right way – which simultaneously has to provide a general view'.[7] Utopianism in the late-Victorian period offered a resolution of the predicament celebrated by Walter Pater, who in 1878 cited Charles Lamb: '"I cannot make these present times", he says once, "present to *me*"'.[8]

'The capacity of utopia to break through the thickness of reality is what interest[s] me', comments Paul Ricoeur.[9] I concur. In this chapter, I interpret

---

5 Dayton 1997, p. 189.
6 Bloch 1986, p. 180.
7 Bloch 1986, pp. 207–08.
8 Pater 1910, p. 111.
9 Ricoeur 1986, p. 309.

News from Nowhere as a solution to the problem posed by 'the thickness of reality', or the darkness of the lived moment, in the later nineteenth-century. Like his contemporaries, Morris objectifies the present in relation to an imaginary history of the future. But in addition, and in contrast to other utopian novels of the 1880s and 1890s, his utopian romance also presents an ideal socialist society that explicitly repudiates or negates the empty present of capitalism. It is this political treatment of time that marks the novel's transformation of the utopian form. Morris's 'epoch of rest' depicts a present characterised by plenitude and transparency. The foreground no longer disappears, as it does for Ruskin when he is travelling by rail. (Perhaps it is no accident that it is while returning by train from a meeting on the future socialist society that our protagonist, the narrator's 'friend', first expresses his utopian frustration: '"If I could but see a day of it," he said to himself; "if I could but see it!"'.)[10] In Nowhere, the present is not alienated, or absent, but present to itself. *News from Nowhere*, in contrast to many of the utopian novels that I have evaluated in previous chapters, breaks the frame of our present, to use Wells's phrase, by dynamically relating it to a redemptive future.

In this chapter, which in effect constructs Morris's fiction as a successful model for the creation of an imaginary future, capable of superseding the characteristic contradictions of utopian politics at the *fin de siècle*, my argument unfolds in two main phases. The next section examines the problem of the perception of the present, proposing a materialist explanation for its impenetrability and opacity in capitalist society. It then tries to theorise utopian thought in terms of its historicising and totalising function, which I read as a response to the 'darkness of the lived moment'. This forms the theoretical basis on which my reading of *News from Nowhere* rests. The following section explores the way in which Morris's utopian fiction depicts a world wherein the present is present to itself. But it also draws attention to the fact that Morris finally questions this fantasy of utopian presence. I conclude with a brief reflection on the possible implications of this interpretation of Morris's utopia for our understanding of his politics.

---

[10] Morris 1912a, p. 4. Subsequent references are given after quotations in the text.

II. Utopia and the present

The present represents a well-nigh insuperable phenomenological problem. Any attempt to capture the presentness of the present results in something like a short-circuit of the logic of cognition. Grasping the present is like trying to stop what William James called 'the wonderful stream of our consciousness', in order to subject it to 'introspective analysis':'[it] is in fact like seizing a spinning top to catch its motion, or trying to turn up the gas quickly enough to see how the darkness looks'.[11] And if we cannot conquer its fundamental resistance to signification, we are forced to accept that a concept of the present has to be produced, constructed.

'*The problem of the present*', as Lukács counselled, must be treated as '*a historical problem*'.[12] So, from the outset, it is important to state that what Bloch describes as 'lack of distance' ('all nearness makes matters difficult', he says, 'and if it is too close, then one is blinded, at least made mute') is characteristic of the history of class society *tout court*.[13] The struggle for existence in a world of unnecessary scarcity and want has condemned the vast majority of human beings to remain within the realm of immediacy. But the perceptual problem of the present in the Victorian period is more specifically the result of the reifying effects of commodity culture under capitalism. Here, I want briefly to explore the preconditions for what Bloch called 'the general collapse of objective contemplation . . . which nearness causes'.[14]

A crisis of representation is endemic to the capitalist mode of production. But this ideological deformation is not simply a species of 'false consciousness', that is to say, the purely mental operation whereby capitalism produces its own misapprehension. As Marx revealed in the first volume of *Capital* (1867), the sense of alienation that haunts human beings is not a hallucination, but, instead, a structural property of their social relations under capitalism. Marx's theory of commodity fetishism represents an attempt to come to terms with the interior hiatus of these relations. It explains that the exploitation of the proletariat, which establishes the foundation of the capitalist mode of production, is systematically concealed by the fact that commodities, the

---

[11] James 1884, p. 3.
[12] Lukács 1971, p. 175.
[13] Bloch 1988, p. 208.
[14] Bloch 1986, p. 296.

products of social labour, function as if they are subject solely to their mutual interrelation in the marketplace. In this way, the social relation between producers assumes 'the fantastic form of a relation between things'. But this 'fantastic form' is not merely the lamination of reality with an illusory relation: it deforms reality itself. For, to the commodified producers, 'the relations connecting the labour of one individual with that of the rest appear, not as direct social relations between individuals at work, but *as what they really are*, material relations between persons and social relations between things'.[15] In sum, as Lefebvre affirms, if the commodity-form 'must inevitably give rise to an opaque society', this opacity is 'a social, or rather, a socio-economic fact'.[16]

Lukács reformulated the 'phantom objectivity' of capitalist relations in terms of 'the phenomenon of reification', the process of alienation whereby the fetishism of the commodity form diffuses into 'capitalist society in all its aspects'. According to him, the rational mechanisation of capitalist production breaks up the labour process and corrodes 'the qualitative, human and individual attributes of the worker'. Under the impact of this atomisation, the worker's activity becomes 'more and more *contemplative*'. And this attitude 'transform[s] the basic categories of man's immediate attitude to the world': in particular, 'time sheds its qualitative, variable, flowing nature; it freezes into an exactly delimited, quantifiable continuum filled with quantifiable "things"'. In these desiccated conditions, the worker cannot totalise or intellectually transcend society. But the reification of consciousness is not restricted to the worker, because 'the objective reality of social existence is *in its immediacy* "the same" for both proletariat and bourgeoisie'. Thus bourgeois consciousness loses sight of the social totality too. Science 'find[s] that the world lying beyond its confines, and in particular the material base which it is its task to understand, *its own concrete underlying reality* lies, methodologically and in principle, *beyond its grasp*'.[17] And this obstruction to the totality of knowledge makes it impossible to ascertain the silent movement of reality. The present time, that is to say, becomes impenetrable, inapprehensible as a moment in history.

---

[15] Marx 1996, p. 84 (emphasis mine).
[16] Lefebvre 1968, p. 63.
[17] Lukács 1971, pp. 83, 88–90, 104, 150.

The reification of consciousness at the *fin de siècle* is graphically illustrated in relation to the commercial sphere by an article on 'The Known and the Unknown in the Economic World', first printed in the *Fortnightly Review* in 1879. 'Not only the future, but even the present, becomes inscrutable in a highly advanced community', proclaims Thomas Cliffe Leslie, the celebrated critic of classical economics: 'the number of employments is so great, each of them is so intricate a business, and affected by such a variety of conditions, the fortunes of the individuals engaged in them are so diverse, that no one dreams of surveying the entire field'. The complexity of the unplanned economy, in spite of attempts to supervise the blind operations of the market, he explains, has produced a commercial situation characterised not so much by 'the depth of the depression', as by 'the sense of being in the dark, and surrounded, as it were, by the unknown'. At the start of the piece, he had expressed his consternation:

> It is the consciousness only of not seeing their way on the part of the people that is new. Trade has long been carried on blindly, and people as little knew what was before them when it was said to be advancing by leaps and bounds as they do now that these are found to have been leaps in the dark. Temporary circumstances have added to the gloom and uncertainty, and it is ascribable in part to a false economic theory; but to get a ray of light we must first recognize that the obscurity of the present crisis has arisen in a great measure from causes inherent in the constitution of the modern economic world.[18]

With considerable eloquence, Leslie describes the effects of commodity fetishism in a climate of acute economic instability. He fails only to emphasise that, if the obscurity of the crisis has arisen from the structural properties of the capitalist economic system, this 'confusion', as he calls it, filters into social relations too, infecting consciousness itself.

The paradox of reification is that it naturalises the present even as it alienates it from human understanding. From the sphere of economics to that of ordinary life, reality is experienced as a frozen plasmic flux that escapes the power of human reflection. The lived moment is like the ocean surface of the planet Solaris in Stanislaw Lem's well-known novel of 1961 – 'a colloidal envelope',

---

[18] Leslie 1888, pp. 221, 225, 235.

fluid but 'obstinate'.[19] Lukács captured this contradictory phenomenon in a polemic with Bloch, proposing that 'when the surface of life is only experienced immediately, it remains opaque, fragmentary, chaotic and uncomprehended'; and, further, that 'what lies on the surface is frozen and any attempt to see it from a higher intellectual vantage-point has to be abandoned'.[20] Utopian thought is an attempt to attain this 'higher intellectual vantage-point', this transcendent perspective: it projects a fictional future from which it estranges the present and tries to totalise the 'untotalizable totality' of capitalist society.

It is the problem of grasping the present in spite of its alienated form with which William Morris and some of his contemporaries grappled in the late-Victorian period. Fredric Jameson summarises the dilemma facing them in one of his accounts of the mechanics of science fiction: 'How to fix this intolerable present of history with the naked eye?'.[21] Utopians at the *fin de siècle* reacted with the anamorphic squint that I outlined in Chapter 1. Utopia pulls away from the patternless forms of the present and tries to reconfigure them from the vantage point of a hoped-for future. This is the process mapped out by Edwin Abbott, the classicist and biblical scholar, in *Flatland: A Romance of Many Dimensions* (1884), undoubtedly the wittiest and most sophisticated meta-utopian fiction of the late nineteenth-century. Abbott's curious novel is a mathematical fable about the political importance of understanding that it is possible to construct a perspective from which society is finally a cultural (and therefore transformable) phenomenon rather than a natural (or unalterable) one.

In Flatland, a two-dimensional realm in which people of all different geometrical shapes, from the lower-class irregular triangle to the upper-class polygon, can grasp their fellow citizens' social status only by feeling their angles (because everybody looks like a straight line when confined to one plane), the alternative perspective is a three-dimensional realm called Spaceland. Abbot's two-dimensional narrator, a solidly middle-class Square, is taken to Spaceland by a Sphere, and there he discovers that the third dimension offers a revolutionary perspective on the limited linear world he has left behind him. 'Let us begin by casting back a glance at the region whence you came',

---

[19] Lem 1971, pp. 18, 78.
[20] Lukács 1977, p. 39.
[21] Jameson 1982, p. 152.

the Sphere counsels. The Square observes his own family, in its 'Pentagonal house', from above: 'I looked below, and saw with my physical eye all that domestic individuality which I had hitherto merely inferred with the understanding. And how poor and shadowy was the inferred conjecture in comparison with the reality which I now beheld!'. Whereas in Flatland figures are reduced to edges, the narrator now sees them as shapes. This peculiar optic has dramatic political implications. He now realises that his wife and children are marked by individual characteristics, and that he is himself more than a mere social abstraction. Furthermore, he can see straight through his social superiors, literally as well as metaphorically. On his return to Flatland, the radicalised Square tries 'to diffuse the Theory of Three Dimensions' to other alienated Flatlanders. 'With the view of evading the Law', he discusses it in an abstract code, speaking 'not of a physical Dimension, but of a Thoughtland whence, in theory, a Figure could look down upon Flatland and see simultaneously the insides of all things'. He fails to evade the Law, however, and is arrested. In prison, he is forced in effect to retreat to the Thoughtland that he has hypothesised, that is to say, to a mental space from which the truth can be inferred but not acted upon. Thoughtland is both a kind of liberation and a further confinement.[22]

Thoughtland, an imaginary perspective from which the darkness of the lived present is alleviated and the character of contemporary society is revealed in historical perspective, is equivalent to utopia. H.G. Wells describes the same interrelationship of utopian and non-utopian perspectives in the present, of telescopic and myopic optics, in the concluding pages of *A Modern Utopia* (1905). The narrator notes that his utopian narrative ends, on its return to the present, *'amidst a gross tumult of immediate realities'*, surrounded by *'a great multitude of little souls and groups of souls as darkened, as derivative as my own'*. This optic corresponds to the perspective of Lineland. But, as he insists, it is unsettled by a flickering anamorphic perception of the total system of which he and his fellow citizens form a part: 'Yet that is not all I see, and I am not altogether bounded by my littleness. Ever and again, contrasting with this immediate vision, come glimpses of a comprehensive scheme, in which these personalities float, the scheme of a synthetic wider being, the great State, mankind, in which we all move and go, like blood corpuscles, like nerve

---

[22] Abbott 1884, pp. 78–9, 96.

cells, it may be at times like brain cells in the body of a man'.[23] This description corresponds to the perspective of Spaceland. Wells explains that the two viewpoints comprise a bifocal optic – like the vision of someone who is simultaneously long-sighted and short-sighted. The utopian capacity for 'looking backwards' from the future is something like this long-sighted perspective. Bloch wrote that 'we need the most powerful telescope, that of polished utopian consciousness, in order to penetrate precisely the nearest nearness'.[24]

This system of perspective forms the premise upon which Morris had founded the narrative practice of *A Dream of John Ball* (1888) in the previous decade. There, the nineteenth-century narrator tells John Ball that he can see the fourteenth-century through the lens of future history: 'And we, looking at these things from afar, can see them as they are indeed; but they who live at the beginning of those times and amidst them, shall not know what is doing around them; they shall indeed feel the plague and yet not know the remedy'.[25] Romance, Morris wrote, 'is the capacity for a true conception of history, a power of making the past part of the present'.[26] But as John Goode argues, for Morris romance also 'becomes a power for seeing the future in the present'.[27] 'Utopian Romance', to cite the subtitle of *News from Nowhere*, fulfils this capacity for history by making the present part of the future too.

Morris also tried 'to realize the face of mediaeval England' in 'The Hopes of Civilization', a lecture first delivered in 1885: 'How strange it would be to us if we could be landed in 14th-century England!'. There was nothing nostalgic about this exclamation. Historicising the past, he wanted also to historicise the present, 'the great commercial epoch in whose *latter* days I would fain hope we are living'. To this end, Morris imagined a people who in the future 'will wonder how we lived in the 14th century'.[28] The inhabitants of Nowhere are a fictional version of this collectivity. The famous account of 'How the Change Came' in *News from Nowhere* is, in effect, a history of the turn of the twentieth-century written in the future perfect tense. In this way,

---

[23] Wells 1905, p. 372. I have de-italicised this passage.
[24] Bloch 1986, p. 12.
[25] Morris 1912b, p. 274.
[26] Morris 1936b, p. 148.
[27] Goode 1971, p. 239.
[28] Morris 1973, p. 163.

[orris may be said to interpret the present from the standpoint of utopian demption.

1. The utopian present

ld Hammond, a professional historian, performs this historiographical inction in *News from Nowhere*. He traces the revolutionary process whereby, me time in the twentieth-century, 'a longing for freedom and equality' was anslated into a force for social transformation (pp. 104–05). In so doing, ₂ penetrates 'the silent movement of real history'.[29] But Hammond is an ₁achronism in Nowhere. He is an anomalous presence precisely because of ₁s passion for making the past part of the present. For if his narrative serves ₁ historicise the late nineteenth-century, then this series of 'tales of the past' ₁nnot interest most of the inhabitants of Nowhere, since they have no sense what Marx styled 'pre-history'. 'The last harvest, the last baby, the last ₁ot of carving in the market-place, is history enough for them', Hammond ₂serves (p. 54). Morris uses this comment to articulate Hammond's criticism the semi-conscious amnesia characteristic of Nowherean citizens. But, gnificantly, he also uses it to emphasise that, in this future socialist society, ₁story itself has been redefined. In Nowhere history is made not in the macro-₁ents of an evolving civilisation but in the micro-processes of daily life. topia, Morris implies, redeems history as the process by which we produce ₁d reproduce ourselves in our everyday lives. So, Morris's utopian romance more than an attempt to grasp the present of capitalist modernity as history. is also an attempt to imagine a communist society in which it is possible ₁ grasp history as the present, that is to say, in which history is simply being. The inhabitants of Nowhere, so Hammond says, are 'assured of peace and ₁ntinuous plenty' (p. 54). As Morris emphasises in his lecture on 'Useful ʹork versus Useless Toil' (1884), 'when revolution has made it "easy to live", ʹhen all are working harmoniously together and there is no one to rob the ʹorker of his time, that is to say, his life; in those coming days there will be ₂ compulsion on us to go on producing things we do not want, no compulsion ₁ us to labour for nothing'. Impossible under capitalism, or any competitive

---

[29] Morris 1914, p. 315.

system, these material and social circumstances are the foundation of a futur
socialist society in which all work is useful and every useful activity is a forn
of work. Work will at last fulfil its fundamental promises – 'hope of rest, hop
of product, hope of pleasure in the work itself', as Morris enumerates them
For when capitalist relations of production are abolished, and labour is mad
'pleasant to everybody', people will be free 'to take a pleasurable interest ir
all the details of life'.[30]

Morris associates these 'details of life' with what he subsequently calls 'th
ornamental part of life': 'We must begin to build up the ornamental part c
life – its pleasures, bodily and mental, scientific and artistic, social an
individual – on the basis of work undertaken willingly and cheerfully, witl
the consciousness of benefiting ourselves and our neighbours with it'. Morris'
celebration of 'social' ornament is based on his assessment of material ornament
He draws a crucial distinction between ornamental objects produced unde
alienated conditions and those produced under disalienated conditions. Ir
capitalist relations of production, 'the workman is compelled to produce
ornament, as he is to produce other wares', and ornament is therefore 'bu
one of the follies of useless toil'.[31] Ornament signifies a pretence of happines
in work, a forced declaration of satisfaction. It camouflages the exploitatior
structural to commodity production under capitalism, and consequentl
reinforces the 'opacity' of social life. In communist society, on the contrary
ornament is an expression of the pleasure of production, and, paradoxically
of the transparency of non-exploitative social relations. And this aestheti
serves as a model for the ethic indicated by Morris's injunction 'to build uj
the ornamental part of life'. In the future socialist society, even the most trivia
aspects of everyday life will serve as an aesthetic pleasure, because they wil
embroider the basic activity of creative labour.

Morris explores his conception of ornament in the episode from *News from
Nowhere* in which William Guest is given a pipe in the little girl's shop. The
pipe is free, like all the products of labour in utopia; but more importantly
it is *ornamental*. It is 'carved out of some hard wood very elaborately, anc
mounted in gold sprinkled with little gems' (p. 217). In Morris's terms, this
implies that it is stamped 'with the impress of pleasure'.[32] In other words

---

[30] Morris 1973, pp. 87, 96–7.
[31] Morris 1973, pp. 100, 102.
[32] Morris 1973, p. 102.

ve are now in a world 'in which the collective labour stored in a given commodity is always and everywhere visible to its consumers and users'.[33] The demise of commodity fetishism means that labour itself is returned from the realm of exchange-value to the realm of use-value. So the split between appearance and reality that is typical of capitalism disappears. Under capitalism, as Marx argues in *Capital*, 'the products of labour become commodities, sensible things which are at the same time supra-sensible'. 'The commodity-form, and the value-relation of the products of labour within which it appears', he continues, 'have absolutely no connection with the physical nature of the commodity and the material [*dinglich*] relations arising out of this'.[34] In utopia, the case is the opposite: the products of labour fully realise their physical properties. Appearance collapses into essence. 'In the happy days when society shall be what it's [*sic*] name means', to use Morris's phrase, the signifier is finally conflated with its signified.[35] *Ceci est une pipe.*

History, to return to an earlier contention, and to cite the title of another well-known lecture by Morris, is in this sense merely 'How We Live'. In Nowhere, history is rendered ordinary. Returned to a people participating in pleasurable labour, it is the opposite of those epic spirals typical of pre-history, as it lurches from crisis to crisis. In Hammond's phrase, it is simply 'the present pleasure of ordinary daily life' (p. 254) – a whole way of life self-consciously felt in all its fibres. In 'Useful Work versus Useless Toil', Morris represents this utopian culture in terms of a holiday:

> How rare a holiday it is for any of us to feel ourselves a part of Nature, and unhurriedly, thoughtfully, and happily to note the course of our lives amidst all the little links of events which connect them with the lives of others, and build up the great whole of humanity.
>
> But such a holiday our whole lives might be, if we were resolute to make all our labour reasonable and pleasant.[36]

In this glimpse of a utopian 'epoch of rest', the totality of social relations is not absent and unrepresentable, as it is under capitalism, but present, and spontaneously apprehended. In his lecture on 'The Society of the Future',

---

[33] Jameson 1999, p. 55.
[34] Marx 1996, p. 165.
[35] Morris 1969, p. 216.
[36] Morris 1973, p. 97.

Morris reaffirms that, in a socialist community, 'the social bond would be habitually and instinctively felt, so that there would be no need to be always asserting it by set forms'.[37] Utopia, as Jameson proposes, is 'a landscape of sheer immanence, in which social life coincid[es] fully with itself, so that the most insignificant situations of its everyday life [are] already in and of themselves fully philosophical'.[38] The present, that is to say, is transparent in Morris's utopia.

News from Nowhere is a fantasy of effortless self-fulfilment. Terry Eagleton has proposed that it is possible to explain utopia as 'a condition in which Freud's "pleasure principle" and "reality principle" would have merged into one, so that social reality itself would be wholly fulfilling'.[39] It is because of something like this lack of conflict that, for a moment, roughly halfway through his stay in Nowhere, Guest enjoys what he refers to as 'a dreamless sleep' (p. 141). Successfully choking down his fears, as he himself phrases it, Guest briefly experiences the pacific harmony of Nowhereans such as Ellen. Ellen is, in fact, the exemplary utopian. She admits to Guest, as they travel up the Thames by boat together, that she does not like 'moving about from one home to another', because 'one gets so used to all the detail of the life about one'; but she also happily contemplates the prospect of 'go[ing] with [him] all through the west country – thinking of nothing' (p. 190). Calm of this sort is not a bestial stasis. As the metaphor of the drifting journey upstream emphasises, Ellen is the model for a kind of dynamic immobility, outlined elsewhere by Morris when he rejects the notion that a state of plenitude necessarily results in stagnation: 'to my mind that would be a contradiction in terms, if indeed we agree that happiness is caused by the pleasurable exercise of our faculties'.[40]

Rest is a familiar trope in utopias of the *fin de siècle*. 'We long to cast from our midst forever the black nightmare of poverty: we yearn for fellowship, for rest, for happiness', wrote the American Leonard Abbott in his book of 1898 on *The Society of the Future*.[41] Utopian fiction of this period often projected what was in effect a mirror-image reversal of life under capitalism. And rest

---

[37] Morris 1973, p. 201.
[38] Jameson 1992, p. 45.
[39] Eagleton 1991, p. 185.
[40] Morris 1973, pp. 202–03.
[41] Abbott 1898, p. 4.

ometimes came to resemble something like Adorno's fantasy of 'universal peace' in his 'Reflections from Damaged Life', *Minima Moralia*: there he proposes that, in a utopian future, doing nothing ('comme une bête') 'might ake the place of process'.[42] Morris had a more dialectical understanding of he utopian state of repose than many of his contemporaries and indeed lescendants. A.L. Morton helpfully compares *News from Nowhere* with W.H. Hudson's *A Crystal Age* (1887), and maintains that 'this time of rest, which or Morris is no more than a temporary and relative pause between periods of marked change . . . is for Hudson unbroken, as far as can be seen, in either direction'.[43] In other words, where Morris sees the 'epoch of rest' as part of history – or, as I have proposed, as its deepening or redemption – Hudson perceives it as a homogeneous, empty space outside history.

In the lecture on 'The Society of the Future', Morris defends his own notion of rest and asks, 'where would be the harm?': 'I remember, after having been ll once, how pleasant it was to lie on my bed without pain or fever, doing nothing but watching the sunbeams and listening to the sounds of life outside; and might not the great world of men, if it once deliver itself from the struggle for life amidst dishonesty, rest for a little after the long fever and be none the worse for it?'.[44] Morris here looks forward to his image of Ellen both attending to the details of life and 'thinking of nothing'. This form of rest is subtly different to that which Morris identifies as 'leisure' in 'The Prospects of Architecture in Civilization' (1881). Under capitalism, leisure is a refuge from work, and Morris confesses that he himself spends part of it 'as a dog does – in contemplation'. Ellen's rest, by contrast, is an extension of the creative, quietly purposive activity of pleasurable labour. It is more closely akin to what Morris calls 'Imaginative Work', because in its peaceful attention to life it bears in its bosom the worth and the meaning of life and the counsel to strive to understand everything'.[45] It is, precisely, 'the pleasurable exercise of our faculties'.[46] Life in Nowhere, as Lionel Trilling once wrote, 'is lived for itself alone, for its own delight in itself. In the life of each individual, the past now exercises no tyranny and the future is not exigent. The present is all,

---

[42] Adorno 1974, p. 157.
[43] Morton 1952, p. 159.
[44] Morris 1973, p. 203.
[45] Morris 1999, pp. 72, 75.
[46] Morris 1973, pp. 202–03.

and it is all-satisfying'.[47] In utopia, real life is no longer absent, as it is in pre-history; it is present.

But it is nonetheless necessary to recall that, before and after the fleeting self-forgetfulness of his 'dreamless sleep', Guest is haunted by 'a vague fear' that he will 'wake up in the old miserable world of worn-out pleasures, and hopes that [are] half-fears' (pp. 141, 153). In this way, the half-forgotten, the repressed, in the form of his own empty present, the present of pre-history, foreshadows its return. If, in Bloch's vocabulary, Morris's 'epoch of rest' embodies '*the utopian primacy of rest*, as the schema of fulfilment, over motion, as the schema of unfulfilled striving for something', then this state of rest is after all simply epochal and impermanent.[48] Socialism, as Morris stressed, 'does not recognise any finality in the progress and aspirations of humanity; and . . . the furthest we can now conceive is only a stage of the great journey of evolution that joins the future and the past to the present'.[49]

In his perceptive essay on Morris, Miguel Abensour addresses this issue of impermanence by proposing that *News from Nowhere* comprises 'a highly original utopian hypothesis on the "hazy realm of non-history", that moment of forgetfulness that alone clears the way for a new history, an amazing history beyond everything it has heretofore told or produced'.[50] But if this interpretation is compelling, it has two problems. First, it fails to grasp the utopian paradox whereby the 'hazy realm of non-history' may in fact be this 'amazing history' to which he refers. Morris is emphatic that our whole life might be a 'holiday' if all our labour is 'reasonable and pleasant', in this way deconstructing the difference between work and play, history and non-history.[51] Second, if it freely acknowledges that, as Ellen puts it, 'happy as we are, times may alter', it fails to recognise that this moment of forgetfulness may itself clear the way for a return to some more alienated, fetishised condition of life. 'We may be bitten with some impulse towards change', muses Ellen, 'and many things may seem too wonderful for us to resist, too exciting not to catch at, if we do not know that they are but phases of what has been before; and withal

---

[47] Trilling 1973, p. 219.
[48] Bloch 1986, p. 825.
[49] Morris 1984, p. 153.
[50] Abensour 1999, p. 134.
[51] Morris 1973, p. 97.

ruinous, deceitful, and sordid' (p. 194). Presumably this refers to the fact that, as Hammond had earlier hinted, the inhabitants of Nowhere are increasingly fearful 'of a possible scarcity in work' (p. 97). Competition may yet upset this realm of 'peace and continuous plenty'. Ellen's comment therefore amounts to an implicit criticism of Hammond, who idealises the past and so opens up the possibility of its return. At the same time, however, it is a guilty admission of her attraction for Guest, who is himself a fragment 'of what has been before', appealing to her precisely because of his emotional complexity, his 'hopes that [are] half-fears' (p. 153).

For Guest is a ghost, and he unsettles the tranquillity of utopia. His very presence is a disruption of the epoch of rest. He is the mark of non-contemporaneity. In his person, the spectre of pre-history haunts the realm of a redemptive history just as the 'ghost of old London' still asserts itself as a centre in Nowhere (p. 33). This is the significance of Dick's conversation with Guest about the cycle of seasons before the feast: '"One thing seems strange to me", said he – "that I must needs trouble myself about the winter and its scantiness, in the midst of the summer abundance. If it hadn't happened to me before, I should have thought it was your doing, Guest; that you had thrown a kind of evil charm over me"' (p. 207). Guest has interrupted the unity of subject and object to which Dick referred a moment ago when he talked of being 'part of it all', part of nature itself, in Nowhere (p. 207). Like an anamorphic mark on a canvas, he unsettles the image of the 'best ornament' of the church in which the harvest is to be celebrated, that is to say, 'the crowd of handsome, happy-looking men and women' wearing 'their gay holiday raiment' (p. 208). As 'the guest of guests' (p. 208), Guest is also the ghost at the feast (as the common etymological root of 'ghost' and 'guest', the word *ghos-ti*, indicates). So the minatory advice that Dick offers Guest in Runnymede, that 'you had better consider that you have got the cap of darkness, and are seeing everything, yourself invisible' (p. 155), is, for a moment, fulfilled quite literally: he watches his physical presence fading quickly from the consciousness of his Nowherean friends, before experiencing his own painful re-apparition in *fin-de-siècle* London. An immaterial presence in Nowhere, he now returns to haunt 'old London'. 'Spectrality', Jameson has written, is 'what makes the present waver: like the vibrations of a heat wave through which the massiveness of the object world – indeed of matter itself – now shimmers like a mirage'. It is in precisely this sense that Morris's protagonist is spectral. He unconsciously announces that 'the living present' – even the utopian present of plenitude and happiness – 'is scarcely as self-sufficient as it claims to be'.[52]

But it is noticeable that Dick draws attention to the fact that he has felt this disturbance before. In the past, old Hammond, representing the link between pre-history and utopia, has probably allowed a sense of the present's possible incompleteness to leak into Dick's consciousness. Guest is therefore not the cause of this spectral effect; he is merely a symptom of it. We might summarise this by saying that he is a sort of symbolic supplement to utopia. That is to say, he conforms to the Derridean logic of supplementarity, whereby an addition also reveals a prior deficiency: 'it comes to compensate for an originary nonself-presence'.[53] Guest's very arrival in Nowhere reveals that the 'filled present' of utopia is not in fact self-sufficient. He has broken through a crack in the outer walls of this world, like the crevice through which Bulwer-Lytton's narrator breaches the hermetic kingdom of the Vril-ya in *The Coming Race*. The appearance of Morris's protagonist in utopia testifies to the ultimate impossibility of complete utopian plenitude. The opaque spot on the lived present in pre-history stains the apparently transparent present of utopia too.

'For ultimately the influence of the lived darkness is not confined to the various foregrounds mentioned above', Bloch remarks in the course of his discussion of this phenomenon; 'but the blind-spot, this not-seeing of the immediately entering Here and Now, also in fact appears in every *realization*'. He clarifies this claim that the present is terminally non-identical to itself with characteristically poetic intensity:

> Everywhere else there is a crack, even an abyss in the realizing itself, in the actuated-topical entrance of what has been so beautifully foreseen, dreamed out; and this abyss is that of the ungrasped existere itself. So the darkness of nearness also gives the *final reason for the melancholy of fulfilment*: no earthly paradise remains on entry without the shadow which the entry still casts over it.[54]

In his utopian fiction, Morris plays with the possibility of a utopian present that is fully present to itself. But he is finally too dialectical to accept the purity of this concept. After all, *News from Nowhere* is a political tract as well

---

[52] Jameson 1999, pp. 38–9.
[53] Derrida 1991, p. 28.
[54] Bloch 1986, p. 299.

as a phenomenological fantasy. It addresses a tight circle of committed readers, at least in its first, serial form of publication. And for these readers, the concept of the utopian present is, crucially, a heuristic possibility. In the words of Robert Musil, 'utopia is not a goal but an orientation'.[55]

IV. Nowhere and the here and now

In his writings for *Commonweal*, as I pointed out in Chapter 2, Morris repeatedly criticised those whom he called 'practical' or 'one-sided' socialists, because 'they do not see except through the murky smoked glass of the present condition of life amongst us'.[56] This notion of what we might call one-dimensional socialism is the basis for his polemical account of *Looking Backward*: 'The only ideal of life which such a man can see is that of the industrious *professional* middle-class men of to-day purified from their crime of complicity with the monopoly class, and become independent, instead of being, as they now are, parasitical'.[57] *News from Nowhere* is, in a dual sense, an attempt to supersede this ideological impasse, and so to render the 'smoked glass of the present' transparent. On the one hand, it is an exercise in clairvoyant historicity: the late nineteenth-century, despite its opacity, is apprehended from the perspective of its future history. On the other hand, it is an exercise in imagining no less than an alternative reality, in the form of a kind of communistic structure of feeling: it recuperates the present by making it present to itself in the utopian future, if only in some incomplete and finally illusory sense. As Bloch says, 'the final will is that to be truly present. So that the lived moment belongs to us and we to it and "Stay awhile" could be said to it' (p. 16).

This 'Stay awhile', which refers to the state for which Goethe's Faust will gladly sell his soul, captures the poignancy and political urgency of Morris's utopia. As William Guest had feared, his dream of Nowhere fades, and he finds himself at home, inferring the following message from Ellen's 'last mournful look': 'Go on living while you may, striving, with whatsoever pain and labour needs must be, to build up little by little the new day of fellowship,

---

[55] Quoted in Suvin 1997, p. 131.
[56] Morris 1994, p. 338.
[57] Morris 1994, p. 421.

and rest, and happiness' (pp. 210–11). All too quickly, Ellen's recommendation recalls the reader of *Commonweal* to the mundane activity of building a socialist movement in late-Victorian London. But it is important to register the fact that the terrain of politics has itself been defamiliarised, and transformed, by the protagonist's dream of the future – just as in daily life the people of whom one has dreamed seem subtly altered the next day. 'Or indeed *was* it a dream?' he wonders (p. 210). For if 'it may be called a vision rather than a dream' (p. 211), if it is symbolic of some inchoate collective consciousness of the post-capitalist society with which the present is already parturient, then the struggle for socialism will have been imperceptibly transfigured by the future.

Socialist politics in the present, according to Morris, are about helping to create those historical conditions of possibility in which the 'great motive-power of the change' – 'a longing for freedom and equality' – coincides with the objective conditions of capitalist crisis described in the discussion of 'How the Change Came' (pp. 104–5). What Guest imports from utopia is a sense of the possibility of that redemptive present, and this in part redeems the present of capitalism from its emptiness. For Morris, finally, as subsequently for Walter Benjamin, 'history is the subject of a structure whose site is not homogeneous, empty time, but time filled by the presence of the now'. William Guest is an allegorical figure for this 'conception of the present as the "time of the now" which is shot through with chips of Messianic time'. For, if he represents a spectral rupture of the utopian present while he is in Nowhere, on his return to Hammersmith he represents a spectral rupture in the capitalist present, as I implied at the end of Chapter 2. And this breach marks out what Benjamin termed 'the strait gate' through which the Messiah, in the form of the moment of revolutionary transformation, might enter history.[58]

When old Hammond tells his kinswoman Clara to 'go and live in the present' during 'The Drive Back to Hammersmith' in *News from Nowhere* (p. 136), he is not simply reassuring her that she must rest in utopia's happy state of plenitude; he is implicitly pressing Guest to return to his present, opening it up to this future.

---

[58] Benjamin 1970, pp. 262–3, 266.

Conclusion

Relating the pre-history of her utopian state in *New Amazonia* (1889), Elizabeth Corbett imagined steadfast anti-colonialists in Ireland resolving after Victoria's reign to liberate their country from British control. To this end, they 'formed themselves into a secret society which embraced nearly all the nation'.[1] This is the deepest social dream of the utopian novelist: a secret society the size of the nation. Almost all of the utopian fantasies of the *fin de siècle*, on the left and right of the political spectrum, have in common a desire to build what might be called a 'Party of Utopia' that will one day expand to such an extent that it is capable of implementing systematic social reform at a stroke. A conspiracy on that scale is no longer a conspiracy; it is a mass movement that has simply been condemned by adverse historical circumstances to a secret existence.

Looking Backward, by far the most popular utopian fiction of the period, came closest to translating this dream into reality. It sold more copies than any novel except *Uncle Tom's Cabin* (1852) in nineteenth-century America. Its political impact has been widely compared to Harriet Beecher Stowe's novel. John Dewey for example claimed in 1934 that 'what *Uncle Tom's Cabin* was to the anti-slavery movement Bellamy's book may well be to the shaping of popular

---

[1] Corbett 1889, p. 30.

opinion for a new social order'.[2] After all, it founded a national political movement. The first Nationalist Club was established in Boston in September 1888, and by February 1891 there were 165 Nationalist clubs distributed across 27 Union states. Their object was 'to propagate Bellamy's ideas as expounded in *Looking Backward*'. Krishan Kumar explains that 'the hope was that by a systematic educating of public opinion Bellamy's ideas could find their way into the mainstream of political life'.[3] Broadly speaking, this is what happened. The Nationalists supported the Populists, who incorporated a number of policies derived from the principles set out in Bellamy's book. They campaigned for them in the presidential election of 1892, and helped to attract as many as one million voters to their candidate, General Weaver. It might be said that behind the People's Party stood the Party of Utopia.

Nationalist organisations were also established in Britain. In July 1890 the Nationalization of Labour Society was formed to promote Bellamy's system. By the autumn, it boasted some two hundred and thirty members, who had bought and sold almost three hundred copies of *Looking Backward* and distributed approximately fourteen thousand pamphlets.[4] It scarcely impacted on the political consciousness of the nation of course, but there is no doubt that the ideas presented in the novel that it promoted did.

Alfred Morris, provincial secretary to the conservative Primrose League for the metropolitan boroughs, wrote a rebuttal to Bellamy's novel that reveals a suspicious awareness of what I have called the Party of Utopia. *Looking Ahead!* (1892), an attempt 'to oppose the advancing tide of Philosophical Socialism', is a fictional portrait of the radical opinions that animated the labour movement in the late 1880s and early 1890s. It claims that the appearance of *Looking Backward* 'came as a godsend to the Socialist leaders, who either could not, or dared not, formulate any definite or connected constructive policy': 'it was a positive fact that the Socialist leaders, when pressed to formulate their policy, were in the habit of referring enquirers to this book, as affording a complete and unanswerable solution'. Pre-eminent among the socialist organisations that treat Bellamy's book as 'a sort of working-man's Bible' is the Social Republican Propaganda Party, which Morris's impressionable

---

[2] Dewey 1934, p. 7.
[3] Kumar 1987, p. 136.
[4] See Marshall 1962, pp. 97–9.

protagonist, a labourer called Sam, impetuously joins. This party, a prototypical Party of Utopia, is composed of secret committees that exist across the world for 'the ostensible purpose of advancing ultra-liberalism'. Their aim is, first, to win over individual soldiers and policemen who might defend the capitalist system, and, second, to drill the international working class so that, 'at a given moment or a given signal, they might act as one man in carrying out the behests of the respective secret committees'. This cacotopian prospect is realized on 21 May 1905, when a kind of mass coup is successfully co-ordinated by the secret committees: 'So admirably had the revolution been organized that, by noon, London was entirely in the hands of the social democratic party'. Amidst social anarchy, Bellamy's ideas are instituted, and the country quickly collapses into a feudal chaos, from which a new capitalist system, it is forcefully implied, must be built from the bottom up.[5]

Morris's fear is that a conspiratorial movement will eventually achieve critical mass among the population at large and so enact its scheme in a single gesture. Ironically, this was not unlike the aspiration underpinning the Primrose League, which was a conservative response to the rise of mass politics after the Second Reform Act of 1867. Neville Kirk explains that 'the Primrose League, formed initially (in 1883) as "a semi-secret society of Conservative gentlemen" (to further the cause of Churchill and his clique), was soon transformed into a mass organisation committed to the defence of the Church and Crown and traditional hierarchies and seeking to enlist the support of those Tory worthies beyond the existing network of clubs and associations'.[6] It was thus the mirror-image of those socialist organisations feared by its members in the late 1880s and early 1890s. The Party of Utopia, it appears, was composed of right-wing as well as left-wing factions. The cacotopias that I reviewed in Chapter 4, with their appeals to a readership capable of reforming the more corrupt aspects of capitalist society in order to preserve it in the face of the spectre of socialist revolution, confirm this impression.

Utopian fiction in the late nineteenth-century is a repository for faith in the capacity of consciousness to conquer social conditions. 'We are that we are because so far it has been impossible to make the rich and poor understand', Robert Blatchford affirmed in *The Sorcery Shop* (1907), after characterising the lamentable

---

Morris 1892, pp. v, 37–39, 49–50, 239.
Kirk 1994, p. 202.

condition of England at the turn of the new century.[7] As we have seen, this idealist attitude to political reform defines the fantasies of conservative authors, contemplating social anarchy, as well as of feminist writers and reformist socialists, half-confident of a peaceful solution to the social conflicts of the *fin de siècle*. A simple shift in consciousness, it is hoped, will make it possible to fulfil a social dream in practice. In his critique of H.G. Wells, Christopher Caudwell commented that 'since he assumes that the relation between mind and environment is perfectly fluid, that the mind can make of the environment anything it pleases, he quite logically considers as his primary task the drawing up of a completely planned Utopia . . . so that this planned Utopia can by his converted readers be brought into being'.[8] This rationale is virtually structural to late-Victorian utopian fiction.

The Party of Utopia that it secretly posits is founded on the readership that it interpellates. It is a scattered assortment of individuals who, by virtue of their reading, have become a mass movement of potential activists. When Hobson praised *Looking Backward*'s impact on 'the great British public', he did so because 'to many thousands of isolated thinkers it offered the first distinctively moral support and stimulus to large projects of structural reform in industry and politics which had hitherto been tainted by association with revolutionary violence'.[9] This testimony to the book's ability to domesticate socialism for the middle classes is, of course, consistent with the claims I made in Chapter 2. But what interests me in the present context is the assertion, implicit in Hobson's statement, that Bellamy collectivised and even united 'many thousands of isolated thinkers'.[10]

This description of an atomised audience uncovering a network of political solidarity in the reception of a book evokes Edwin Abbott's meditation on utopian thinking in *Flatland*, a novel to which I referred in Chapter 5. Trapped in a cell at the end of the novel, where he has been incarcerated for holding seditious opinions, Abbott's narrator, 'A Square', who has experienced the third dimension, and who has consequently perceived the limitations of his two-dimensional world, complains that he is 'absolutely destitute of converts',

---

[7] Blatchford 1907, p. xiv.
[8] Caudwell 1938, p. 87.
[9] Hobson 1898, p. 180.
[10] On the reception in Britain of *Looking Backward*, in the context of a collective act of consumption, see Beaumont 2003.

and wonders whether 'the millennial Revelation has been made to me for nothing'. In this dispirited frame of mind, he is reduced to hoping that his memoirs, 'in some manner, I know not how, may find their way to the minds of humanity in Some Dimension, and may stir up a race of rebels who shall refuse to be confined to limited Dimensionality'.[11] All utopian fiction is premised on the same hope that it will somehow find sympathetic readers who can stir up a race of rebels, or of partisans at least. And all utopian fiction is premised, like the Square's social dream, on the idealist assumption that, if enough people become the advocates of an alternative future, they have already started to bring it into being.

But this remains mere hope, mere assumption. As Abbott's narrator is forced to admit when he pauses to consider his faith in this race of rebels, 'that is the hope of my brighter moments'. In his darker moments, he lacks any confidence in himself and reflects that 'all the substantial realities of Flatland itself, appear no better than the offspring of a diseased imagination, or the baseless fabric of a dream'. In the absence of a collective movement, capable of verifying his belief that there is a third dimension in which the everyday world acquires unimaginable richness and depth, he is like one of the many thousands of isolated thinkers, dreaming of a new social order, described by Hobson in his article on *Looking Backward*. The Square's memoirs, which constitute *Flatland* itself, are therefore like a desperate conspiratorial message that has been smuggled out of his prison cell. It is almost impossible to predict who will read them and how they will be interpreted, but they appeal to an ideal readership all the same. They are written for 'the minds of humanity in Some Dimension', a collective audience that can stir up the race of rebels. The Square does not ask his imaginary readers to free him so much as to create a well-nigh universal audience for the book's basic idea, that we are 'all alike the Slaves of our respective Dimensional prejudices'.[12] For once we all discover that we are the slaves of a limited world-view, we are no longer the slaves of a limited world-view. An entire race of rebels is the utopian state for which it has conspired. A secret society the size of the nation is the nation.

---

[11] Abbott 1884, p. 100.
[12] Ibid.

Utopian fiction dreams that the diffusion of its ideas in the present will create the conditions necessary for instituting its ideal society in the future. In this way, it can conceive a revolutionary transformation by evolutionary means. In *Looking Backward*, for example, Dr. Leete tells West that 'popular sentiment' supported the capitalist corporations because the people 'came to realize their necessity as a link, a transition phase, in the evolution of the true industrial system'.[13] Bellamy's book is itself the preliminary attempt to forge in the present the consensus that it imagines will transform society in the future. It appeals not to particular readers but to a readership. And it hopes that this readership comprises an incipient community of Nationalists that will ultimately encompass entire sections of the population. Of course, as I explained in the concluding remarks of Chapter 3, under capitalism almost any readership is in practice a *public introuvable*. Consequently, the readership of a utopian novel is almost inevitably a notional aggregate of individual readers, not unlike Hobson's thousands of thinkers. But its political aspirations require it to invest in the hope that some less atomised readership is possible. It must assume, as Sartre did, that 'the human race is at the horizon of the concrete and historical group of its readers', and that its 'real public' can be expanded to the limits of its 'virtual public'.[14]

The utopian assumption that the mind can make of the environment anything it pleases, and that it is therefore of pressing political importance to draft ideas that can be realised by a popular movement in the future, is an effect of what I have called a utopian structure of feeling. I have attempted to characterise the social and cultural preconditions of this structure of feeling throughout this book, but it seems appropriate to recapitulate them in the present context. The *fin de siècle* was a time when society appeared to be on the point of structural transformation: the capitalist system was metamorphosing in the face of sustained economic crisis; the working class was emerging as an organised historical force; and a kind of counter-culture, defined by middle-class and lower-middle-class intellectuals who, unconfidently enough, were beginning to question the ideology of progress that they had inherited from the mid-Victorian age, tried to come to terms with the metabolic impact of modernity. In these circumstances, the future seemed to acquire

---

[13] Bellamy 1888, p. 79.
[14] Sartre 1950, pp. 58, 61.

a uniquely plastic quality. And utopian ideas consequently assumed an inflationary importance. The subjective conditions for social reformation outran its objective conditions of possibility. Despite the unprecedented potential of the forces of production, the relations of production militated against systemic change. So, the social dreams of the late nineteenth-century centred for the most part on the superstructure. Instead of depicting a class conflict capable of transforming the organising structures of society, along the lines thrown up by the political convulsion of the Paris Commune, they depicted a gradual victory over the hearts and minds of the middle classes. Utopian fiction, in this context, posited its readers as a kind of evolutionary vanguard.

William Morris, whom I have treated throughout this account of utopian thinking, implicitly and explicitly, as an exception to the pattern cut out by his contemporaries, is not entirely immune to criticism of this kind. His materialist attitude to history is sometimes contradicted by an idealist attitude to the political requirements of the present. In the *Manifesto of the Socialist League* (1885), for example, Morris and Bax stressed above all the role performed by 'the education of the people' in 'the advancement of the Cause'. 'Industry in learning its principles, industry in teaching them, are most necessary to our progress', its account of socialist doctrine concluded; 'but to these we must add if we wish to avoid speedy failure, frankness and fraternal trust in each other, and single-hearted devotion to the religion of Socialism'.[15] The notion of a 'religion of socialism' was attractive to middle-class individuals associated with the late-Victorian counter-culture not least because it implied the necessity of an intellectual priesthood, a hieratic élite whose historical vocation is to administer socialist ideas to the people.

There is, however, a crucial distinction between Morris's understanding of the role of the political vanguard and that of other utopians in the period. This can perhaps be most clearly illustrated with reference to the final paragraph of his lecture on 'Art under Plutocracy' (1883), a portion of which I quoted at the end of Chapter 2:

> Organized brotherhood is that which must break the spell of anarchical Plutocracy. One man with an idea in his head is in danger of being considered a madman; two men with the same idea in common may be foolish, but

---

[15] Morris 1996, p. 8.

can hardly be mad; ten men sharing an idea begin to act, a hundred draw attention as fanatics, a thousand and society begins to tremble, a hundred thousand and there is war abroad, and the cause has victories tangible and real; and why only a hundred thousand? Why not a hundred million and peace upon the earth? You and I who agree together, it is we who have to answer that question.[16]

Morris dreams, like so many of his contemporaries in the movement for social reform, of the diffusion of progressive ideas among the people, to the point at which they acquire a popular democratic mandate. But unlike his contemporaries, he perceives that, even in these subjective conditions, the objective conditions of society cannot be reformed as if by universal fiat. Capitalist society itself is not, after all, an aggregate of individuals, but an historical formation in which the interests of the ruling class are more or less successfully managed. It has to be altered by acting together and not merely by thinking together. According to Morris, systematic change requires class struggle. This is the process of revolutionary transformation that he relates in the chapter on 'How the Change Came' in *News from Nowhere*. There, the working class acts collectively, in its own interest, because it has nothing to lose but its chains. 'Socialist opinion', with which 'the huge mass [has] been leavened', serves to direct the workers' 'animal necessities and passions' from the destruction of the old society to the task of creating 'a system of life founded on equality and Communism' – but on its own it is not an historical force.[17]

Utopian fiction takes on a different function within this dialectical and materialist framework. Morris does not inflate the role of ideas in the outcome of class conflict. So his utopia is a heuristic intervention in the ongoing dialogue about the future of society at the *fin de siècle*. His utopia is not a goal but an orientation within the struggle against capitalism. It does not identify its readership as, necessarily, the nucleus of the society of which it dreams. The readers of *Commonweal* are instead the precursors of those 'declared Socialists' that will guide the 'huge mass' of working people when the revolution occurs.[18]

---

[16] Morris 1973, pp. 84–5.
[17] Morris 1912a, pp. 125, 128.
[18] Morris 1912a, p. 125.

Morris, for whom, as Miguel Abensour argues, 'the first and most important milieu to be addressed is the extremely limited circle of radical readers of a theoretically and politically engaged journal', stands virtually alone in the late nineteenth-century as an inspiring instance of the aspiration 'to transform utopian writing into a necessarily partial and provisional moment of revolutionary practice within a specific group'.[19]

The opening chapter of *News from Nowhere* makes this plain when it describes 'a brisk conversational discussion', at a meeting of the Socialist League, 'as to what would happen on the Morrow of the Revolution'. This debate – 'at which there were six persons present, and consequently six sections of the party were represented' – 'finally shad[es] off into a vigorous statement by various friends of their views on the future of the fully-developed new society'.[20] The dream of Nowhere that is subsequently narrated is a belated contribution to this discussion. 'The moment of revolutionary practice belongs as such to the recipients no less than to the producer', as Abensour rightly insists, 'since the recipients are encouraged to propose their own utopia, to inscribe written utopia elsewhere than on paper, to criticize it and take a step beyond the written word'.[21] This is the utopian praxis with which Morris opposes the pragmatic utopianism of his contemporaries. *News from Nowhere* is primarily an intercession in the political discussions of revolutionary socialists at the end of the nineteenth-century; but it is also an ornately written letter of rejection which makes it clear that, despite answering Bellamy's social dream with a social dream of his own, Morris cannot countenance becoming a member of the Party of Utopia.

[19] Abensour 1999, pp. 128–29.
[20] Morris 1912a, p. 3.
[21] Abensour 1999, p. 128.

References

[Abbott, Edwin A.] A Square 1884, *Flatland: A Romance of Many Dimensions*, London: Seeley.

Abbott, Leonard D. 1898, *The Society of the Future*, Girard, Kansas: Wayland.

Abensour, Miguel 1999, 'William Morris: The Politics of Romance', translated by Max Blechman, in *Revolutionary Romanticism*, edited by Max Blechman, San Francisco: City Lights.

Adorno, Theodor 1974, *Minima Moralia: Reflections from Damaged Life*, translated by E.F.N. Jephcott, London: New Left Books.

Adorno, Theodor W. 1997 [1970], *Aesthetic Theory*, revised translation, translated by Robert Hullot-Kentor, London: Athlone.

Agulhon, Maurice 1981 [1979], *Marianne into Battle: Republican Imagery and Symbolism in France, 1789–1880*, translated by Janet Lloyd, Cambridge: Cambridge University Press.

Albinski, Nan Bowman 1988, *Women's Utopias in British and American Fiction*, London: Routledge.

Allan, James McGrigor 1890, *Woman Suffrage Wrong: In Principle, And Practice: An Essay*, London: Remington.

Allen, Grant 1895, *The British Barbarians*, London: Lane.

'An Appeal Against Female Suffrage' 1889, *Nineteenth Century*, 148 (June): 781–88.

Anderson, Perry 1980, *Arguments within English Marxism*, London: New Left Books.

Anderson, Perry 1991, 'Origins of the Present Crisis', in *English Questions*, London: Verso.

Anderson, Perry 2004, 'The River of Time', *New Left Review*, II, 26: 67–77.

'An Echo from the Mersey' 1891, letter to the editor, *Nationalization News*, 1 (1 November): 125–26.

'An Ex-M.P.' 1885, *A Radical Nightmare: or, England Forty Years Hence*, London: Field and Tuer, Simpkin, Marshall.

'An Ex-Revolutionist' 1893, *'England's Downfall:' or, the Last Great Revolution*, Second Edition, London: Digby and Long.

Annual Register 1872, *The Annual Register: A Review of Public Events at Home and Abroad, for the Year 1871*, London: Rivingtons.

Anonymous 1857, *Imaginary History of the Next Thirty Years*, London: Sampson Low.

Anonymous 1871a, 'Paris Vignettes', *All the Year Round*, 6 (23 September): 390–94.

Anonymous 1871b, 'Of the Commune and On Communism', *Leisure Hour: A Family Journal of Instruction and Recreation*, 20 (30 September): 621–24.

Anonymous 1872, 'Glimpses of the Future', *Blackwood's Edinburgh Magazine*, 112: 282–305.

Anonymous 1884, [review of Maxime du Camp, *Les convulsions de Paris* and Lissagaray, *L'Histoire de la Commune de 1871*,] *Edinburgh Review*, 159 (January): 82–120.

Anonymous 1889, 'Women's Suffrage: A Reply', *Fortnightly Review*, 271 (July): 123–39.

Anonymous 1892, *The Doom of the County Council of London*, London: Allen.

Anonymous 1894a, 'Recollections of the Commune of Paris', *Blackwood's Edinburgh Magazine*, 155 (January): 1–14.

Anonymous 1894b, 'Character Note. "The New Woman"', *Cornhill Magazine*, 136 (October): 365–68.

Anonymous 1898, 'What the People Read XI. – A Wife', *Academy*, 53 (12 March): 293–94.

Anonymous 1977 [1873], [review of Edward Maitland, *By and By: An Historical Romance of the Future*], *Science-Fiction Studies*, 4: 311–14.

Arnold, Matthew 1895, *Letters of Matthew Arnold 1848–1888*, Volume Two, edited by George W.E. Russell, London: Macmillan.

Arnold, Matthew 1965 [1869], *Culture and Anarchy*, in *The Complete Prose Works of Matthew Arnold*, Volume 5, edited by R.H. Super, Ann Arbor: University of Michigan Press.

'A Vicar of the Church of England' 1871, 'At Paris, Just Before the End', *Fraser's Magazine*, 4 (August): 230–48.

Barrère, C. 1971, *The Story of the Commune, by 'A Communalist'*, London: Chapman and Hall.

Bauman, Zygmunt 1976, *Socialism: The Active Utopia*, London: Allen and Unwin.

Bax, E. Belfort 1891, *Outlooks from the New Standpoint*, London: Swan Sonnenschein.

Beaumont, Matthew 2003, 'William Reeves and Late Victorian Radical Publishing: Unpacking the Bellamy Library', *History Workshop Journal*, 55: 91–110.

Beaumont, Matthew 2004, 'Reinterpreting Oscar Wilde's Concept of Utopia: 'The Soul of Man Under Socialism', *Utopian Studies*, 15: 13–29.

Bebel, August 1885 [1879], *Woman in the Past, Present and Future*, translated by H.B. Adams Walther, London: Modern Press.

Becker, Lydia E. 1889, *A Reply to the Protest which Appeared in the 'Nineteenth Century Review', June, 1889*, Manchester: Women's Suffrage Journal.

Beetham, David 1987, 'Reformism and the "Bourgeoisification" of the Labour Movement', in *Socialism and the Intelligentsia: 1880–1914*, edited by Carl Levy, London: Routledge and Kegan Paul.

Bellamy, Edward 1888, *Looking Backward: 2000–1887*, Boston: Ticknor.

Benjamin, Walter 1970 [1940], 'Theses on the Philosophy of History', in *Illuminations*, translated by Harry Zohn, London: Cape.

Benjamin, Walter 1979 [1937], 'Edward Fuchs, Collector and Historian', in *One-Way Street and Other Writings*, translated by Edmund Jephcott and Kingsley Shorter, London: New Left Books.

Benjamin, Walter 1999 [1927–40], *The Arcades Project*, translated by Howard Eiland and Kevin McLaughlin, Cambridge, MA.: Belknap Press and Harvard University Press.

Berens, E.H. and I. Singer 1894, *The Story of My Dictatorship*, London: Bliss, Sands and Foster.

Berneri, Marie-Louise 1951, *Journey Through Utopia*, Boston: Beacon Press.

Bertall [Charles Albert d'Arnoux] 1874, *The Communists in Paris 1871: Types, Physiognomies, Characters, With Explanatory Text by 'An Englishman/Eye-Witness of the Scenes and Events of that Year'*, Paris: Buckingham.

Besant, Annie 1889, 'Industry under Socialism', in *Fabian Essays in Socialism*, London: The Fabian Society.

Besant, Walter 1882, *The Revolt of Man*, London: Blackwood.

Blain, Virginia, Patricia Clements and Isobel Grundy (eds.) 1990, *The Feminist Companion to Literature in English: Women Writers from the Middle Ages to the Present*, London: Batsford.

Bland, Lucy 1995, *Banishing the Beast: English Feminism and Sexual Morality 1885–1914*, Harmondsworth: Penguin.

Blatchford, Robert 1893, *Merrie England*, Manchester: Clarion Press.

Blatchford, Robert 1907, *The Sorcery Shop: An Impossible Romance*, Manchester: Clarion Press.

Bloch, Ernst 1986 [1959], *The Principle of Hope*, translated by Neville Plaice, Stephen Plaice and Paul Knight, Cambridge, MA.: MIT Press.

Bloch, Ernst 1988 [1956], 'On the Present in Literature', in *The Utopian Function of Art and Literature: Selected Essays*, translated by Jack Zipes and Frank Mecklenburg, Cambridge, MA.: MIT Press.

Booth, General 1890, *In Darkest England and the Way Out*, London: Int. Headquarters of the Salvation Army.

Boumelha, Penny 1982, *Thomas Hardy and Women: Sexual Ideology and Narrative Form*, Brighton: Harvester Press.

Bourdieu, Pierre 1993, 'The Market of Symbolic Goods', in *The Field of Cultural Production: Essays on Art and Literature*, translated by Randal Johnson, Cambridge: Polity.

Bowman, Sylvia E. 1962, 'Edward Bellamy, The American Prophet (1850–1898)', in *Edward Bellamy Abroad: An American Prophet's Influence*, edited by Sylvia E. Bowman et al., New York: Twayne.

Bradlaugh, Charles 1884, *How Are We to Abolish the Lords?*, London: Freethought Press.

Briggs, Asa 1963, *Victorian Cities*, London: Odhams Press.

Briggs, Caroline Ashurst [n.d.], *A Letter from an Englishwoman to Englishwomen*, London: National Society for Women's Suffrage.

Britton, Norman 1884, 'New Heaven and a New Earth', *Progress*, 4: 113–22.

Buck-Morss, Susan 1989, *The Dialectics of Seeing: Walter Benjamin and the Arcades Project*, Cambridge, MA.: MIT Press.

Bulwer-Lytton, Edward 1871, *The Coming Race*, Edinburgh and London: Blackwood.

Burgess, Anthony 1978, 'Cacotopia', in *1985*, London: Hutchinson.

Carpenter, Edward 1885, *England's Ideal: A Tract*, Manchester: Heywood.

Carpenter, Edward 1896, *Love's Coming-Of-Age: A Series of Papers on the Relations of the Sexes*, Manchester: Labour Press.

Carpenter, Edward 1916, *My Days and Dreams: Being Autobiographical Notes*, London: Allen and Unwin.

Carr, E.H. 1969, 'Editor's Introduction', in N. Bukharin and E. Preobrazhensky, *The ABC of Communism*, translated by Eden and Cedar Paul, Harmondsworth: Penguin.

Caudwell, Christopher 1938, 'H.G. Wells: A Study in Utopianism', in *Studies in a Dying Culture*, London: Lane.

Chesney, G.T. 1871, *The Battle of Dorking: Reminiscences of a Volunteer*, London: Blackwood.

Chesterton, Gilbert K. 1917, *Utopia of Usurers and Other Essays*, New York: Boni and Liveright.

Chilton, H. Herman 1892, *Woman Unsexed: A Novel*, London: Foulsham.

Clapperton, Jane Hume 1885, *Scientific Meliorism and the Evolution of Happiness*, London: Kegan Paul, Trench.

Clapperton, J.H. 1888, *Margaret Dunmore: or, A Socialist Home*, London: Swan Sonnenschein, Lowerey.

Clarke, I.F. 1958, 'The Nineteenth-Century Utopia', *Quarterly Review*, 296: 80–91.

Clarke, I.F. 1979, *The Pattern of Expectation 1644–2001*, London: Cape.

Clarke, I.F. 1995, 'Introduction: The Paper Warriors and their Fights of Fantasy', in *The Tale of the Next Great War, 1871–1914: Fictions of Future Warfare and of Battles Still-to-come*, edited by I.F. Clarke, Liverpool: Liverpool University Press.

Collini, Stefan 1979, *Liberalism and Sociology: L.T. Hobhouse and Political Argument in England 1880–1914*, Cambridge: Cambridge University Press.

Corbett, Mrs George 1889, *New Amazonia: A Foretaste of the Future*, London: Tower.

Corbett, Mrs George 1893, *Mrs Grundy's Victims*, London: Tower.

Corbett, Elizabeth T. 1995 [1869], 'My Visit to Utopia', in *Daring to Dream: Utopian Fiction by United States Women before 1950*, edited by Carol F. Kessler, New York: Syracuse University Press.

Crackanthorpe, Hubert 1894, 'Reticence in Literature: Some Roundabout Remarks', *The Yellow Book: An Illustrated Quarterly*, 2 (July): 259–69.

Creighton, Louise 1889, 'The Appeal Against Female Suffrage: A Rejoinder', *Nineteenth Century*, 150 (August): 347–54.

Crowder, Diane Griffin 1993, 'Separatism and Feminist Utopian Fiction', in *Sexual Practice/Textual Theory: Lesbian Cultural Criticism*, edited by Susan J. Wolfe and Julia Penelope, Oxford: Blackwell.

Cunningham, Gail 1978, *The New Woman and the Victorian Novel*, London: Macmillan.

Cunningham, William 1879, 'The Progress of Socialism in England', *Contemporary Review*, 34 (January): 245–60.

Dayton, Tim 1997, 'The Mystery of Pre-History: Ernst Bloch and Crime Fiction', in *Not Yet: Reconsidering Ernst Bloch*, edited by Jamie Owen Daniel and Tom Moylan, London: Verso.

Davidson, Thomas 1888, *The Moral Aspects of the Economic Question: A Lecture Read before the Fellowship of the New Life*, New York, London: Reeves.

de Laveleye, Émile 1884 [1881], *The Socialism of To-Day*, translated by Goddard H. Orpen, London: Field and Tuer.

de Man, Paul 1983, 'Literary History and Literary Modernity', in *Blindness and Insight: Essays in the Rhetoric of Contemporary Criticism*, Revised Edition, Minneapolis: University of Minnesota Press.

Dentith, Simon 1990, 'News from Nowhere: The Rhetoric of Utopianism in the Writing of William Morris and Edward Carpenter', in *A Rhetoric of the Real: Studies in Post-Enlightenment Writing from 1790 to the Present*, London: Harvester Wheatsheaf.

Derrida, Jacques 1991, 'Speech and Phenomena', in *A Derrida Reader: Between the Blinds*, edited by Peggy Kamuf, London: Harvester Wheatsheaf.

Derrida, Jacques 1994 [1993], *Specters of Marx: The State of the Debt, the Work of Mourning, and the New International*, translated by Peggy Kamuf, London: Routledge.

Dewey, John 1934, 'A Great American Prophet', *Common Sense* 3, 4 (April).

Dicey, Edward 1871, 'Paris after the Peace', *The Fortnightly Review*, 15 (1 April): 485–94.

Dickens, Charles 1854, *Hard Times. For These Times*, London: Bradbury and Evans.

Dilke, M.M. 1889, 'The Appeal Against Female Suffrage: A Reply II', *Nineteenth Century*, 149 (July): 97–103.

Dix, Gertrude 1900, *The Image Breakers*, London: Heinemann.

Dixie, Lady Florence 1890, *Gloriana; or, The Revolution of 1900*, London: Henry.

Dobb, Maurice 1963 [1946], *Studies in the Development of Capitalism*, Revised Edition. London: Routledge and Kegan Paul.

Donnelly, Ignatius ['Edmund Boisgilbert'] 1891 [1890], *Caesar's Column: A Story of the Twentieth Century*, London: Ward, Lock.

Draper, Hal 1992, 'The Two Souls of Socialism', in *Socialism from Below*, edited by E. Haberkern, New Jersey: Humanities Press.

Eagleton, Terry 1976, *Myths of Power: A Marxist Study of the Brontës*, London: Macmillan.

Eagleton, Terry 1990, *The Ideology of the Aesthetic*, Oxford: Blackwell.

Eagleton, Terry 1991, *Ideology: An Introduction*, London: Verso.

Egerton, George 1894, 'The Regeneration of Two', in *Discords*, London: Lane.

Eley, Geoff 1996, 'Intellectuals and the German Labor Movement', in *Intellectuals and Public Life: Between Radicalism and Reform*, edited by Leon Fink, Stephen T. Leonard and Donald M. Reid, Ithaca: Cornell University Press.

Ellis, Havelock 1890, *The New Spirit*, London: Bell.

Ellis, Havelock 1894, *Man and Woman: A Study of Human Secondary Sexual Characters*, London: Scott.

Ellis, Havelock 1900, *The Nineteenth Century: A Dialogue in Utopia*, London: Richards.

Engels, Frederick 1883, 'The Book of Revelation', *Progress*, 2 (August): 112–16.

Engels, Frederick 1933, *Germany: Revolution and Counter-Revolution*, London: Lawrence.

Engels, Frederick 1984 [1887]. 'Preface to the Second Edition of *The Housing Question*', in Karl Marx and Frederick Engels, *On Reformism: A Collection*, Moscow: Progress.

Engels, Frederick 1989 [1880], *Socialism: Utopian and Scientific*, in Karl Marx and Frederick Engels, *Collected Works*, Volume Twenty-Four, London: Lawrence and Wishart.

Engels, Frederick 1990 [1888], 'Preface to the 1888 English Edition' [of the *Communist Manifesto*], in *Collected Works*, Volume Twenty-Six, London: Lawrence and Wishart.

Engels, Frederick 1998, 'Supplement and Addendum to Volume 3 of *Capital*', in *Collected Works*, Volume Thirty-Seven, London: Lawrence and Wishart.

Ethelmer, Ellis [Elizabeth Wolstenholme] 1893, 'Index to Notes', in *Woman Free*, London: Women's Emancipation Union.

[Fairfield, Charles] 1884, *The Socialist Revolution of 1888, By an Eye-Witness*, London: Hamson.

Falkiner, C. Litton 1885, *The New Voyage to Utopia*, Dublin: University Press.

Fawcett, Millicent Garrett 1874, *Tales in Political Economy*, London: Macmillan.

Fawcett, Millicent Garrett, 'The Appeal Against Female Suffrage: A Reply', *19th Century*, 149 (July): 86–96.

Felski, Rita 1995, *The Gender of Modernity*, Cambridge, MA.: Harvard University Press.

Ferns Chris 1999, *Narrating Utopia: Ideology, Gender, Form in Utopian Literature*, Liverpool: Liverpool University Press.

Flint, Kate 1993, *The Woman Reader 1837–1914*, Oxford: Clarendon Press.

Foote, G.W. 1886, 'Social Dreams', *Progress*, 6: 189–94.

Ford, Isabella O. 1895, *On the Threshold*, London: Arnold.

Fourier, Charles 1996 [1808], *The Theory of the Four Movements*, edited by Gareth Stedman Jones and Ian Patterson, Cambridge: Cambridge University Press.

Freedman, Carl 2000, *Critical Theory and Science Fiction*, Hanover, NH.: Wesleyan University Press.

Frye, Northrop 1973, 'Varieties of Literary Utopias', in *Utopias and Utopian Thought*, edited by Frank E. Manuel, London: Souvenir Press.

Gale, Frederick ['Lord Macaulay's New Zealander'] 1867 ['3867'], *The History of the English Revolution of 1867*, edited by 'Wykehamicus Friedrick', London: King.

Gibson, William 1872, *Paris During the Commune, 1871: Being Letters from Paris and its Neighbourhood, Written Chiefly During the Time of the Second Siege*, London: Whittaker.

Gilbert, W.S. 1893, *Utopia (Limited); or, The Flowers of Progress*, London: Chappell.

Gilbert, Sandra and Susan Gubar 1989, *No Man's Land: The Place of the Woman Writer in the Twentieth Century*, Volume Two ('Sexchanges'), New Haven: Yale University Press.

Gissing, George 1893, *The Odd Women*, Volume Three, London: Lawrence and Bullen.

Gleig, Charles 1898, *When All Men Starve: Showing How England Hazarded Her Naval Supremacy, and the Horrors which Followed the Interruption of Her Food Supply*, London: Lane.

Goncourt, Edmund and Jules Goncourt 1969 [1959], *Paris under Siege, 1870–1871: From the Goncourt Journal*, edited and translated by George J. Becker, Ithaca: Cornell University Press.

Goode, John 1971, 'William Morris and the Dream of Revolution', in *Literature and Politics in the 19th Century*, edited by John Lucas, London: Methuen.

Goode, John 1976, 'Woman and the Literary Text', in *The Rights and Wrongs of Women*, edited by Juliet Mitchell and Ann Oakley, Harmondsworth: Penguin.

Gorst, Harold E. 1898, 'The Struggle Against Woman', in *Sketches of the Future*, London: MacQueen.

Goschen George 1891, *The Use of Imagination in Study and in Life: An Address Delivered at Edinburgh University, November 19th, 1891*, Edinburgh: Harrison.

Gramsci, Antonio 1985, 'Indirect Sources: "Utopias" and So-called "Philosophical Novels"', in *Selections from Cultural Writings*, translated by William Boelhower, London: Lawrence and Wishart.

Gramsci, Antonio 1971 [1929–35], 'Problems of Marxism', in *Selections from the Prison Notebooks of Antonio Gramsci*, translated by Quintin Hoare and Geoffrey Nowell-Smith, London: Lawrence and Wishart.

Greenblatt, Stephen 1980, *Renaissance Self-Fashioning from More to Shakespeare*, Chicago: University of Chicago Press.

Grenfell, Alice 1895, 'Contemporary English Socialists and Women', *Shafts*, 6 (September): 81–82.

Griffith, George [George Chetwynd Griffith Jones] 1893, *The Angel of the Revolution: A Tale of the Coming Terror*, London: Tower.

Gronlund, Laurence 1892, *The Cooperative Commonwealth in its Outlines: An Exposition of Modern Socialism*, edited by G.B. Shaw, London: Reeves.

Hall, Stuart and Bill Schwarz 1985, 'State and Society, 1880–1930', in *Crises in the British State 1880–1930*, edited by Mary Layoun and Bill Schwarz, London: Hutchinson, in association with the CCCS, University of Birmingham.

Hansard's Parliamentary Debates

Hapgood, Lynne 2000, '"Is this Friendship?": Eleanor Marx, Margaret Harkness and the Idea of Socialist Community', in *Eleanor Marx (1855–1898): Life, Work, Contexts*, edited by John Stokes, Hants.: Ashgate.

Harrison, Frederic 1871, 'The Revolution of the Commune', *Fortnightly Review*, 15 (1 May): 556–79.

Harrison, Royden (ed.) 1971, *The English Defence of the Commune 1871*, London: Merlin Press.

Harrison, Royden 1987, 'Sidney and Beatrice Webb', in *Socialism and the Intelligentsia 1880–1914*, edited by Carl Levy, London: Routledge and Kegan Paul.

Harvey, David 1985, 'Monument and Myth: The Building of the Basilica of the Sacred Heart', in *Consciousness and the Urban Experience: Studies in the History and Theory of Capitalist Urbanization*, Volume One, Oxford: Blackwell.

Harvey, David 1990, *The Condition of Postmodernity: An Enquiry into the Origins of Cultural Change*, Oxford: Blackwell.

Haweis, Mrs H.R. 1900, 'Women as Writers', in *Words to Women: Addresses and Essays*, London: Burnet and Isbister.

Hay, William Delisle 1880 [n.d.], *The Doom of the Great City; Being the Narrative of a Survivor, Written A.D. 1942*, London: Newman.

Hayens, Herbert 1897, *Paris at Bay: A Story of the Siege and the Commune*, London: Blackie.

Hemyng, Bracebridge 1871 [n.d.], *The Commune in London; or, Thirty Years Hence: A Chapter of Anticipated History*, London: Clarke.

Henty, G.A. 1895, *A Woman of the Commune*, London: White.

Hewlett, Maurice 1973, 'A Materialist's Paradise', in *William Morris: The Critical Heritage*, edited by Peter Faulkner, London: Routledge and Kegan Paul.

Hobsbawm, E.J. 1962, *The Age of Capital, 1848–1875*, London: Weidenfeld and Nicolson.

Hobsbawm, E.J. 1964, 'The Fabians Reconsidered', in *Labouring Men: Studies in the History of Labour*, London: Weidenfeld and Nicolson.

Hobsbawm, E.J. 1968, *Industry and Empire: An Economic History of Britain since 1750*, London: Weidenfeld and Nicolson.

Hobsbawm, E.J. 1987, *The Age of Empire, 1875–1914*, London: Weidenfeld and Nicolson.

Hobsbawm, Eric 1998 [1980], 'Socialism and the Avant-Garde, 1880–1914', in *Uncommon People: Resistance, Rebellion and Jazz*, London: Weidenfeld and Nicolson.

Hobson, J.A. 1898, 'Edward Bellamy and the Utopian Romance', *Humanitarian*, 13: 179–89.

Holderness, Graham 1987, 'Anarchism and Fiction', in *The Rise of Socialist Fiction 1880–1914*, edited by H. Gustav Klaus, Brighton: Harvester Press.

Hook, Sydney 1936, 'Marx on Bentham and Utilitarianism', in *From Hegel to Marx: Studies in the Intellectual Development of Karl Marx*, London: Gollancz.

Howard, E. 1898, *To-Morrow: The Peaceful Path to Real Reform*, London: Swan Sonnenschein.

Howard, Ebeneezer 1926, 'Ebeneezer Howard: The Originator of the Garden City Idea', in *Garden Cities and Town Planning* 16 (July): 132–34.

Hudson, W.H. 1887, *A Crystal Age*, London: Fisher Unwin.

Hume, Fergus 1891, *The Year of Miracle: A Tale of the Year One Thousand Nine Hundred*, London: Routledge.

Hyndman, H.M. 1881, 'Dawn of a Revolutionary Epoch', *Nineteenth Century*, 9: 1–18.

Hyndman, H.M. 1883, *The Historical Basis of Socialism in England*, London: Kegan Paul, Trench.

Hyndman, H.M. 1884, 'Revolution and Reform', *To-Day*, 2 (August): 181–82.

Hyndman, H.M. 1890, *General Booth's Book Refuted*, London: Justice.

Jackson, Holbrook 1913, *The Eighteen Nineties: A Review of Art and Ideas at the Close of the Nineteenth Century*, London: Richards.

James, Edward 1995, 'Science Fiction by Gaslight: An Introduction to English-Language Science Fiction in the Nineteenth Century', in *Anticipations: Essays on Early Science Fiction and it Precursors*, edited by David Seed, Liverpool: Liverpool University Press.

James, William 1884, 'On Some Omissions of Introspective Psychology', *Mind: A Quarterly Review of Psychology and Philosophy*, 9 (January): 1–26.

Jameson, Fredric 1977, 'Reflections in Conclusion', in Ernst Bloch et al., *Aesthetics and Politics*, London: New Left Books.

Jameson, Fredric 1981, *The Political Unconscious: Narrative as a Socially Symbolic Act*, London: Methuen.

Jameson, Fredric 1982, 'Progress versus Utopia; or, Can We Imagine the Future?', *Science-Fiction Studies*, 9: 147–58.

Jameson, Fredric. 1991, *Postmodernism: or, The Cultural Logic of Late Capitalism*, London: Verso.

Jameson, Fredric 1992a, 'Reification and Utopia in Mass Culture', in *Signatures of the Visible*, London: Routledge.

Jameson, Fredric 1992b, 'Totality as Conspiracy', in *The Geopolitical Aesthetic: Cinema and Space in the World System*, London: BFI.

Jameson, Fredric 1994, *The Seeds of Time*, New York: Columbia University Press.

Jameson, Fredric 1999, 'Marx's Purloined Letter', in *Ghostly Demarcations: A Symposium on Jacques Derrida's Spectres of Marx*, edited by Michael Sprinker, London: Verso.

Jameson, Fredric 2004, 'The Politics of Utopia', *New Left Review*, II, 25: 35–54.

Jefferies, Richard 1885, *After London: or, Wild England*, London: Cassell.

Jellinek, Frank 1937, *The Paris Commune of 1871*, London: Gollancz.

Jenkins, Edward 1873, *Little Hodge*, London: King.

Kaufmann, Rev. M. 1879, *Utopias; or, Schemes of Social Improvement, from Sir Thomas More to Karl Marx*, London: Kegan Paul.

Kautsky, Karl 1910, *The Class Struggle*, translated by William E. Bohn, Chicago: Kerr.

Kautsky, Karl 1983, *Karl Kautsky: Selected Political Writings*, translated by Patrick Goode, London: Macmillan.

Kern, Stephen 1983, *The Culture of Time and Space 1880–1918*, Cambridge, MA.: Harvard University Press.

Kiernan, V.G. 1989, 'Tennyson, King Arthur and Imperialism', in *Poets, Politics and the People*, edited by Harvey J. Kaye, London: Verso.

Kilvert, Francis 1944, *Kilvert's Diary 1870–1879: Selections from the Diary of the Rev. Francis Kilvert*, edited by William Plomer, London: Cape.

Kingsman, A. 1872, *Over Volcanoes: or, Through France and Spain in 1871*, London: King.

Kirk, Neville 1994, *Labour and Society in Britain and the USA*, Volume Two ('Challenge and Accommodation, 1850–1939'), Aldershot: Scolar Press.

Kocka, Jürgen, *Industrial Culture and Bourgeois Society: Business, Labor, and Bureaucracy in Modern Germany*, Oxford: Berghahn.

Kranidis, Rita S. 1995, *Subversive Discourse: The Cultural Production of Late Victorian Feminist Novels*, New York: St. Martin's Press.

Kumar, Krishan 1987, *Utopia and Anti-Utopia in Modern Times*, Oxford: Blackwell.

Lacan, Jacques 1992, *The Ethics of Psychoanalysis 1959–60: The Seminar of Jacques Lacan*, translated by Dennis Potter, London: Tavistock/Routledge.

Lafargue, Paul 1883, 'The "Spectre Rouge" Trick: Its Use in French Politics', *Progress*, 2 (August): 102–05.

Lafargue, Paul 1907a, 'Socialism and the Intellectuals', in *The Right To Be Lazy and Other Studies*, translated by C.H. Kerr, Chicago: Kerr.

Lafargue, Paul 1907b, 'The Socialist Ideal', in *The Right To Be Lazy and Other Studies*, translated by C.H. Kerr, Chicago: Kerr.

Lamazou, Pierre Henri 1872, *The Place Vendôme and La Roquette: The First and Last Acts of the Commune (1871)*, translated by C.F. Audley, London: Burns, Oates.

Landes, David S. 1969, *The Unbound Prometheus: Technological Change and Industrial Development in Western Europe from 1750 to the Present*, Cambridge: Cambridge University Press.

Lazarus, Henry 1894, *The English Revolution of the Twentieth Century: A Prospective History*, edited by Henry Lazarus, London: Fisher Unwin.

Lefebvre, Henri 1968, *The Sociology of Marx*, translated by Norbert Guterman, London: Allen Lane.

Leighton, John 1871, *Paris Under the Commune: or, The Seventy-Three Days of the Second Siege. With Numerous Illustrations, Sketches Taken on the Spot, and Portraits (From the Original Photographs)*, London: Bradbury, Evans.

Leith, James A. 1978, 'The War of Images Surrounding the Commune', in *Images of the Commune/Images de la Commune*, edited by James A. Leith, Montréal: McGill-Queen's University Press.

Lem, Stanislaw 1971 [1961], *Solaris*, translated by Joanna Kilmartin and Steve Cox, London: Faber and Faber.

Lenin, V.I. 1968 [1916], *Imperialism, The Highest Stage of Capitalism (A Popular Outline)*, in *Selected Works*, Moscow: Progress.

Leslie, Thomas Edward Cliffe 1888 [1879], 'The Known and the Unknown in the Economic World', in *Essays in Political Economy*, Second, Revised Edition, edited by J.K. Ingram and C.F. Bastable, London: Longmans, Green.

L'Estrange, Miles 1892, *What We Are Coming To*, Edinburgh: Douglas.

Levitas, Ruth 1990, *The Concept of Utopia*, Syracuse: Syracuse University Press.

Lewes, Darby 1995, *Dream Revisionaries: Gender and Genre in Women's Utopian Fiction 1870–1920*, Tuscaloosa: University of Alabama Press.

Lidsky, Paul 1970, *Les écrivains contre la commune*, Paris: Maspero.

Löwy, Michael 1979 [1976], *Georg Lukács: From Romanticism to Bolshevism*, translated by Patrick Camiller, London: New Left Books.

Löwy, Michael 1993, 'Rosa Luxemburg's Conception of "Socialism or Barbarism"', translated by Paul Le Blanc, in *On Changing the World: Essays in Political Philosophy, from Karl Marx to Walter Benjamin*, New Jersey: Humanities Press.

Lukács, Georg 1971 [1923], 'Reification and the Consciousness of the Proletariat', in *History and Class Consciousness: Studies in Marxist Dialectics*, translated by Rodney Livingstone, London: Merlin.

Lukács, Georg 1977 [1938], 'Realism in the Balance', translated by Rodney Livingstone, in Ernst Bloch et al., *Aesthetics and Politics*, translated by Ronald Taylor et al., London: New Left Books.

Lukács, Georg 1989 [1937], *The Historical Novel*, translated by Hannah and Stanley Mitchell, London: Merlin Press.

Macaulay, Thomas Babington 1982, *The Selected Letters of Thomas Babington Macaulay*, edited by Thomas Pinney, Cambridge: Cambridge University Press.

Mannheim, Karl 1936 [1929–31], *Ideology and Utopia: An Introduction to the Sociology of Knowledge*, translated by Louis Wirth and Edward Shils, London: Kegan Paul, Trench, Trübner.

Manuel, Frank 1973, 'Towards a Psychological History of Utopias', in *Utopias and Utopian Thought*, edited by Frank Manuel, London: Souvenir Press.

Manuel, Frank and Fritzie P. Manuel 1979, *Utopian Thought in the Western World*, Oxford: Blackwell.

March, Thomas 1896, *The History of the Paris Commune of 1871*, London: Swan Sonnenschein.

Marcuse, Herbert 1956, *Eros and Civilization: A Philosophical Inquiry into Freud*, London: Routledge and Kegan Paul.

Marshall, Peter 1962, 'A British Sensation', in *Edward Bellamy Abroad: An American Prophet's Influence*, edited by Sylvia E. Bowman et al., New York: Twayne.

Marx, Karl and Frederick Engels 1934, *Correspondence 1846–1895: A Selection with Commentary and Notes*, translated by Dona Torr, London: Lawrence.

Marx, Karl and Frederick Engels 1971, *On the Paris Commune*, Moscow: Progress.

Marx, Karl and Frederick Engels 1975a [1844], 'Contribution to the Critique of Hegel's Philosophy of Law', in Karl Marx and Frederick Engels, *Collected Works*, Volume Three, London: Lawrence and Wishart.

Marx, Karl and Frederick Engels 1975b [1845], *The Holy Family (1845)*, in Karl Marx and Frederick Engels, *Collected Works*, Volume Four, London: Lawrence and Wishart.

Marx, Karl and Frederick Engels 1976a [1845–6], *The German Ideology*, in Karl Marx and Frederick Engels, *Collected Works*, Volume Five, London: Lawrence and Wishart.

Marx, Karl and Frederick Engels 1976b [1847], *The Poverty of Philosophy*, in Karl Marx and Frederick Engels, *Collected Works*, Volume Six, London: Lawrence and Wishart.

Marx, Karl and Frederick Engels 1976c [1848], *Manifesto of the Communist Party*, in Karl Marx and Frederick Engels, *Collected Works*, Volume Six, London: Lawrence and Wishart.

Marx, Karl and Frederick Engels 1984, *On Reformism: A Collection*, Moscow: Progress.

Marx, Karl 1986 [1871], *The Civil War in France*, in Karl Marx and Frederick Engels, *Collected Works*, Volume Twenty-Two, London: Lawrence and Wishart.

Marx, Karl 1987 [1859], 'Preface to *A Contribution to the Critique of Political Economy*', in Karl Marx and Frederick Engels, *Collected Works*, Volume Twenty-Nine, London: Lawrence and Wishart.

Marx, Karl 1989 [1875], *Critique of the Gotha Programme*, in Karl Marx and Frederick Engels, *Collected Works*, Volume Twenty-Four, London: Lawrence and Wishart.

Marx, Karl 1996 [1867], *Capital*, Volume One, in Karl Marx and Frederick Engels, *Collected Works*, Volume Thirty-Five, London: Lawrence and Wishart.

Marx Aveling, Edward and Eleanor Marx Aveling 1886, *The Woman Question*, London: Swan Sonnenschein, Le Bas and Lowrey.

Masterman, C.F.G. 1905, *In Peril of Change: Essays Written in Time of Tranquillity*, London: Fisher Unwin.

Masterman, C.F.G. 1909, *The Condition of England*, London: Methuen.

Mayer, Arno 1975, 'The Lower Middle Class as Historical Problem', *Journal of Modern History*, 47: 409–36.

Meier, Paul 1978, *William Morris: The Marxist Dreamer*, Volume One, translated by Frank Gubb, Brighton: Harvester Press.

Miller, Jane Eldridge 1994, *Rebel Women: Feminism, Modernism and the Edwardian Novel*, London: Virago.

Morgan, Arthur E. 1944, *Edward Bellamy*, New York: Columbia University Press.

Morgan-Cockerell, Mrs 1896, 'Is the New Woman a Myth?', *The Humanitarian*, 8, 5 (May): 339–50.

Morris, Alfred 1892, *Looking Ahead! A Tale of Adventure (Not by the Author of 'Looking Backward')*, Second Edition, London: Henry.

Morris, William 1912a [1891], *News from Nowhere; or, An Epoch of Unrest* [sic]: *Being Some Chapters from a Utopian Romance*, in *The Collected Works of William Morris*, Volume Sixteen, London: Longmans Green.

Morris, William 1912b, *A Dream of John Ball*, in *The Collected Works of William Morris*, Volume Sixteen, London: Longmans Green.

Morris, William 1914 [1884], 'Architecture and History', in *The Collected Works of William Morris*, Volume Twenty-Two, London: Longmans Green.

Morris, William 1915a [1886], 'Dawn of a New Epoch', in *The Collected Works of William Morris*, Volume Twenty-Three, London: Longmans Green.

Morris, William 1915b [1886], *The Pilgrims of Hope*, in *The Collected Works of William Morris*, Volume Twenty-Four, London: Longmans Green.

Morris, William 1936a [1893], 'More's *Utopia*: Foreword by William Morris', in *William Morris: Artist, Writer, Socialist*, Volume One, edited by May Morris, Oxford: Blackwell.

Morris, William 1936b [1889], 'Address at the Twelfth Annual Meeting of the Society for the Protection of Ancient Buildings, 3 July 1889', in *William Morris, Artist, Writer, Socialist*, Volume Two, edited by May Morris, Oxford: Blackwell.

Morris, William 1969 [1887], '[The Present Outlook in Politics]', in *The Unpublished Lectures of William Morris*, edited by Eugene D. LeMire, Detroit: Wayne State University Press.

Morris, William 1973, *Political Writings of William Morris*, edited by A.L. Morton, London: Lawrence and Wishart.

Morris, William 1984 [1894], 'A Theory of Life', in *William Morris: News from Nowhere and Selected Writings and Designs*, edited by Asa Briggs, Harmondsworth: Penguin.

Morris, William 1987, *Collected Letters of William Morris*, Volume Two, edited by Norman Kelvin, Princeton: Princeton University Press.

Morris, William 1994, *Political Writings: Contributions to Justice and Commonweal 1883–1890*, edited by Nicholas Salmon, Bristol: Thoemmes.

Morris, William 1996, *Journalism: Contributions to Commonweal, 1885–1890*, edited by Nicholas Salmon, Bristol: Thoemmes.

Morris, William 1999 [1881], 'The Prospects of Architecture in Civilization', in *William Morris on Art and Socialism*, edited by Norman Kelvin, New York: Dover.

Morton, A.L. 1952, *The English Utopia*, London: Lawrence and Wishart.

Morton, A.L. 1990, 'Utopia Yesterday and Today', in *History and the Imagination: Selected Writings of A.L. Morton*, edited by Margot Heinemann and Willie Thompson, London: Lawrence and Wishart.

Moylan, Tom 2000, *Scraps of the Untainted Sky: Science Fiction, Utopia, Dystopia*, Boulder: Westview Press.

Mumford, Lewis 1923, *The Story of Utopias: Ideal Commonwealths and Social Myths*, London: Harrap.

Nellist, Brian 1995, 'Imagining the Future: Predictive Fiction in the Nineteenth Century', in *Anticipations: Essays on Early Science Fiction and it Precursors*, edited by David Seed, Liverpool: Liverpool University Press.

Nordau, Max 1895, *Degeneration*, London: Heinemann.

North, Delaval 1887, *The Last Man in London*, London: Hodder and Stoughton.

Novotny, Helga 1994 [1989], *Time: The Modern and Postmodern Experience*, translated by Neville Plaice, Cambridge: Polity.

Oakehurst, William 1891, *The Universal Strike of 1899*, London: Reeves.

O' Brien, M.D. 1892, *Socialism Tested by Facts: Being an Account of Certain Experimental Attempts to carry out Socialistic Principles and containing a Criticism of 'Looking Backward' and the 'Fabian Essays'*, London: Liberty and Property Defence League.

Pankhurst, E. Sylvia, *The Suffrage Movement: An Intimate Account of Persons and Ideals*, London: Longmans, Green.

Pater, Walter 1910 [1878], 'Charles Lamb', in *Appreciations: With an Essay on Style*, London: Macmillan.

Perrycoste, F.H. ['A Free Lance'] 1894, *Towards Utopia (Being Speculations in Social Evolution)*, London: Swan Sonnenschein.

Pfaelzer, Jean 1984, *The Utopian Novel in America 1886–1896: The Politics of Form*, Pittsburgh: University of Pittsburgh Press.

Pierson, Stanley 1973, *Marxism and the Origins of British Socialism: The Struggle for a New Consciousness*, Ithaca: Cornell University Press.

Pierson, Stanley 1979, *British Socialists: The Journey from Fantasy to Politics*, Cambridge, MA.: Harvard University Press.

'Pioneer 363' 1896, 'Is the So-called "New Woman" a Modern Prodigy?', *Shafts*, 4 (January): 146–7.

Porter, Linn Boyd 1903 [1890], *Riverfall*, London: Fisher Unwin.

Poulantzas, Nicos 1975, *Classes in Contemporary Capitalism*, translated by David Fernbach, London: New Left Books.

Presley, James T. 1873, 'Bibliography of Utopias and Imaginary Travels and Histories', *Notes and Queries*, fourth series, 12 (12 July): 22–23.

Ricoeur, Paul 1986, *Lectures on Ideology and Utopia*, New York: Columbia University Press.

Roberts J.M. 1973, 'The Paris Commune from the Right', in *The English Historical Review*, Supplement Six, London: Longman.

Ross, Kristin 1988, *The Emergence of Social Space: Rimbaud and the Paris Commune*, London: Macmillan.

Rowbotham, Sheila 1972, *Women, Resistance and Revolution*, London: Allen Lane.

Rowbotham, Sheila 1977, 'Edward Carpenter: Prophet of the New Life', in Sheila Rowbotham and Jeffrey Weeks, *Socialism and the New Life: The Personal and Sexual Politics of Edward Carpenter and Havelock Ellis*, London: Pluto Press.

Rowbotham, Sheila 1997, *A Century of Women: The History of Women in Britain and the United States*, London: Viking.

Ruskin, John 1906 [1872], *The Eagle's Nest: Ten Lectures on the Relation of Natural Science to Art*, in *The Works of John Ruskin*, Library Edition, Volume Twenty-Two, edited by E.T. Cook and Alexander Wedderburn, London: Allen.

Ruskin, John 1907 [1871], 'Charitas', in *Fors Clavigera*, Volume One, in *The Works of John Ruskin*, Library Edition, Volume Twenty-Seven, edited by E.T. Cook and Alexander Wedderburn, London: Allen.

Ruskin, John 1909, *The Letters of John Ruskin, 1827–1869*, in *The Works of John Ruskin*, Library Edition, Volume Thirty-Six, edited by E.T. Cook and Alexander Wedderburn, London: Allen.

[Salisbury, Lord] 1871, 'The Commune and the Internationale', *Quarterly Review*, 131 (October): 549–80.

Samuel, Raphael 1985, 'The Vision Splendid', *New Socialist*, 27: 24–8.

Sargent, Lyman Tower 1988, *British and American Utopian Literature, 1516–1985: An Annotated, Chronological Bibliography*, New York: Garland.

Sartre, Jean-Paul 1950, *What is Literature?*, translated by Bernard Frechtman, London: Methuen.

Schivelbusch, Wolfgang 1980, *The Railway Journey: Trains and Travel in the 19th Century*, translated by Anselm Hollo, Oxford: Blackwell.

Schreiner, Olive 1926, *From Man to Man; or, Perhaps Only*, London: Fisher Unwin.

Schreiner, Olive 1988, *Olive Schreiner Letters, I: 1871–1899*, edited by Richard Rive, Oxford: Oxford University Press.

Schulkind, Eugene 1972, 'Introduction', in *The Paris Commune of 1871: The View from the Left*, edited by Eugene Schulkind, London: Cape.

Shaw, G. Bernard 1892, *The Fabian Society: What It Has Done; & How It Has Done It*, London: Fabian Society.

Showalter, Elaine 1978, *A Literature of Their Own: British Women Novelists from Brontë to Lessing*, London: Virago.

Showalter, Elaine 1987, *The Female Malady: Women, Madness, and English Culture 1830–1980*, London: Virago.

Showalter, Elaine 1991, *Sexual Anarchy: Gender and Culture at the Fin de Siècle*, London: Bloomsbury.

Smith, F.B. 1972, 'Some British Reactions to the Commune', in *Paradigm for Revolution? The Paris Commune 1871–1971*, edited by Eugene Kamenka, Canberra: Australian National University Press.

Smith, Goldwin 1886, *False Hopes; or, Fallacies, Socialistic and Semi-Socialistic, Briefly Answered*, London: Cassell.

Sorel, Georges 1916, *Reflections on Violence*, translated by T.E. Hulme, London: Allen and Unwin.

Stacey, Enid 1897, 'A Century of Women's Rights', in *Forecasts of the Coming Century, by a Decade of Writers*, edited by Edward Carpenter, Manchester: Labour Press.

Stanley, William 1903, *The Case of The Fox; Being his Prophecies under Hypnotism of the Period Ending A.D. 1950: A Political Utopia*, London: Truslove and Hanson.

Stead, William T. 1894, *If Christ Came to Chicago! A Plea for the Union of All Who Love in the Service of All Who Suffer*, London: Office of Review of Reviews.

Stedman Jones, Gareth 1971, *Outcast London: A Study in the Relationship between Classes in Victorian Society*, Oxford: Clarendon Press.

Stedman Jones, Gareth 1983, 'Working-Class Culture and Working-Class Politics in London, 1870–1900: Notes on the Remaking of a Working Class', in *Languages of Class: Studies in English Working-Class History, 1832–1982*, Cambridge: Cambridge University Press.

Sutherland, John 1991, *Mrs. Humphry Ward: Eminent Victorian, Pre-Eminent Edwardian*, Oxford: Oxford University Press.

Suvin, Darko 1983, *Victorian Science Fiction in the UK: The Discourses of Knowledge and of Power*, Boston: Hall.

Suvin, Darko 1997, 'Locus, Horizon, and Orientation: The Concept of Possible Worlds as a Key to Utopian Studies', in *Not Yet: Reconsidering Ernst Bloch*, edited by Jamie Owen Daniel and Tom Moylan, London: Verso.

Suvin, Darko 2001, 'Afterword', in *Learning from Other Worlds*, edited by Patrick Parrinder, Liverpool: Liverpool University Press.

Swanwick, Anna 1888, *An Utopian Dream and How It May Be Realized*, London: Kegan Paul, Trench.

Sypher, Eileen 1993, *Wisps of Violence: Producing Public and Private Politics in the Turn-of-the-Century British Novel*, London: Verso.

Taylor, Barbara 1983, *Eve and the New Jerusalem: Socialism and Feminism in the Nineteenth Century*, London: Virago.

'The Journeyman Engineer' 1871, 'The English Working Classes and the Paris Commune', *Fraser's Magazine*, 4 (July): 62–8.

Thomas, John L. 1967, 'Introduction', in Edward Bellamy, *Looking Backward 2000–1887*, edited by John L. Thomas, Cambridge, MA.: Belknap Press.

Tchernuishevsky, Nikolai G. 1886 [1863], *A Vital Question; or, What Is to Be Done?*, translated by Nathan Haskell Dole and S.S. Skidelsky, New York: Crowell.

Thompson, E.P. 1977 [1955], *William Morris: Romantic to Revolutionary*, Revised Edition, London: Merlin.

Trevelyan, G.M. 1944, *English Social History: A Survey of Six Centuries, Chaucer to Queen Victoria*, London: Longmans, Green.

Trilling, Lionel 1973, 'Aggression and Utopia: A Note on William Morris's *News from Nowhere*', *The Psychoanalytic Quarterly*, 42, 2: 214–25.

Trotsky, Leon 1966, *The Intelligentsia and Socialism*, translated by Brian Pearce, London: New Park.

Tuke, James Hack 1871, *A Visit to Paris in the Spring of 1871, on behalf of the War Victim's Fund of the Society of Friends, Being a Lecture Delivered at the Town Hall, Hitchin, April 4, 1871*, London: Kitto.

Walkowitz, Judith 1986, 'Science, Feminism and Romance: The Men and Women's Club 1885–1889', *History Workshop Journal*, 21: 37–59.

Waters, Mrs John 1881, *A Young Girl's Adventures in Paris*, London: Remington.

Watlock, W.A. 1886, *The Next 'Ninety-Three: or, Crown, Commune, and Colony, Told in a Citizen's Diary*, London: Field and Tuer.

Watson, Henry Crocker Marriot 1890, *The Decline and Fall of the British Empire: or, The Witch's Cavern*, London: Trischler.

Waugh, Arthur 1894, 'Reticence in Literature', *Yellow Book*, 1 (April): 201–19.

Weeks, Jeffrey 1984, 'The Fabians and Utopia', in *Fabian Essays in Socialist Thought*, edited by Ben Pimlott, London: Heinemann.

Wegner, Philip E. 2002, *Imaginary Communities: Utopia, the Nation, and the Spatial Histories of Modernity*, Berkeley: University of California Press.

Welch, Edgar 1882, *The Monster Municipality, or, Gog and Magog Reformed. A Dream. By 'Grip'*, London: Sampson Low, Marston, Searle and Rivington.

Wells, David A. 1890, *Recent Economic Changes and their Effect on the Production and Distribution of Wealth and the Well-Being of Society*, London: Longmans, Green.

Wells, H.G. 1898, *The War of the Worlds*, London: Heinemann.

Wells, H.G. 1905, *A Modern Utopia*, London: Chapman and Hall.

Wells, H.G. 1936, *The Croquet Player: A Story*, London: Chatto and Windus.

Wells, H.G. 1980a, 'About Sir Thomas More', in *H.G. Wells's Literary Criticism*, edited by Patrick Parrinder and Robert M. Philmus, Brighton: Harvester Press.

Wells, H.G. 1980b [1938], 'Fiction about the Future', in *H.G. Wells's Literary Criticism*, edited by Patrick Parrinder and Robert M. Philmus, Brighton: Harvester Press.

West, Rebecca 1982 [1912], 'So Simple', in *The Young Rebecca: Writings of Rebecca West 1911–17*, edited by Jane Marcus, London: Macmillan.

Williams, Raymond 1973, *The Country and the City*, London: Chatto and Windus.

Williams, Raymond 1977, *Marxism and Literature*, Oxford: Oxford University Press.

Wolfe, Willard 1975, *From Radicalism to Socialism: Men and Ideas in the Formation of Fabian Socialist Doctrines, 1881–1889*, New Haven: Yale University Press.

Wollstonecraft, Mary 1792, *A Vindication of the Rights of Woman: with Strictures on Political and Moral Subjects*, London: Johnson.

W.R.G. 1871, 'Suum Cuique. The Moral of the Paris Catastrophe', *Fraser's Magazine*, 4 (July): 115–34.

Yeo, Stephen 1977, 'A New Life: The Religion of Socialism in Britain, 1883–1896', *History Workshop Journal*, 4: 5–56.

Woods, Robert Archery 1892, *English Social Movements*, London: Swan, Sonnenschein.

Yeo, Stephen 1980, 'State and Anti-State: Reflections on Social Forms and Struggles from 1850', in *Capitalism, State Formation and Marxist Theory: Historical Investigations*, edited by Philip Corrigan, London: Quartet.

Žižek, Slavoj 1997, 'Multiculturalism; Or, the Cultural Logic of Multinational Capitalism', *New Left Review*, I, 225: 28–51.

INDEX

CPSIA information can be obtained
at www.ICGtesting.com
Printed in the USA
JSHW040232090221
11732JS00001B/3